THE

WAYFARER'S

HANDBOOK

A Field Guide for
THE INDEPENDENT TRAVELER

EVAN S. RICE

BLACK DOG
& LEVENTHAL
PUBLISHERS

Conversions between the imperial and metric measurement systems are rounded to the nearest applicable degree. • This book is intended to be apolitical. Any implications to the contrary are unintentional. • Definitions included will provide only the applicable definition, not the complete definition. • Some archaic spellings used in older quotes have been updated for the ease of the reader. • Every effort has been made to ensure the accuracy of the information contained herein. Information is intended to be accurate as of January 1, 2017.

Please direct any questions, corrections, or suggestions to:
Evan@thewayfarershandbook.com

BLACK DOG & LEVENTHAL PUBLISHERS
HACHETTE BOOK GROUP
1290 Avenue of the Americas • New York, NY 10104
www.hachettebookgroup.com • www.blackdogandleventhal.com

First Edition: April 2017

Black Dog & Leventhal Publishers is an imprint of Hachette Books, a division of Hachette Book Group. The Black Dog & Leventhal Publishers name and logo are trademarks of Hachette Book Group, Inc.

The publisher is not responsible for websites (or their content) that are not owned by the publisher.

The Hachette Speakers Bureau provides a wide range of authors for speaking events. To find out more, go to www.HachetteSpeakersBureau.com or call (866) 376-6591.

Print book interior design by Paul Kepple & Max Vandenberg at HEADCASE DESIGN
www.headcasedesign.com

Library of Congress Cataloging-in-Publication Data
Names: Rice, Evan S., author. • Title: The wayfarer's handbook: a field guide for the independent traveler / Evan S. Rice. • Description: New York, NY: Black Dog & Leventhal, 2017. • Identifiers: LCCN 2016034511| ISBN 9780316271349 (hardback) | ISBN 9781478915317 (audio download) | ISBN 9780316271356 (e-book) • Subjects: LCSH: Travelers. | Tourism. | BISAC: TRAVEL / Reference. • Classification: LCC G155.A1 R496 2017 | DDC 910.92--dc23 LC record available at https://lccn.loc.gov/2016034511

ISBNs: 978-0-316-27134-9 (hardcover), 978-0-316-27135-6 (ebook)

Printed in the U.S.A.

WOR

10 9 8 7 6 5 4 3 2 1

INTRODUCTION

W HEN I WAS 25, I left my job and booked a one-way ticket to Kenya. By the time I returned home almost ten months later, I had become enchanted by the road. I discovered countless treasures sprinkled throughout the world: lovely communities of kind people, beautiful and bizarre wildlife, delicious street foods, wonderful little mountain villages, bustling rainbow-colored markets, and so much more.

In seeking out these gems of nature and culture and unexpectedness, I also found a group of people who chose to experience life in a way that I didn't know was possible. Independent travelers, of all ages, who went to wondrous places for indeterminate amounts of time, driven by reasons that even they didn't seem to understand. They were so effortless in their movements: relaxed but aware, self-reliant but blissfully aimless, improvising their own spontaneous paths through the world. And best of all, they were free. Truly, completely free, in a world that increasingly opposes that notion.

The people I met out there weren't perfect. It's tempting to imagine that the road is full of noble citizens of the earth, all strictly adhering to some alternative but deeply ethical philosophy. The reality is that the itinerant lifestyle attracts all types: doctors and drunks, soldiers and hippies, the devoutly religious and the unabashedly hedonistic. They were united by only one idea: the refusal to mindlessly adhere to societally imposed concepts of how to live life. They recognized, and rejected, the absurdity of things like being told to choose a lifelong career path when you're in your early twenties or limiting the act of exploration to corporate vacations. For all their flaws, I came to deeply respect that choice.

The lifestyle they, and now I, so passionately preach is not for everyone. Independent travel is a personal decision, unique to every person who makes the critical choice to explore a new place. For some, that means a weeklong trek up a mountain. For others, it's about wandering the world for years at a time, picking up seasonal jobs along the way. All are equally valid forms of exploration. It has become increasingly fashionable among the backpacking set to romanticize the act of travel at the expense of others, to deride anyone less adventurous as "conformist" and in doing so subtly imbue oneself with some kind of enlightenment. This is a comforting but false superiority; to judge others based on your own goals is reductive and foolish. Worse, it misses the point of *independent* travel entirely. The specifics of how a person chooses to explore the world are irrelevant, all that matters is having the autonomy and knowledge to make that choice for oneself.

I wrote this book because I suspect there are many people, my fellow Americans especially, who are as uninformed as I once was. People perhaps unhappy in their work or unsure of what they want from life or simply curious about the world, who are completely unaware of how accessible independent travel is. So many daydream about travel but consider it vaguely implausible, like some unrealistic hobby that they are inexplicably not lucky enough to be able to participate in. But there are roving bands of independent travelers of all different kinds out there, right now, staring at some horizon, wondering what's beyond it. The dream of this book is to encourage you in the idea that, if you so choose, you can be one of them.

Even after these few years on the road, I am not some expert traveler. I spend money foolishly, have no sense of direction, am terrible with languages, and have found myself in more calamitous circumstances of my own making than anyone I know. But being "good" at traveling is neither the point of this book nor the point of travel. There is a terrible, pervasive misconception that you need to be uniquely skilled (or prepared or wealthy or strong or brave) to explore the world. Nothing could be further from the truth—I am living proof of that fact. Even this very book, which is among the more cavalier in attitude currently on the market, errs wholly on the side of caution and is full of bits of advice for situations that you will hopefully never encounter. In short, you don't need this or any book to travel. Talking with locals and other travelers, not reading books or websites, will always be your most accurate and interesting source of information. This is meant simply as a small collection of notes, tips, and stories that might help you avoid some common pitfalls or keep you entertained on a long bus ride. Everything you truly need is already out there.

The world is a far safer place than most people give it credit for. There is money to be made in peddling fear, and that business is, and always will be, flourishing. Entire industries are built on the idea that something unknown is something fundamentally dangerous. And while there are unsafe places, to be sure, there is a much scarier fate to consider. If you give into the paranoia incited by those who promote terror and dread, you will voluntarily imprison yourself in your tiny corner of the world, cut off from countless amazing experiences. That outcome, not meeting some menacing thug in a dark alley, is the one you should fear. It is infinitely more common.

The best piece of advice I could ever hope to provide is, simply, "Go." The world has never been safer, easier, and cheaper to explore than it is right now. Be free, be curious, disappear, have an adventure. Once you start seeing things, you will realize just how much there is to see. Go seek your own treasures and you too will be joyfully overwhelmed by what you find.

—EVAN S. RICE
Baltimore, MD
2016

For all its material advantages, the sedentary life has left us edgy, unfulfilled. Even after 400 generations in villages and cities, we haven't forgotten. The open road still softly calls, like a nearly forgotten song of childhood. We invest far-off places with a certain romance. This appeal, I suspect, has been meticulously crafted by natural selection as an essential element in our survival. Long summers, mild winters, rich harvests, plentiful game—none of them lasts forever. It is beyond our ability to predict the future. Catastrophic events have a way of sneaking up on us, of catching us unaware. Your own life, or your band's, or even your species' might be owed to a restless few—drawn, by a craving they can hardly articulate or understand, to undiscovered lands and new worlds.

—CARL SAGAN
Pale Blue Dot, 1994

COUNTRIES OF THE WORLD

THERE IS NO official, universally agreed upon set of criteria or internationally accepted authority for determining what constitutes a "country." Some governments choose to recognize certain geographic regions as "countries," others do not, all for a host of complex historical and geopolitical reasons. There are principalities, commonwealths, colonies, dependencies, provinces, constituent countries, free-association states, municipalities, special administrative regions, overseas territories, tribal homelands, confederacies, unincorporated territories, and many more such ambiguously termed regions, all of which enjoy varying degrees of independence, none of which adhere to internationally consistent definitions. There are micronations, disputed territories, unrecognized states, breakaway republics, and seceding communities, each with constantly fluctuating levels of international recognition and support.

At the time of this writing, there are 206 National Olympic Committees, 209 FIFA member states, 234 country calling codes, 249 International Organization for Standardization country codes, 256 registered country Internet domains, and countless more official-sounding global listings of geographic regions—and hardly any of them agree on how many countries there are in the world.

For the purposes of this book, in an attempt to minimize confusion and remain as apolitical as possible, only the 193 United Nations member states and Vatican City will be considered "countries."

Any statistics, comparisons, reference listings, and infographics contained in the book are based on this number of countries unless otherwise noted.

Notes on Countries of the World (pages 2–17)

1 ››› For countries with multiple official currencies, only information concerning the most widely used currency is provided.

2 ››› Time zones listed in Coordinated Universal Time (UTC). Information provided only for mainland and nearby islands (<100 miles/161 kilometers) of country in question; see next page for time zones of officially designated dependencies and external territories. See page 223 for more information on time zones.

3 ››› Also known as Burma.

4 ››› Nauru does not have an official capital; government offices are located in Yaren District.

Key

* Administrative capital   ** Commercial capital   *** Judiciary capital   **** Legislative capital
• Seat of Government   " Some or all of the region observes Daylight Savings Time (DST)

COMMON NAME	OFFICIAL NAME	CAPITAL(S)	COUNTRY CODE
Afghanistan	Islamic Republic of Afghanistan	Kabul	93
Albania	Republic of Albania	Tirana	35
Algeria	People's Democratic Republic of Algeria	Algiers	21
Andorra	Principality of Andorra	Andorra la Vella	37
Angola	Republic of Angola	Luanda	24
Antigua and Barbuda	Antigua and Barbuda	Saint John's	1-26
Argentina	Argentine Republic	Buenos Aires	54
Armenia	Republic of Armenia	Yerevan	37
Australia	Commonwealth of Australia	Canberra	61
Austria	Republic of Austria	Vienna	43
Azerbaijan	Republic of Azerbaijan	Baku	99
Bahamas	Commonwealth of The Bahamas	Nassau	1-24
Bahrain	Kingdom of Bahrain	Manama	97
Bangladesh	People's Republic of Bangladesh	Dhaka	88
Barbados	Barbados	Bridgetown	1-24
Belarus	Republic of Belarus	Minsk	37
Belgium	Kingdom of Belgium	Brussels	32
Belize	Belize	Belmopan	50
Benin	Republic of Benin	Porto-Novo	22
Bhutan	Kingdom of Bhutan	Thimphu	97
Bolivia	Plurinational State of Bolivia	La Paz,* Sucre ***,****	59
Bosnia and Herzegovina	Bosnia and Herzegovina	Sarajevo	38
Botswana	Republic of Botswana	Gaborone	26
Brazil	Federative Republic of Brazil	Brasília	5
Brunei	Brunei Darussalam	Bandar Seri Begawan	67

OFFICIAL CURRENCY	CURRENCY SYMBOL[1]	TIME ZONE(S)[2]	VOLTAGE	OUTLET TYPE
Afghan afghani	AFN ؋	+04:30	220 V	C/F
Albanian lek	ALL Lek	+01:00 *	230 V	C/F
Algerian dinar	DZD دج	+01:00	230 V	C/F
Euro	EUR €	+01:00 *	230 V	C/F
Angolan kwanza	AOA Kz	+01:00	220 V	C
East Caribbean dollar	XCD $	−04:00	230 V	A/B
Argentine peso	ARS $	−03:00	220 V	I
Armenian dram	AMD դ	+04:00	230 V	C/F
Australian dollar	AUD $	+08:00 to +10:00 *	230 V	I
Euro	EUR €	+01:00 *	230 V	C/F
Azerbaijani manat	AZN ман	+04:00 *	220 V	C/F
Bahamian dollar	BSD $	−05:00 *	120 V	A/B
Bahraini dinar	BHD .د.ب	+03:00	230 V	G
Bangladeshi taka	BDT Tk	+06:00	220 V	A/C/D/ G/K
Barbadian dollar	BBD $	−04:00	115 V	A/B
New Belarusian ruble	BYN Br	+03:00	220 V	C/F
Euro	EUR €	+01:00 *	230 V	C/E
Belize dollar	BZD BZ$	−06:00	110 V/220 V	A/B/G
West African CFA franc	XOF CFA	+01:00	220 V	C/E
Bhutanese ngultrum	BTN Nu.	+05:30	230 V	C/D/G
Bolivian boliviano	BOB $b	−04:00	230 V	A/C
Bosnia and Herzegovina convertible mark	BAM KM	+01:00 *	230 V	C/F
Botswana pula	BWP P	+02:00	230 V	D/G
Brazilian real	BRL R$	−05:00 to −02:00 *	127 V/ 220 V	C/N
Brunei dollar	BND $	+08:00	240 V	G

ᵛᵛᵛ *continued* ᵛᵛᵛ

COMMON NAME	OFFICIAL NAME	CAPITAL(S)	COUNT CODE
Bulgaria	Republic of Bulgaria	Sofia	359
Burkina Faso	Burkina Faso	Ouagadougou	226
Burundi	Republic of Burundi	Bujumbura	257
Cabo Verde	Republic of Cabo Verde	Praia	238
Cambodia	Kingdom of Cambodia	Phnom Penh	855
Cameroon	Republic of Cameroon	Yaoundé	237
Canada	Canada	Ottawa	1
Central African Republic	Central African Republic	Bangui	236
Chad	Republic of Chad	N'Djamena	235
Chile	Republic of Chile	Santiago	56
China	People's Republic of China	Beijing	86
Colombia	Republic of Colombia	Bogotá	57
Comoros	Union of the Comoros	Moroni	269
Congo, Republic of	Republic of the Congo	Brazzaville	242
Costa Rica	Republic of Costa Rica	San José	506
Côte d'Ivoire	Republic of Côte d'Ivoire	Yamoussoukro	225
Croatia	Republic of Croatia	Zagreb	385
Cuba	Republic of Cuba	Havana	53
Cyprus	Republic of Cyprus	Nicosia	357
Czechia	Czech Republic	Prague	420
Congo, Democratic Republic of	Democratic Republic of the Congo	Kinshasa	243
Denmark	Kingdom of Denmark	Copenhagen	45
Djibouti	Republic of Djibouti	Djibouti	253
Dominica	Commonwealth of Dominica	Roseau	1-76
Dominican Republic	Dominican Republic	Santo Domingo	1-80 1-82 1-84

OFFICIAL CURRENCY	CURRENCY SYMBOL[1]	TIME ZONE(S)[2]	VOLTAGE	OUTLET TYPE
Bulgarian lev	BGN лв	+02:00 *	230 V	C/F
West African CFA franc	XOF CFA	±0:00	220 V	C/E
Burundian franc	BIF FBu	+02:00	220 V	C/E
Cape Verdean escudo	CVE Esc	−0:100	230 V	C/F
Cambodian riel	KHR ៛	+07:00	230 V	A/C/G
Central African CFA franc	XAF FCFA	+01:00	220 V	C/E
Canadian dollar	CAD $	−08:00 to −03:30 *	120 V	A/B
Central African CFA franc	XAF FCFA	+01:00	220 V	C/E
Central African CFA franc	XAF FCFA	+01:00	220 V	C/D/E/F
Chilean peso	CLP $	−05:00	220 V	C/L
Chinese renminbi (yuan)	CNY ¥	+08:00	220 V	A/C/I
Colombian peso	COP $	−05:00	110 V	A/B
Comorian franc	KMF KMF	+03:00	220 V	C/E
Central African CFA franc	XAF FCFA	+01:00	230 V	C/E
Costa Rican colón	CRC ₡	−06:00	120 V	A/B
West African CFA franc	XOF CFA	±0:00	220 V	C/E
Croatian kuna	HRK kn	+01:00 *	230 V	C/F
Cuban peso	CUP ₱	−03:00 *	110 V/220 V	A/B/C/L
Euro	EUR €	+02:00 *	230 V	G
Czech koruna	CZK Kč	+01:00 *	230 V	C/E
Congolese franc	CDF FC	+01:00, +02:00	220 V	C/D/E
Danish krone	DKK kr	+01:00 *	230 V	C/E/F/K
Djiboutian franc	DJF Fdj	+03:00	220 V	C/E
East Caribbean dollar	XCD $	−04:00	230 V	D/G
Dominican peso	DOP RD$	−04:00	120 V	A/B/C

∨∨∨ continued ∨∨∨

COMMON NAME	OFFICIAL NAME	CAPITAL(S)	COUN COD
Ecuador	Republic of Ecuador	Quito	593
Egypt	Arab Republic of Egypt	Cairo	20
El Salvador	Republic of El Salvador	San Salvador	503
Equatorial Guinea	Republic of Equatorial Guinea	Malabo	240
Eritrea	State of Eritrea	Asmara	29
Estonia	Republic of Estonia	Tallinn	372
Ethiopia	Federal Democratic Republic of Ethiopia	Addis Ababa	25
Fiji	Republic of Fiji	Suva	679
Finland	Republic of Finland	Helsinki	35
France	French Republic	Paris	33
Gabon	Gabonese Republic	Libreville	24
Gambia	Republic of The Gambia	Banjul	220
Georgia	Georgia	Tbilisi	99
Germany	Federal Republic of Germany	Berlin	49
Ghana	Republic of Ghana	Accra	23
Greece	Hellenic Republic	Athens	30
Grenada	Grenada	Saint George's	1-47
Guatemala	Republic of Guatemala	Guatemala City	50
Guinea	Republic of Guinea	Conakry	22
Guinea-Bissau	Republic of Guinea-Bissau	Bissau	24
Guyana	Co-operative Republic of Guyana	Georgetown	59
Haiti	Republic of Haiti	Port-au-Prince	50
Honduras	Republic of Honduras	Tegucigalpa	50
Hungary	Hungary	Budapest	36
Iceland	Republic of Iceland	Reykjavík	35
India	Republic of India	New Delhi	91

OFFICIAL CURRENCY	CURRENCY SYMBOL[1]	TIME ZONE(S)[2]	VOLTAGE	OUTLET TYPE
United States dollar	USD $	−05:00	120 V	A/B
Egyptian pound	EGP £	+02:00	220 V	C/F
United States dollar	USD $	−06:00	120 V	A/B
Central African CFA franc	XAF FCFA	+01:00	220 V	C/E
Eritrean nakfa	ERN ናቕፋ	+03:00	230 V	C/L
Euro	EUR €	+03:00 *	230 V	C/F
Ethiopian birr	ETB Br	+03:00	220 V	C/F
Fijian dollar	FJD $	+12:00	240 V	I
Euro	EUR €	+02:00 *	230 V	C/F
Euro	EUR €	+01:00 *	230 V	C/E
Central African CFA franc	XAF FCFA	+01:00	220 V	C
Gambian dalasi	GMD D	± 0:00	230 V	G
Georgian lari	GEL GEL	+04:00	220 V	C/F
Euro	EUR €	+01:00 *	230 V	C/F
Ghanaian cedi	GHS ¢	± 0:00	230 V	D/G
Euro	EUR €	+02:00 *	230 V	C/F
East Caribbean dollar	XCD $	−04:00	230 V	G
Guatemalan quetzal	GTQ Q	−06:00	120 V	A/B
Guinean franc	GNF FG	± 0:00	220 V	C/F/K
West African CFA franc	XOF CFA	± 0:00	220 V	C
Guyanese dollar	GYD $	−03:00	120/240 V	A/B/ D/G
Haitian gourde	HTG G	−05:00 *	110 V	A/B
Honduran lempira	HNL L	−06:00	120 V	A/B
Hungarian forint	HUF Ft	+01:00 *	230 V	C/F
Icelandic króna	ISK kr	± 0:00	230 V	C/F
Indian rupee	INR ₹	+05:30	230 V	C/D/M

vvv continued vvv

COMMON NAME	OFFICIAL NAME	CAPITAL(S)	COU CO
Indonesia	Republic of Indonesia	Jakarta	6
Iran	Islamic Republic of Iran	Tehran	9
Iraq	Republic of Iraq	Baghdad	9(
Ireland	Ireland	Dublin	35
Israel	State of Israel	Jerusalem	97
Italy	Italian Republic	Rome	3
Jamaica	Jamaica	Kingston	1-8
Japan	Japan	Tokyo	8
Jordan	Hashemite Kingdom of Jordan	Amman	9(
Kazakhstan	Republic of Kazakhstan	Astana	7
Kenya	Republic of Kenya	Nairobi	25
Kiribati	Republic of Kiribati	Tarawa	6(
Kuwait	State of Kuwait	Kuwait City	9(
Kyrgyzstan	Kyrgyz Republic	Bishkek	9(
Laos	Lao People's Democratic Republic	Vientiane	85
Latvia	Republic of Latvia	Riga	3
Lebanon	Lebanese Republic	Beirut	9(
Lesotho	Kingdom of Lesotho	Maseru	2(
Liberia	Republic of Liberia	Monrovia	2
Libya	State of Libya	Tripoli	2
Liechtenstein	Principality of Liechtenstein	Vaduz	4
Lithuania	Republic of Lithuania	Vilnius	3
Luxembourg	Grand Duchy of Luxembourg	Luxembourg City	3
Macedonia	Republic of Macedonia	Skopje	3
Madagascar	Republic of Madagascar	Antananarivo	2

OFFICIAL CURRENCY	CURRENCY SYMBOL[1]	TIME ZONE(S)[2]	VOLTAGE	OUTLET TYPE
Indonesian rupiah	IDR Rp	+07:00 to +09:00	230 V	C/F
Iranian rial	IRR ﷼	+03:30 *	230 V	C/F
Iraqi dinar	IQD ع.د	+03:00	230 V	C/D/G
Euro	EUR €	± 0:00 *	230 V	G
Israeli new shekel	ILS ₪	+02:00 *	230 V	C/H
Euro	EUR €	+01:00 *	230 V	C/F/L
Jamaican dollar	JMD J$	−05:00	110 V	A/B
Japanese yen	JPY ¥	+09:00	100 V	A/B
Jordanian dinar	JOD JOD	+02:00 *	230 V	C/D/F/ G/J
Kazakhstani tenge	KZT ЛВ	+05:00, +06:00	220 V	C/F
Kenyan shilling	KES KSh	+03:00	240 V	G
Australian dollar	AUD $	+12:00 to +14:00	240 V	I
Kuwaiti dinar	KWD د.ك	+03:00	240 V	G
Kyrgyzstani som	KGS ЛВ	+06:00	220 V	C/F
Lao kip	LAK ₭	+07:00	230 V	A/B/C/ E/F
Euro	EUR €	+03:00 *	230 V	C/F
Lebanese pound	LBP £	+02:00 *	230 V	C/D/G
Lesotho loti	LSL L, M	+02:00	220 V	M
Liberian dollar	LRD $	± 0:00	120 V	A/B
Libyan dinar	LYD LD, د.ل	+02:00	230 V	C/L
Swiss franc	CHF CHF	+01:00 *	230 V	C/J
Euro	EUR €	+02:00 *	230 V	C/F
Euro	EUR €	+01:00 *	230 V	C/F
Macedonian denar	MKD ден	+01:00 *	230 V	C/F
Malagasy ariary	MGA Ar	+03:00	220 V	C/E

∨∨∨ continued ∨∨∨

COMMON NAME	OFFICIAL NAME	CAPITAL(S)	COUNTRY CODE
Malawi	Republic of Malawi	Lilongwe	265
Malaysia	Malaysia	Kuala Lumpur	60
Maldives	Republic of Maldives	Malé	960
Mali	Republic of Mali	Bamako	223
Malta	Republic of Malta	Valletta	356
Marshall Islands	Republic of the Marshall Islands	Majuro	692
Mauritania	Islamic Republic of Mauritania	Nouakchott	222
Mauritius	Republic of Mauritius	Port Louis	230
Mexico	United Mexican States	Mexico City	52
Micronesia	Federated States of Micronesia	Palikir	691
Moldova	Republic of Moldova	Chişinău	373
Monaco	Principality of Monaco	Monaco	377
Mongolia	Mongolia	Ulaanbaatar	976
Montenegro	Montenegro	Podgorica	382
Morocco	Kingdom of Morocco	Rabat	212
Mozambique	Republic of Mozambique	Maputo	258
Myanmar[3]	Republic of the Union of Myanmar	Naypyidaw	95
Namibia	Republic of Namibia	Windhoek	264
Nauru	Republic of Nauru	Yaren District[4]	674
Nepal	Federal Democratic Republic of Nepal	Kathmandu	977
Netherlands	Kingdom of the Netherlands	Amsterdam, The Hague•	31
New Zealand	New Zealand	Wellington	64
Nicaragua	Republic of Nicaragua	Managua	505
Niger	Republic of Niger	Niamey	227

OFFICIAL CURRENCY	CURRENCY SYMBOL[1]	TIME ZONE(S)[2]	VOLTAGE	OUTLET TYPE
Malawian kwacha	MWK MK	+02:00	230 V	G
Malaysian ringgit	MYR RM	+08:00	240 V	G
Maldivian rufiyaa	MVR Rf	+05:00	230 V	C/D/G/ J/K/L
West African CFA franc	XOF CFA	± 0:00	220 V	C/E
Euro	EUR €	+01:00 *	230 V	G
United States dollar	USD $	+10:00	120 V	A/B
Mauritanian ouguiya	MRO UM	± 0:00	220 V	C
Mauritian rupee	MUR Rs	+04:00	230 V	C/G
Mexican peso	MXN $	−08:00 to −05:00 *	127 V	A/B
United States dollar	USD $	+10:00, +11:00	120 V	A/B
Moldovan leu	MDL MDL	+02:00 *	230 V	C/F
Euro	EUR €	+01:00 *	230 V	C/E/F
Mongolian tugrik	MNT ₮	+07:00, +08:00 *	230 V	C/E
Euro	EUR €	+01:00	230 V	C/F
Moroccan dirham	MAD د.م.	± 0:00 *	220 V	C/E
Mozambican metical	MZN MT	+02:00	220 V	C/F/M
Myanma kyat	MMK K	+06:30	230 V	A/C/D/ G/I
Namibian dollar	NAD $	+02:00 *	220 V	D/M
Australian dollar	AUD $	+12:00	240 V	I
Nepalese rupee	NPR Rs	+05:45	230 V	C/D/M
Euro	EUR €	+01:00 *	230 V	C/F
New Zealand dollar	NZD $	+12:00, +12:45 *	230 V	I
Nicaraguan córdoba	NIO C$	−06:00	120 V	A/B
West African CFA franc	XOF CFA	+01:00	220 V	C/D/ E/F

▾▾▾ continued ▾▾▾

COMMON NAME	OFFICIAL NAME	CAPITAL(S)	COUN CODE
Nigeria	Federal Republic of Nigeria	Abuja	234
North Korea	Democratic People's Republic of Korea	Pyongyang	850
Norway	Kingdom of Norway	Oslo	47
Oman	Sultanate of Oman	Muscat	968
Pakistan	Islamic Republic of Pakistan	Islamabad	92
Palau	Republic of Palau	Ngerulmud	680
Panama	Republic of Panama	Panama City	507
Papua New Guinea	Independent State of Papua New Guinea	Port Moresby	675
Paraguay	Republic of Paraguay	Asunción	59
Peru	Republic of Peru	Lima	51
Philippines	Republic of the Philippines	Manila	63
Poland	Republic of Poland	Warsaw	48
Portugal	Portuguese Republic	Lisbon	35
Qatar	State of Qatar	Doha	974
Romania	Romania	Bucharest	40
Russia	Russian Federation	Moscow	7
Rwanda	Republic of Rwanda	Kigali	250
Saint Kitts and Nevis	Federation of Saint Kitts and Nevis	Basseterre	1-869
Saint Lucia	Saint Lucia	Castries	1-758
Saint Vincent and the Grenadines	Saint Vincent and the Grenadines	Kingstown	1-784
Samoa	Independent State of Samoa	Apia	685
San Marino	Republic of San Marino	City of San Marino	37
Saõ Tomé and Príncipe	Democratic Republic of Saõ Tomé and Príncipe	São Tomé	23
Saudi Arabia	Kingdom of Saudi Arabia	Riyadh	966
Senegal	Republic of Senegal	Dakar	22

OFFICIAL CURRENCY	CURRENCY SYMBOL[1]	TIME ZONE(S)[2]	VOLTAGE	OUTLET TYPE
Nigerian naira	NGN ₦	+01:00	230 V	D/G
North Korean won	KPW ₩	+09:00	220 V	C
Norwegian krone	NOK kr	+01:00 *	230 V	C/F
Omani rial	OMR ريال	+04:00	240 V	G
Pakistani rupee	PKR Rs	+05:00	230 V	C/D
United States dollar	USD $	+09:00	120 V	A/B
United States dollar	USD $	−05:00	120 V	A/B
Papua New Guinean kina	PGK K	+10:00	240 V	I
Paraguayan guarani	PYG Gs	−04:00 *	220 V	C
Peruvian nuevo sol	PEN S/.	−05:00	220 V	A/C
Philippine peso	PHP ₱	+08:00	220 V	A/B/C
Polish złoty	PLN zł	+01:00 *	230 V	C/E
Euro	EUR €	± 0:00 *	230 V	C/F
Qatari riyal	QAR ريال	+03:00	240 V	G
Romanian leu	RON lei	+02:00 *	230 V	C/F
Russian ruble	RUB ₽	+02:00 to +12:00	220 V	C/F
Rwandan franc	RWF RF	+02:00	230 V	C/J
East Caribbean dollar	XCD $	−04:00	230 V	D/G
East Caribbean dollar	XCD $	−04:00	230 V	G
East Caribbean dollar	XCD $	−04:00	110 V/ 230 V	A/B/G
Samoan tala	WST WS$	−11:00 *	230 V	I
Euro	EUR €	+01:00 *	230 V	C/F/L
Saõ Tomé and Príncipe dobra	STD Db	± 0:00	230 V	C/F
Saudi riyal	SAR ريال	+03:00	230 V	G
West African CFA franc	XOF CFA	± 0:00	230 V	C/D/ E/K

ᵛᵛᵛ *continued* ᵛᵛᵛ

COMMON NAME	OFFICIAL NAME	CAPITAL(S)	COUN CO
Serbia	Republic of Serbia	Belgrade	38
Seychelles	Republic of Seychelles	Victoria	24
Sierra Leone	Republic of Sierra Leone	Freetown	23
Singapore	Republic of Singapore	Singapore	6
Slovakia	Slovak Republic	Bratislava	42
Slovenia	Republic of Slovenia	Ljubljana	38
Solomon Islands	Solomon Islands	Honiara	67
Somalia	Federal Republic of Somalia	Mogadishu	25
South Africa	Republic of South Africa	Pretoria,* Bloemfontein,*** Cape Town****	2
South Korea	Republic of Korea	Seoul	8
South Sudan	Republic of South Sudan	Juba	21
Spain	Kingdom of Spain	Madrid	3
Sri Lanka	Democratic Socialist Republic of Sri Lanka	Colombo,** Sri Jayewardenep-ura Kotte****	9
Sudan	Republic of the Sudan	Khartoum	24
Suriname	Republic of Suriname	Paramaribo	59
Swaziland	Kingdom of Swaziland	Mbabane,* Lobamba***	26
Sweden	Kingdom of Sweden	Stockholm	4
Switzerland	Swiss Confederation	Bern	4
Syria	Syrian Arab Republic	Damascus	96
Tajikistan	Republic of Tajikistan	Dushanbe	99
Tanzania	United Republic of Tanzania	Dar es Salaam, Dodoma****	25
Thailand	Kingdom of Thailand	Bangkok	6
Timor-Leste	Democratic Republic of Timor-Leste	Dili	67
Togo	Togolese Republic	Lomé	22

OFFICIAL CURRENCY	CURRENCY SYMBOL[1]	TIME ZONE(S)[2]	VOLTAGE	OUTLET TYPE
Serbian dinar	RSD Дин.	+01:00*	230 V	C/F
Seychellois rupee	SCR Rs	+04:00	240 V	G
Sierra Leonean leone	SLL Le	±0:00	230 V	D/G
Singapore dollar	SGD $	+08:00	230 V	G
Euro	EUR €	+01:00*	230 V	C/E
Euro	EUR €	+01:00*	230 V	C/F
Solomon Islands dollar	SBD $	+11:00	230 V	G/I
Somali shilling	SOS S	+03:00	220 V	C
South African rand	ZAR R	+02:00	230 V	C/D/ M/N
South Korean won	KRW ₩	+09:00	220 V	C/F
South Sudanese pound	SSP £	+03:00	230 V	C/D
Euro	EUR €	+01:00*	230 V	C/F
Sri Lankan rupee	LKR Rs	+05:30	230 V	D/G
Sudanese pound	SDG SDG	+02:00	230 V	C/D
Surinamese dollar	SRD $	−03:30	127 V/ 230 V	A/B/ C/F
Swazi lilangeni	SZL SZL	+02:00	230 V	M
Swedish krona	SEK kr	+01:00*	230 V	C/F
Swiss franc	CHF CHF	+01:00*	230 V	C/J
Syrian pound	SYP £	+02:00*	220 V	C/E/L
Tajikistani somoni	TJS TJS	+06:00	220 V	C/F
Tanzanian shilling	TZS TSh	+03:00	230 V	D/G
Thai baht	THB ฿	+07:00	220 V	A/B/ C/O
United States dollar	USD $	+09:00	220 V	C/E/F/I
West African CFA franc	XOF CFA	±0:00	220 V	C

ᵛᵛᵛ continued ᵛᵛᵛ

COMMON NAME	OFFICIAL NAME	CAPITAL(S)	COUN COD
Tonga	Kingdom of Tonga	Nuku'alofa	676
Trinidad and Tobago	Republic of Trinidad and Tobago	Port of Spain	1-86
Tunisia	Republic of Tunisia	Tunis	216
Turkey	Republic of Turkey	Ankara	90
Turkmenistan	Turkmenistan	Ashgabat	993
Tuvalu	Tuvalu	Funafuti	688
Uganda	Republic of Uganda	Kampala	256
Ukraine	Ukraine	Kiev	380
United Arab Emirates	United Arab Emirates	Abu Dhabi	97
United Kingdom	United Kingdom of Great Britain and Northern Ireland	London	44
United States of America	United States of America	Washington, DC	1
Uruguay	Oriental Republic of Uruguay	Montevideo	59
Uzbekistan	Republic of Uzbekistan	Tashkent	99
Vanuatu	Republic of Vanuatu	Port Vila	67
Vatican City	Vatican City State	Vatican City	39
Venezuela	Bolivarian Republic of Venezuela	Caracas	58
Vietnam	Socialist Republic of Vietnam	Hanoi	84
Yemen	Republic of Yemen	Sanaa	96
Zambia	Republic of Zambia	Lusaka	26
Zimbabwe	Republic of Zimbabwe	Harare	26

OTHER

The following is a list of independent states that have defined territories, functioning governments, and permanent populations but that are neither member states of the United Nations nor globally recognized as countries. Though some maintain significant international support, the political status and control of these areas remains heavily disputed. Only states that have been officially recognized by at least one UN member state are included.

OFFICIAL CURRENCY	CURRENCY SYMBOL[1]	TIME ZONE(S)[2]	VOLTAGE	OUTLET TYPE
Tongan pa'anga	TOP T$	+13:00	240 V	I
Trinidad and Tobago dollar	TTD TT$	−04:00	115 V	A/B
Tunisian dinar	TND د.ت	+01:00	230 V	C/E
Turkish lira	TRY ₺	+02:00 "	230 V	C/F
Turkmenistani new manat	TMT m	+05:00	220 V	C/F
Australian dollar	AUD $	+12:00	230 V	I
Ugandan shilling	UGX USh	+03:00	240 V	G
Ukrainian hryvnia	UAH ₴	+03:00 "	230 V	C/F
UAE dirham	AED د.إ	+04:00	230 V	G
Great Britain pound (sterling)	GBP £	±0:00 "	230 V	G
United States dollar	USD $	−05:00 to −10:00 "	120 V	A/B
Uruguayan peso	UYU $U	−03:00 "	220 V	C/F/L
Uzbekistani som	UZS лв	+06:00	220 V	C/F
Vanuatu vatu	VUV Vt	+11:00	230 V	I
Euro	EUR €	+01:00 "	230 V	C/F/L
Venezuelan bolívar	VEF Bs	−04:00	120 V	A/B
Vietnamese dong	VND ₫	+07:00	220 V	A/C/D
Yemeni rial	YER ريال	+03:00	230 V	A/D/G
Zambian kwacha	ZMW ZK	+02:00	230 V	C/D/G
United States dollar	USD $	+02:00	240 V	D/G

Notes on Other States (pages 18–19)

1 ››› For countries with multiple official currencies, only information concerning the most widely used currency is provided.

2 ››› Time zones listed in Coordinated Universal Time (UTC).

Key

" Some or all of the region observes Daylight Savings Time (DST)

ᵛᵛᵛ continued ᵛᵛᵛ

COMMON NAME	OFFICIAL NAME	CAPITAL(S) or ADMINISTRATIVE CENTER	COUN COD
Palestinian Territories	Palestinian Territories	East Jerusalem	970
Kosovo	Republic of Kosovo	Pristina	383
Sahrawi Arab Democratic Republic	Sahrawi Arab Democratic Republic	Laayoune	212
Taiwan	Republic of China	Taipei	886
Abkhazia	Republic of Abkhazia	Sukhumi	840
South Ossetia	Republic of South Ossetia	Tskhinvali	995
Northern Cyprus	Turkish Republic of Northern Cyprus	North Nicosia	90

ASSOCIATED TERRITORIES

The following is a list of territories that are in some way associated with a specific country and therefore not considered to be fully independent states. It is important to note that these areas, many of which are relatively small islands, operate under wide-ranging levels of autonomy. Some are entirely controlled by their associated countries and essentially function as distant nationalized communities while others are completely separate, self-governing societies that maintain only basic economic relations with a larger nearby country.

COMMON NAME	OFFICIAL NAME	SOVEREIGNTY, ADMINISTRATION, or ASSOCIATION	CAPITAL(S) ADMINISTRA CENTER
Akrotiri and Dhekelia	Sovereign Base Areas of Akrotiri and Dhekelia	United Kingdom	Episkop Cantonme
American Samoa	Territory of American Samoa	United States	Pago Pag
Anguilla	Anguilla	United Kingdom	The Valle
Aruba	Aruba	Netherlands	Oranjesta
Ashmore and Cartier Islands	Territory of Ashmore and Cartier Islands	Australia	Canberr
Bermuda	Bermuda	United Kingdom	Hamilto
Bonaire	Bonaire	Netherlands	Kralendi
Bouvet Island	Bouvet Island	Norway	Oslo
British Indian Ocean Territory	British Indian Ocean Territory	United Kingdom	London

UN RECOGNITION	OFFICIAL CURRENCY[1]	CURRENCY SYMBOL	VOLTAGE	OUTLET TYPE	TIME ZONE(S)[2]
136	Israeli new sheqel	ILS ₪	230 V	C/H	+02:00 "
110	Euro	EUR €	230 V	C/F	+01:00 "
47	Sahrawi peseta	EHP Pts	230 V	C/F	±0:00
20	New Taiwan dollar	TWD NT$	110 V	A/B	+08:00
4	Russian ruble	RUB ₽	220 V	C/F	+03:00
4	Russian ruble	RUB ₽	220 V	C/F	+03:00
1	Turkish lira	TRY ₺	230 V	G	+02:00 "

Notes on Associates Territories (pages 18–23)

1 ››› For territories with multiple official currencies, only information concerning the most widely used currency is provided.

2 ››› Time zones listed in Coordinated Universal Time (UTC).

3 ››› The three atolls of Tokelau—Atafu, Nukunonu, and Fakaofo—each maintain its own administrative center.

Key

" Some or all of the region observes Daylight Savings Time (DST)

COUNTRY CODE	OFFICIAL CURRENCY[1]	CURRENCY SYMBOL	VOLTAGE	OUTLET TYPE	TIME ZONE(S)[2]
357	Euro	EUR €	230 V	G	+02:00 "
1-684	United States dollar	USD $	120 V	A/B/F/I	–11:00
1-264	East Caribbean dollar	XCD $	110V	A/B	–04:00
297	Aruban florin	AWG ƒ	120 V	A/B/F	–04:00
No permanent population					+08:00
1-441	Bermudian dollar	BMD $	120 V	A/B	–04:00 "
599	United States dollar	USD $	127 V	A/C	–04:00
No permanent population					+1:00
246	United States dollar	USD $	230V	G	+06:00

✓✓✓ continued ✓✓✓

COMMON NAME	OFFICIAL NAME	SOVEREIGNTY, ADMINISTRATION, or ASSOCIATION	CAPITAL(S) or ADMINISTRATIVE CENTER
British Virgin Islands	British Virgin Islands	United Kingdom	Road Town
Cayman Islands	Cayman Islands	United Kingdom	George Town
Christmas Island	Territory of Christmas Island	Australia	Flying Fish Cove
Clipperton Island	Clipperton Island	France	Paris
Cocos (Keeling) Islands	Territory of Cocos (Keeling) Islands	Australia	West Island
Cook Islands	Cook Islands	New Zealand	Avarua
Coral Sea Islands	Coral Sea Islands Territory	Australia	Canberra
Curaçao	Curaçao	Netherlands	Willemstad
Falkland Islands (Islas Malvinas)	Falkland Islands (Islas Malvinas)	United Kingdom	Stanley
Faroe Islands	Faroe Islands	Denmark	Tórshavn
French Guiana	French Guiana	France	Cayenne
French Polynesia	Territory of French Polynesia	France	Papeete
French Southern and Antarctic Lands	Territory of the French Southern and Antarctic Lands	France	Paris
Gibraltar	Gibraltar	United Kingdom	Gibraltar
Greenland	Greenland	Denmark	Nuuk
Guadeloupe	Department of Guadeloupe	France	Basse-Terre
Guam	Territory of Guam	United States	Hagåtña
Guernsey	Bailiwick of Guernsey	United Kingdom	Saint Peter Port
Heard Island and McDonald Islands	Territory of Heard Island and McDonald Islands	Australia	Canberra
Hong Kong	Hong Kong Special Administrative Region of the People's Republic of China	China	Hong Kong
Isle of Man	Isle of Man	United Kingdom	Douglas
Jan Mayen	Jan Mayen	Norway	Oslo
Jersey	Bailiwick of Jersey	United Kingdom	Saint Helier
Macau	Macau Special Administrative Region	China	Macau

COUNTRY CODE	OFFICIAL CURRENCY[1]	CURRENCY SYMBOL	VOLTAGE	OUTLET TYPE	TIME ZONE(S)[2]
1-284	United States dollar	USD $	110V	A/B	−04:00
1-345	Cayman Islands dollar	KYD $	120 V	A/B	−05:00
61	Australian dollar	AUD $	230 V	I	+07:00
No permanent population					−08:00
61	Australian dollar	AUD $	230 V	I	+06:30
682	New Zealand dollar	NZD $	240 V	I	−10:00
No permanent population					+10:00
599	Netherlands Antillean guilder	ANG ƒ	127 V	A/B	−04:00
500	Falkland Islands pound	FKP £	240 V	G	−03:00
298	Faroese króna	DKK kr	230 V	C/E/F/K	± 0:00 *
594	Euro	EUR €	220 V	C/D/E	−03:00
689	Central Pacific franc	XPF F	220 V	A/B/C/E	−9:00 to −10:00
No permanent population					+04:00, +05:00
350	Gibraltar pound	GIP £	230 V	C/G	+01:00 *
299	Danish krone	DKK kr	230 V	C/E/F/K	± 0:00 to +04:00*
590	Euro	EUR €	230 V	C/E	−04:00
1-671	United States dollar	USD $	110V	A/B	+10:00
44	Guernsey pound	GBP £	230 V	C/G	± 0:00 *
No permanent population					+05:00
852	Hong Kong dollar	HKD HK$	220 V	G	+08:00
44	Isle of Man pound	GBP £	230 V	C/G	± 0:00 *
47	Norwegian krone	NOK kr	220 V	C/E/F/V	+1:00 *
44	Pound sterling	GBP £	230 V	C/G	± 0:00 *
853	Macanese pataca	MOP MOP$	220 V	G	+08:00

ᐯᐯᐯ *continued* ᐯᐯᐯ

COMMON NAME	OFFICIAL NAME	SOVEREIGNTY, ADMINISTRATION, or ASSOCIATION	CAPITAL(S) ADMINISTRATION CENTER
Martinique	Department of Martinique	France	Fort-de-Fra...
Mayotte	Department of Mayotte	France	Mamoudz...
Montserrat	Montserrat	United Kingdom	Plymouth
New Caledonia	Territory of New Caledonia and Dependencies	France	Nouméa
Niue	Niue	New Zealand	Alofi
Norfolk Island	Territory of Norfolk Island	Australia	Kingston
Northern Mariana Islands	Commonwealth of the Northern Mariana Islands	United States	Saipan
Pitcairn Islands	Pitcairn, Henderson, Ducie, and Oeno Islands	United Kingdom	Adamstow...
Puerto Rico	Commonwealth of Puerto Rico	United States	San Juar...
Réunion	Department of Reunion	France	Saint-Den...
Saba	Saba	Netherlands	The Botto...
Saint Barthelemy	Saint Barthelemy	France	Gustavia
Saint Helena	Saint Helena, Ascension, and Tristan da Cunha	United Kingdom	Jamestow...
Saint Martin	Collectivity of Saint Martin	France	Marigot
Saint Pierre and Miquelon	Territorial Collectivity of Saint Pierre and Miquelon	France	Saint-Pier...
Sint Eustatius	Sint Eustatius	Netherlands	Oranjesta...
Sint Maarten	Sint Maarten	Netherlands	Philipsbu...
South Georgia and the South Sandwich Islands	South Georgia and the South Sandwich Islands	United Kingdom	King Edwa... Point
Svalbard	Svalbard	Norway	Longyearby...
Tokelau	Tokelau	New Zealand	Multiple
Turks and Caicos Islands	Turks and Caicos Islands	United Kingdom	Cockbur... Town
U.S. Minor Outlying Islands	United States Minor Outlying Islands	United States	Washingto... DC
U.S. Virgin Islands	Virgin Islands of the United States	United States	Charlott... Amalie
Wallis and Futuna	Territory of the Wallis and Futuna Islands	France	Matā'ut...

COUNTRY CODE	OFFICIAL CURRENCY[1]	CURRENCY SYMBOL	VOLTAGE	OUTLET TYPE	TIME ZONE(S)[2]
596	Euro	EUR €	220 V	C/D/E	−04:00
262	Euro	EUR €	230 V	C/E	+03:00
1-664	East Caribbean dollar	XCD $	230 V	A/B	−04:00
687	Central Pacific franc	XPF F	220 V	C/F	+11:00
683	New Zealand dollar	NZD $	230 V	I	−11:00
672	Australian dollar	AUD $	230 V	I	+11:30
1-670	United States dollar	USD $	120 V	A/B	+10:00
64	New Zealand dollar	NZD $	230 V	I	−08:00
1-787, 1-939	United States dollar	USD $	120 V	A/B	−04:00
262	Euro	EUR €	230 V	C/E	+04:00
599	United States dollar	USD $	110 V	A/B	−04:00
590	Euro	EUR €	220 V	C/E	−04:00
290, 247	Saint Helena pound	SHP £	230 V	G	±0:00
590	Euro	EUR €	220 V	C/E	−4:00
508	Euro	EUR €	220 V	E	−03:00 "
599	United States dollar	USD $	110/220 V	A/B/C/F	−04:00
1-721	Netherlands Antillean guilder	ANG ƒ	110 V	A/B	−04:00
No permanent population					−02:00
47	Norwegian krone	NOK kr	220 V	C/E/F/V	+1:00 "
690	New Zealand dollar	NZD $	230 V	I	+13:00
1-649	United States dollar	USD $	120 V	A/B	−04:00
No permanent population					+12:00 to −05:00
1-340	United States dollar	USD $	110V	A/B	−04:00
681	Central Pacific franc	XPF F	220 V	C/E	+12:00

BRING A SNACK

Never journey without something to eat in your pocket,
if only to throw to the dogs when attacked.

—E. S. BATES,
Touring in 1600, 1912

IN DEVELOPED COUNTRIES, thanks to the advent of delivery services and perpetually open convenience stores, some sort of food is almost always available to those willing to pay for it. It is important to note that this is not the case in the rest of the world. Shops and restaurants in foreign countries may have wildly different hours of operation, may be unexpectedly closed for religious or cultural reasons, or just may be far less accessible than what most travelers are used to. For this reason, it is good practice to always have a reserve stash of nonperishable food hidden deep in your bag, wrapped in plastic to avoid detection by animals or insects. These backup snacks will come in handy when you arrive in some small, distant town late at night and find every single shop closed.

TRAVELIN' BAND

METALLICA BECAME THE first band in history to perform on all seven continents after playing a show at Carlini Base in Antarctica in December 2013. To prevent sound waves from damaging the fragile environment, the show, called Freeze 'Em All, was played without the use of speakers. Instead the sound was transmitted to the 120-person audience via wireless headphones.

A GOLDEN TICKET

It soon became apparent that the public was smarter than we were.

—ROBERT CRANDALL,

Former American Airlines president and chairman, on AAirpass, an unlimited airline ticket American Airlines began selling in 1981 for $250,000. Customer Steve Rothstein purchased an AAirpass in 1987 and is estimated to have flown 10,000 flights, earned 40 million frequent flier miles, and cost the company $21 million dollars.

AN UNEXPECTED ARRIVAL

Are you from the sun or the moon?

—First words said to Arctic explorers Sirs John Ross and William Parry, through an interpreter named John Sacheuse, by a group of Inuit people living near Baffin Bay in 1818 in what is now Greenland, who were under the impression that they were the only people on earth.

ISLAND[3]

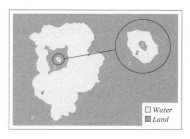

1   *Vulcan Point*
2   *Main Crater Lake*
3   *Taal Volcano Island*
4   *Taal Lake*
5   *Luzon Island*

☐ Water
■ Land

Vulcan Point in the Philippines is

	an island	on a lake	on an island	on a lake	on an island.
	Vulcan Point	*Main Crater Lake*	*Taal Volcano Island*	*Taal Lake*	*Luzon Island*
14°0′33.6″ N, 120°59′46.0″ E	4,556 yd²	.45 mi²	8.8 mi²	90.4 mi²	40,420 mi²
	3,809 m²	1.17 km²	22.8 km²	234.2 km²	104,687 km²

A larger island on a lake on an island on a lake on an island was recently discovered using satellite technology at 69°47′34.8″ N, 108°14′27.6″ W in northern Canada. The area is so remote however that neither the island itself, nor the surrounding lake, nor the larger surrounding island, nor the even larger surrounding lake, has a widely recognized name. All of these unnamed lakes and islands are located on Victoria Island, which is also referred to by its traditional Inuit name of Kitlineq. The smallest island is roughly four acres (1.6 hectares) in area and has probably never been visited by humans.

A COMMUNICATION MILESTONE

IN OCTOBER 1910, six men and a cat named Kiddo attempted to cross the Atlantic Ocean in an airship. They were led by aeronaut Walter Wellman and their ship was the *America*, which was essentially a gondola attached to a massive balloon filled with hydrogen. It was the first of its kind to carry a wireless radio set.

After launching from Atlantic City, Kiddo, apparently unaccustomed to the wonders of flying, began frantically scratching and clawing at crew members. The ship was being followed by a motorboat full of reporters and the crew quickly concocted a plan in which they would lower down the terrified Kiddo in a canvas bag to the boat below them.

This prompted first engineer Melvin Vaniman to transmit a message—probably the first air-to-ground communication ever sent:[1]

"Roy come and get this goddam cat!"

But despite their best efforts, the seas were too rough to safely complete the transfer, and poor Kiddo was forced to stay aboard the *America*. He soon settled down though, and "began to behave himself fairly well," according to the crew.

Unfortunately, Wellman, Kiddo, and crew never actually made it to Europe. After three days and more than 1,300 miles (2,092 kilometers), they were forced to abandon their ship near Bermuda and take refuge in the lifeboat. The steamship *Trent* quickly picked them up and they returned to New York as celebrities, having set aerial distance records despite falling short of their goal. Kiddo—renamed Trent as a tribute to their rescuers—was given a gilded cage at popular department store Gimbels and lived out the rest of his days with Wellman's daughter Edith. He never flew again.

1 ››› Some historians believe that J. D. A. McCurdy sent the first air-to-ground transmission from a biplane near Long Island, New York, in August of 1910.

STRAP UP

WHEN TRAVELING IN unsafe areas, get in the routine of always sticking your arm or leg through a strap of your backpack whenever you're not wearing it to prevent theft.

THE OUTSIDERS

A NY TRAVELER WHO'S spent enough time in a sufficiently foreign place knows that sometimes your very identity can seem to undergo a sort of mutation. You are no longer yourself, you are *gringo* or *mzungu* or *farang* and you cannot escape being viewed in that context. There were many other *gringos* and *wazungu* and *farangs* before you; those words inevitably carry the weight of long histories.

Below is a collection of such words. It is by no means complete; there are hundreds more words in hundreds more strange languages, but all follow a similar progression. They begin as highly literal descriptions of what local people understood particular groups of strangers to be: gods, ghosts, fools, drunks, heathens, or simply peculiar people with oddly colored hair or skin. Then they evolve past their specific descriptive origins to include anyone meeting a far more general set of characteristics.

CAVEATS

Note that while some of these terms are essentially friendly greetings commonly directed at foreign visitors, others have become politically incorrect in certain contexts, and still others are sometimes considered offensive racial slurs. Almost all depend heavily on context and the intent of the speaker. Further, be aware that these are phonetic English spellings of foreign words and therefore spellings vary from source to source. Lastly, these are all old words; some are ancient. Many were in use for centuries before ever being written down. The subtleties of their meaning have changed over time and, as their use spread to new communities, many began to take on new, location-specific implications. The list below is intended to be a curated selection of current usage and meaning, not a comprehensive resource for definition or etymology.

TERM	PLACE, *LANGUAGE*, or **PEOPLE**	LITERAL MEANING	COLLOQUIAL MEANING
A dohk a	Taiwan	"Pointed nose"	White person
Ajam	*Arabic*	"One who is illiterate in language"	Stranger
Ajnabi	*Arabic*	"Stranger" or "Someone to avoid"	Foreigner
Ang Mo	*Hokkien*	"Red hair"	Foreigner
Barang	Cambodia	"Frank"	Westerner or foreigner

▾▾▾ *continued* ▾▾▾

TERM	PLACE, LANGUAGE, or PEOPLE	LITERAL MEANING	COLLOQUIAL MEANING
Blan	*Haitian Creole*	"White"	Foreigner
Bolillo	Mexico	"Bread"	White or pale-skinned person
Bule	Indonesia	"Albino"	White person
Cheechaco	Alaska	"Newcomer"	Outsider
Dim-dim	Trobriand Islands	"Someone very different"	White man
Falang	Laos	"Frank"	Westerner or foreigner
Farang	Thailand	"Frank"	Westerner or foreigner
Faranji	Ethiopia	"Frank"	Westerner or foreigner
Ferengi	Middle East	"Frank"	Westerner or foreigner
Gaijin	Japan	"Outside person"	Foreigner
Gharib	*Arabic*	"From the West"	Stranger
Gora	*Hindi*	"White"	White man
Gringo	*Spanish*	"Greek" (origin disputed)	White person or foreigner
Gubba	**Aboriginal Australians**	"Government man"	White person
Gweilo	*Cantonese*	"Ghost man"	Foreigner
Haole	Hawaii	"Breathless"	White people
I-matang	Kiribati	"Person from Matang"	Foreigner
Indlebe zikhayi langa	**Zulu**	"Those whose ears glow in the sun"	White people
Kabloonak	**Inuit**	"People with bushy eyebrows"	Non-Inuit
Kafir	*Arabic*	"Nonbeliever"	Outsider
Kaivalagi	Fiji	"From the land of foreigners"	White person
Laleo	*Korowai*	"Ghost-demons"	Outsiders
Lǎowài	*Mandarin*	"Always outsider"	Foreigner

TERM	PLACE, LANGUAGE, or **PEOPLE**	LITERAL MEANING	COLLOQUIAL MEANING
Mat Salleh	Malaysia	"Mad sailor"	White people
Mundele	Democratic Republic of Congo	"White"	White person
Murdele	West Africa	"Men from the sea"	White people
Mzungu	East Africa	"Aimless wanderer"	White person
Nasrani	*Arabic*	"Christian"	Foreigner
Obroni	Ghana	"A person from beyond the horizon"	Foreigner
Orang puteh	Malaysia	"White person"	White person
Oyibo	Nigeria	"Peeled skin"	White person
Pākehā	***Maori***	"White or pale in appearance"	Foreigner
Pālagi	Samoa	"From the sky"	Foreigner
Papa'a	*Cook Islands Maori*	"Four layers of clothing"	Foreigner
Pariwat	**Munduruku**	"Prey"	Outsiders
Poken	New Caledonia	"English spoken"	White people
Tây	Vietnam	"Westerner"	Foreigner
Toubab	Central and West Africa	"Doctor"	White person or traveler
Tuluk	***Eskimo***	"Englishman"	Foreigner
Umlungu	***Zulu***	"People who practice magic"	White people
Vazaha	Madagascar	"Person or thing not from Madagascar"	Foreigner
Vulagi	Fiji	"Sky spirit"	Visitor
Waegukin	South Korea	"Outside country person"	Foreigner
Wàiguórén	*Mandarin*	"Outlander"	Foreigner
Wasi'chus	**Lakota Indians**	"Takes the fat" or "greedy person"	White man
Yáng guǐzi	*Mandarin*	"Western devil"	Foreigner
Yurak siki	*Quechuan*	"White rear end"	White person

HOW TO ESCAPE A RIPTIDE

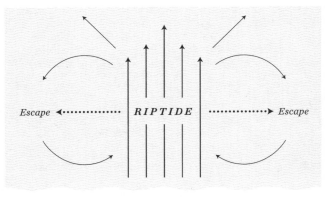

Escape ⬅················ *RIPTIDE* ················➡ *Escape*

Beach

"IT'S GREEK TO ME"

MANY SCHOLARS BELIEVE that the phrase "it's Greek to me" originated from European monks who were transcribing text in the Middle Ages. Very few of these scribes knew how to read Greek and therefore began to write the Latin phrase *Graecum est; non potest legi* ("It is Greek; it cannot be read") next to Greek words they encountered in the manuscripts they were translating. Referring to something indecipherable as "Greek" became commonplace and William Shakespeare incorporated this newly popular phrase into one of his plays.

> *Casca: . . . those that understood him smiled at one another and*
> *shook their heads; but, for mine own part, it was Greek to me.*
>
> —WILLIAM SHAKESPEARE,
> *The Tragedy of Julius Caesar*, 1599

But while Greek became the designated language of confusion in England, other countries chose their own descriptors of misunderstanding. Some cultures naturally gravitated toward the foreign language its people found the most alien, which is partially why *Chinese* is the most globally common substitute for *Greek* in the phrase. In other instances, the history between two nations played a part. Rhyme or cadence also often shaped the phrasing; certain words just sounded good together. Whatever the source of a particular idiom, the end result is a wonderful linguistic diversity of people describing misunderstanding by referencing a foreign language. Below is just a small sample of the incredible global variety of such expressions.

LANGUAGE	TRANSLATED PHRASE
Arabic	*"Are you speaking Hindi?"*
Bulgarian	*"You're speaking to me in Patagonian."*
Czech	*"This is like a Spanish village to me."*
Danish	*"That sounds like a town in Russia to me."*
Esperanto[1]	*"It's Volapük[1] to me."*
Finnish	*"It's all Hebrew to me."*
French	*"To me, it's Javanese."*
German	*"That seems like Spanish to me."*
Greek	*"This strikes me as Chinese."*
Italian	*"To me, this is Aramaic."*
Mandarin[2]	*"That sounds like bird language."*
Portuguese	*"You are speaking Latin."*
Turkish	*"I am French to this topic."*

1 ›› Constructed or "invented" languages.

2 ›› It's interesting to note that while Chinese is by far the most referenced language in these types of phrases, the Chinese languages themselves are some of the few on earth that don't specifically mention a foreign tongue. Along with "bird language" Mandarin speakers often refer to "heavenly language" and "ghost script"; native speakers of Cantonese commonly call text that they don't understand "chicken intestines."

━━━━━◆━━━━━

DON'T BE THAT PERSON

A class of men who are exceedingly tiresome are those who, having traveled, talk of nothing but their adventures, the countries which they have seen or traversed, the dangers, whether real or fictitious, which they have encountered, repeating the same things [a] hundred times over.

— ST. JOHN BAPTIST DE LA SALLE,
French priest and Catholic saint, 1695

THE RED LIST

THE INTERNATIONAL UNION for Conservation of Nature is the global authority on issues of conservation. The organization publishes the IUCN Red List, the world's most comprehensive catalogue of the status of threatened species. Below are summary descriptions, current number of species, and examples of each category throughout the world.

EXTINCT (EX)

No known individuals remaining

....

855
SPECIES

Atlas Bear
* Elephant Bird
Golden Toad
Labrador Duck
Thylacine
Toolache Wallaby

EXTINCT IN THE WILD (EW)

Captive individuals survive, no free-living natural populations

....

68
SPECIES

Barbary Lion
Butterfly Splitfin
Catarina Pupfish
Hawaiian Crow
* Scimitar Oryx
Socorro Dove

CRITICALLY ENDANGERED (CR)

Faces an extremely high risk of extinction in the near future

....

5,107
SPECIES

* Axolotl
Brazilian Merganser
Chinese Alligator
Gharial
Kakapo
Vaquita

ENDANGERED (CR)

Faces a very high
risk of extinction in
the near future

....

7,602
SPECIES

Bonobo

Dhole

*Japanese Crane

Rothschild's
Giraffe

Takhi

Volcano Rabbit

VULNERABLE (VU)

Faces a high risk
of extinction in the
medium-term

....

11,219
SPECIES

Clouded Leopard

Dugong

Gaur

*Humboldt Penguin

Mountain Zebra

Takin

NEAR THREATENED (NT)

May be considered
threatened in
the future

....

5,323
SPECIES

Blue-billed Duck

Emperor Goose

Maned Wolf

*Narwhal

Reddish Egret

White Rhinoceros

LEAST CONCERN (LC)

No immediate
threat to the survival
of the species

....

39,053
SPECIES

Cougar

Grey Wolf

Meerkat

Milk Shark

Olive Baboon

*Scarlet Macaw

A TRAVEL CODE TO EMULATE

MORITZ THOMSEN HAS been called "the finest American writer you've never heard of." Born rich, he served in World War II and then slowly began to reject the millionaire lifestyle his family tried to push on him. After a failed stint as a pig farmer (he couldn't bring himself to actually slaughter the pigs), he joined the Peace Corps when he was 48 and was sent to Ecuador. He never looked back. He lived out his days there, making a few more (mostly failed) attempts at farming while writing books and articles. His 1969 memoir *Living Poor: A Peace Corps Chronicle* is widely considered one of the most accurate descriptions of what it's like to serve in the Peace Corps. His writing was praised for, above all else, its unflinching honesty about the realities of living in poverty. He died in Guayaquil in 1991.

These are some of the travel guidelines he followed, which any traveler would do well to emulate:

> *Dollar meals if I can find them; five dollar hotels, if they still exist.*
> *No guided tours, no visits to historical monuments, or old churches.*
> *No taxis, no mixed drinks in fancy bars. No hanging around places*
> *where English might be spoken.*
> —*The Saddest Pleasure: A Journey on Two Rivers, 1990*

LANGUAGE ABILITY

STANDARDIZED LANGUAGE PROFICIENCY levels allow educators and employers to precisely identify how well a person knows a given language. These types of standards can indicate general knowledge or how well a person speaks, listens, reads, or writes.

There is no global, or even national, agreement on how to standardize language proficiency. There are currently dozens of sets of general language standards, along with countless numbers of language-specific tests, certificates, degrees, and scales.

Below is a chart comparing some of the world's most widely used general language proficiency standards, along with brief descriptions and the estimated hours of instruction necessary to achieve each level.

The specifics of these levels, the estimated hours of instruction, and the relationships between the standards themselves vary slightly from source to source and are dependent upon the language in question.

	DESCRIPTION	HOURS	ACTFL[1]	ILR[2]	CEFR[3]
Beginner	Can understand and use familiar everyday expressions	—	Novice *Low/Mid/High*	0/0+	A1
	Can understand sentences and frequently used expressions	180–200	Intermediate *Low/Mid/High*	1	A2
Intermediate	Can deal with most situations likely to arise while traveling	350–400	Intermediate *High*	1+	B1
	Can understand the main ideas of complex text	500–600	Advanced *Low/Mid/High*	2/2+	B2
Advanced	Can use language flexibly and effectively for social, academic, and professional purposes	700–800	Superior	3/3+	C1
	Can express him/herself spontaneously, very fluently, and precisely	1,000–1,200	Distinguished	4/4+/5	C3

1 ››› **A**merican **C**ouncil on the **T**eaching of **F**oreign **L**anguages
   The most commonly used set of standards in American academia
2 ››› **I**nteragency **L**anguage **R**oundtable
   A set of standards developed and used by the US government
3 ››› **C**ommon **E**uropean **F**ramework of **R**eference for **L**anguages
   A widely used set of standards for the European languages

PERCEPTION IS REALITY

In this world there is always danger for those who are afraid of it.

— GEORGE BERNARD SHAW,

Irish playwright

THE TRAVEL BUG

fern·weh (FEIRN-veyh) *German*

noun. Literally "far-sickness," as in the opposite of homesickness. A longing for travel in unknown territories.

From the German *fern* ("far") and *weh* ("woe" or "sickness")

A German word whose closest English equivalent is probably wanderlust, *fernweh* is a condition familiar to any traveler sitting at home, staring at a map of some far-off land. *Fernweh* is the travel bug, the itchy feet, the inner desire to strike out into the world and find a totally foreign place. Danish author Hans Christian Andersen was a well-known sufferer of this affliction and explained the concept in an 1856 letter:

> *When the snow melts, the stork arrives, and the first steamships race off, then I feel the painful travel unrest.*

COUNTRY PRONUNCIATION GUIDE

COUNTRY	PRONUNCIATION
Bhutan	*boo-TAN*
Chile	*CHEE-leh*
Côte d'Ivoire	*COAT-dee-vwar*
Djibouti	*jih-BOOT-ee*
Eritrea	*air-ih-TREE-uh*
Gabon	*ga-BAHN*
Guinea-Bissau	*GIN-ee bih-SOU*
Kyrgyzstan	*keer-gih-STAN*
Laos	*Lous*
Lesotho	*luh-SOE-toe*
Liechtenstein	*LIHKT-en-shtine*
Maldives	*MALL-deevz*
Mauritania	*mawr-uh-TAY-nee-uh*
Mauritius	*mawr-RIH-shuhs*
Nauru	*nah-OO-roo*
Niger	*NY-jur*
Papua New Guinea	*PA-pyoo-uh noo GIH-nee*
Qatar	*KAH-tur*
Saint Kitts and Nevis	*NEE-vis*

```
Saint Lucia . . . . . . . . . . . . . . . . . . . . . . . . . . . . . . . . . . . . . . . . . . . LOO-shuh
Saõ Tomé and Príncipe . . . . . . . . . . . . . . . sou-too-MAY/PREEN-see-pee
Sri Lanka . . . . . . . . . . . . . . . . . . . . . . . . . . . . . . . . . . . . . . . sree-LAHNG-kuh
Seychelles . . . . . . . . . . . . . . . . . . . . . . . . . . . . . . . . . . . . . . . . . say-SHELL
Tajikistan . . . . . . . . . . . . . . . . . . . . . . . . . . . . . . . . . . . . . tah-jih-kih-STAN
Tanzania . . . . . . . . . . . . . . . . . . . . . . . . . . . . . . . . . . . . . tan-zuh-NEE-uh
Timor-Leste . . . . . . . . . . . . . . . . . . . . . . . . . . . . . . . . . TEE-moor LESS-tay
```

Pronunciation information from inogolo.com

THE MAD TRAVELER'S DISEASE

dro·mo·ma·nia (drom-o-MANE-ee-uh)

noun. A sudden uncontrollable impulse to wander or travel.
From the Greek *dromos* ("running") and *mania* ("insanity")

Also known as traveling fugue and mad traveler's disease, *dromomania* was a psychological disorder first diagnosed by French doctors in the late 19th century. Sufferers were said to be unable to resist abandoning their jobs, families, and homes in pursuit of new travel experiences, often giving little or no warning of their departure. Thankfully, *dromomania* is no longer recognized as a mental illness by the American Medical Association or any other prominent medical body.

WIDE OPEN SPACES

G REENLAND'S NORTHEAST Greenland National Park is larger than 164 countries. Its name in Greenlandic is *Kalaallit Nunaanni nuna eqqissisimatitaq* and it covers 375,291 square miles (971,999 square kilometers). The human population is now zero, down from a high of 40 in the mid-1980s.

Key

■ = Northeast Greenland National Park

OVERCHARGED

Base Fare x (Passenger Weight + Luggage Weight) = Ticket Price

—Pricing formula used by Samoa Air, the world's first and only airline to charge passengers by weight. The small-scale airline services ten destinations throughout Samoa and American Samoa, which have some of highest rates of obesity in the world.

A ROYAL MISUNDERSTANDING

FOR AN OUTSIDER, the relationship between a nation's public and its royal family can be difficult to understand. Many travelers hail from countries where royalty is either nonexistent or generally thought of as an inconsequential relic from a bygone era.

It is important for travelers to note, however, that the citizens of many countries genuinely adore their nation's monarchs. They sing their praises and pray for their health and paste their pictures everywhere. Some even believe royalty to be infallible or semi-divine. Admittedly, there are certain countries in which this type of allegiance is required by law and brutally enforced. But in many cases the affection of the public is surprisingly sincere. And in nations where such honest, fanatical devotion to royalty is common, citizens may be deeply offended if they perceive visitors acting in a disrespectful manner.

With this in mind, it's best to always be particularly conscientious of your actions when it comes to anything involving a country's monarchy (or government for that matter). It's not unheard of for travelers to receive harsh jail sentences for crimes as innocuous as spray-painting over billboards of royals. There have also been situations where Facebook pages and blog posts, meant as harmless jokes, have led to serious accusations of "insulting the monarchy." Even completely unintentional insults can have dire consequences. Royal faces often adorn a country's currency, for instance, and many people believe that currency should therefore be treated with a certain level of respect. Most travelers are unaware of this custom, leading to unexpectedly violent confrontations with offended locals when money is crumpled, dropped, or stepped on. In short, many travelers expect all cultures to be as indifferent toward royalty as their own. This is a mistaken assumption that can lead to heated misunderstandings.

KEEP IT CHEAP

I T ' S   B E S T   N O T to bring expensive flip-flops or sunglasses on long trips. These are two of the most commonly lost or stolen traveler items and cheap substitute pairs of both items are available almost everywhere. Bring too valuable a pair of either and you'll be stressed out every time you go for a swim. Leave the pricy stuff at home and you'll have one less thing to worry about.

THE LANGUAGE OF LANGUAGE

A person who speaks:		is		also known as a	
	one language		monolingual		monoglot
	one language and part of another		sesquilingual		–
	two languages		bilingual		diglot
	multiple languages		multilingual		polyglot

THE KIWIS

T HE   KIWI   IS a small flightless bird native to New Zealand. They grow to anywhere from 3 to 9 pounds (1.4 to 4.1 kilograms) in weight and hold the distinction for laying the largest eggs of any bird in relation to their size. They are semi-nocturnal and almost always mate for life.

In the late 19th century New Zealand military badges began to feature images of the bird and, during World War I, *kiwi* became an informal nickname for New Zealand soldiers. This, along with the international popularity of Kiwi shoe polish, led to the kiwi becoming a symbol of national pride, as well as a way to refer to anyone from New Zealand.

ROUGH RATE

250,000,000,000,000 Zimbabwean dollars = 1 US dollar

—"Exchange rate" offered by the Reserve Bank of Zimbabwe to citizens still holding reserves of Zimbabwean dollars in 2015, as part of the process to legally discontinue the currency. After shortsighted economic policies resulted in hyperinflation, the currency became essentially worthless. The country began regularly using American dollars and South African rand in 2009.

TRYING TRANSLATIONS

yo·ko me·shi (YO-ko MEH-she)   *Japanese*

noun. The stress that accompanies trying to speak a foreign language
From the Japanese *yoko* ("horizontal") and *meshi* ("cooked rice")

Anyone who has ever stammered in front of a bewildered local, trying desperately to string together a few intelligible words in a confusing foreign tongue, knows the feeling of *yoko meshi*. The literal translation of this Japanese phrase roughly equates to "a meal eaten sideways." This is a tongue-in-cheek reference to the fact that the Japanese writing system is traditionally written vertically, while most other writing systems are written horizontally.

PROOF OF ONWARD TRAVEL

T**HE OFFICIAL VISA** requirements of almost every country in the world include something about "proof of onward travel." While they're happy for travelers to come for a visit, most governments want assurances that these visitors will eventually move on to somewhere else. It's this same logic that motivates many nations to list minimum amounts of money each traveler should have. A traveler who suddenly doesn't have the resources to leave a place can result in significant expenses for a country. At worst, they might become unregistered alien citizens. Thus, most nations want to ensure that tourists will cross the border, spend all the money they're willing to spend, and promptly move on without incident.

Though this policy logically appeals to many governments, it clashes with the freewheeling philosophy of most independent travelers. For many, lacking a plan is a core commandment of their traveling religion and a country's visa application requiring such foresight is akin to blasphemy. Deciding how, when, and in which direction one might leave a country an entire month (or three) in advance is almost unthinkable. Who knows where you'll end up? Many would argue that not knowing is the very point of the whole experience.

Luckily, as prevalent as this restrictive proof of onward travel policy is, it's also one of the most rarely enforced visa requirements out there. Border guards are generally more concerned with things like illegal substances, visa fees, passport expiration dates, and vaccination requirements. This doesn't mean "onward ticket" issues never arise, but they are rare.

When these issues do come up, it's often because the border guard has a specific reason to demand proof of an onward ticket. For this reason, it's essential to be prepared and confident. The guard will likely ask how long you plan to stay in the country and where you're going next. Even if you are unsure about your plans, it's best to try to answer both questions quickly, as specifically as possible, and confidently.

"Twenty-two days, then I'm going to Namibia."
"Two weeks, and then I'm flying to Bangkok."
"I'll be leaving for Peru on the ninth, three weeks from today."

Note that these responses don't explicably state that you have a ticket, just that you have a potential plan. It's always best to only lie as much as you need to. You're not under oath and you weren't asked whether you had a ticket with you. Most guards will only want to see an actual ticket if you seem unsure. Don't give them any reason to think your plans aren't definite and they will likely wave you through.

It is possible however, that the issue will escalate. Some countries are simply stricter than others and some border crossings ask every single traveler to show proof of onward travel as standard practice. Furthermore, any given guard might be new, bored, curious, mean, or hoping to get bribed. Some things are out of your control and these are the official requirements after all. So, if you accidentally admit that you don't yet have a plan, or the guard senses that something is amiss and demands to see a ticket you don't actually possess, or you simply get unlucky for whatever reason, don't fret. All is not lost.

If a border guard is adamant about seeing physical proof of a ticket that you simply do not have, be calm, humble, and very apologetic.

⌄⌄⌄ *continued* ⌄⌄⌄

Explain that you're just a simple traveler and emphasize that you have absolutely no intention of staying in this great country that you've heard so many wonderful things about any longer than this kind border guard allows. Pull out a map, point to a different border, and offer a plan—even if a tentative one—for how and when you intend to leave the country in just a few short weeks. Present any itineraries or important-looking documents that you're carrying as evidence that you don't intend on becoming an illegal resident.

These strategies should get you through most borders. When it comes to dealing with this issue however, borders are actually often easier to navigate than the other enforcer of the proof of onward travel policy: airlines. It may seem odd that an airline would be so concerned with enforcing a country's entry requirements but they do so with good reason: if a passenger is denied entry into their destination country, they become the airline's responsibility. So, if a passenger flies from the United States to New Zealand and is denied entry because they don't have proof of onward travel, the airline has to pay for that passenger's flight back to the United States. Therefore, it's in the airline's best interest to be absolutely sure that every passenger will be allowed into their destination country. They are completely within their rights to deny you from getting on the plane if they aren't fully convinced you will meet a country's entry requirements.

IF ALL ELSE FAILS OR TO BE SURE YOU GET THROUGH

If you find yourself dealing with a particularly strict border guard, or an airline employee adhering to this restrictive policy, or you simply want to ensure that this won't become an issue in the first place, you are left with the following two options:

BUY SOMETHING CHEAP	BUY SOMETHING REFUNDABLE
Bus, train, boat, or hot air balloon: buy whatever the cheapest onward ticket is that shows that you'll be leaving the country within your allowed time period. These tickets are often available at the border but sometimes must be arranged beforehand.	*Many companies offer highly expensive, fully refundable plane or train tickets. This will satisfy the proof of onward travel requirement but remember to read the fine print. There are often confusing conditions, time limits, or hidden fees when it comes to actually getting the refund.*

THE QUEEN'S PAPERS

A LL BRITISH PASSPORTS are issued in the name of the queen, therefore Queen Elizabeth II herself does not require a passport for international travel. All other members of the royal family do need passports however.

THE TWO-WALLET SYSTEM

The traveler with nothing on him sings in the thief's face.

—JUVENAL,
Roman poet, c. 125 AD

DAY WALLET

USE: Carried at all times

MATERIAL: Straw or cheap canvas

FOR: Small amounts of local currency, tickets, and anything else you'll need in the course of a day. Should be just big enough to occasionally hold an ATM card for a cash run or an ID for a night out.

TRAVEL WALLET

USE: Locked in the safe at hotel or hostel, carried only on travel days

MATERIAL: Leather or high-quality fabric

FOR: Reserve currency, ID, passport, ATM card, credit cards, insurance cards, any other important tickets or documents. Zip closures and security chains are nice features to have. Sacrifice comfort and style for security.

THE ART OF DECLINING

Τ HE MOST USEFUL word in the traveler's vocabulary might be *no*. When you're in a part of the world where locals are constantly approaching you in the street, offering everything from trinkets to prostitutes, it can seem like a large part of your day is spent turning down energetic sales pitches. In addition to the desperate salesmen, there are scammers, children, beggars, and plainly curious people, all of whom may wish to spend more time with you than you wish to spend with them. As cruel as it may sound, you will need to reject almost all of these people as efficiently as possible. Yet, there is an art to declining, especially when you're in a foreign and unfamiliar place. Possessing a good *no* is a valuable tool in the traveler's arsenal, one that allows you to enjoy even the busiest of places hassle-free and unconcerned.

A truly effective denial of something should be firm but polite. Decline too lightly and you risk wasting valuable time and money. Do so too harshly and you might offend someone. Hit the right pitch and tone with your words and you'll send the salesman away defeated but unoffended.

Here are some tips to mastering the art of saying *no*.

ACKNOWLEDGE

If you see someone directly approaching you, don't pretend not to notice them. This will only require that they get even physically closer to you before starting their pitch of whatever it is they're selling. Don't immediately launch into an angry rejection of your own, however, especially if they have yet to speak. Simply acknowledge their presence and prepare yourself to reject.

JUST SAY NO

Smile pleasantly, raise your arms, slightly bent, in front of you with your palms out, and say something along the lines of "No, no thanks, no" in the local language. Don't act arrogant, but also don't seem like you were ever considering a possible purchase. You're going for "apologetic but confident" rather than "susceptible and nervous" or worse, "condescending and angry."

KEEP IT PEACEFUL

Always keep the vibe of the interaction light. Knowingly smile to imply that you've played this game before—even if you're annoyed by the frequency of these interactions or offended by someone offering you something illegal. It's important to remember that you're outnumbered and that crime is often more prevalent in places with large amounts of vendors. Getting angry won't solve anything.

KEEP MOVING

Stopping and engaging with someone implies that you're at least somewhat interested in what they're offering. It also allows other vendors to gather around you, awaiting their turn. A common tactic used to make travelers stop walking is to shout questions ("Where are you from?") or funny exclamations ("I love USA!") or ultra-cheap "joke" offers ("Four watches for one dollar!")—anything to elicit a reaction. There's also the age-old method of a seller extending a hand and introducing themselves, under the guise of simply wanting to meet a foreigner. All of these should be responded to with the pleasant but confident declination detailed above.

DON'T BE SORRY

If you've acted appropriately, don't be fooled into thinking you've offended someone. A last-ditch tactic to grab the interest of a traveler is for the seller to feign indignation that you wouldn't even consider their products or shake their hand. This plays on your fear of offending a local and tries to make you feel guilty for rejecting a poor vendor simply trying to provide for their family. Do not fall prey to this manipulation. The selling of anything involves frequent rejection no matter what nationality you are. Street salesmen are rejected hundreds of times a day and the fact that you in particular weren't interested in a purchase is not particularly discouraging to a given vendor, regardless of how they might act. They only want you to feel in the wrong so that you might be compelled to buy something as a way of apology. But if you've declined their offer in an assured but polite tone then you have nothing to apologize for.

LET YOURSELF LIVE

I'm having enjoyment. And I made a promise to myself that I would not consider enjoyment a sin. I take a pleasure into inquiring into things. I've never been content to pass a stone without looking under it. And it is a black disappointment to me that I can never see the far side of the moon.

—JOHN STEINBECK,
American author, *East of Eden*, 1952

TRAVEL FREEDOM RANKING

T HE NUMBER OF countries that holders of the following passports can enter without a pre-arranged visa:

153	Germany
152	Sweden
151	Finland, France, Switzerland, Spain, South Korea, United Kingdom
150	Belgium, Denmark, Italy, Japan, Netherlands, Norway, Singapore, United States
149	Austria, Luxembourg, Portugal
~	
30	Somalia
29	Syria
28	Iraq
27	Pakistan
23	Afghanistan

ALTITUDE SICKNESS

A MYSTERIOUS THREAT

Altitude sickness is the riptide of the mountains: an invisible, persistently underestimated, subtly lethal danger that many people aren't fully informed about.

Humans are adversely affected by the lack of oxygen available at high altitudes and this can induce a variety of serious medical issues. However, beyond identifying this basic root cause, medical professionals actually have relatively little understanding of what is occurring in the body of someone severely affected by altitude.

QUALITY, NOT QUANTITY

The air at high altitudes is not fundamentally different (the earth's air is composed of 20.95 percent oxygen no matter where you are), it's simply more spread out. The decreased atmospheric pressure means the air is less compressed, which in turn means that climbers breathe in fewer oxygen molecules.

WHO'S AFFECTED

One of the many mysteries of altitude sickness is that there doesn't seem to be any rhyme or reason as to who's affected. A few studies have indicated that older people are less susceptible, but this may just be because they have more experience and sense in dealing with altitude. Following that same idea, some sources consider males ages 16 to 25 to be the most at risk of altitude sickness simply because they often believe themselves to be in superior physical shape, think that they won't be affected by altitude, and then end up overexerting themselves. The reality is that the only reliable altitude sickness risk indicator is altitude itself: how high up a person is, how quickly they've ascended, and how much time they've spent at a given altitude.

PREVENTION IS KEY

Ascend Responsibly: By far the most important thing a person can do to prevent altitude sickness is to ascend gradually and without overexerting oneself. Many experts recommend the "climb high, sleep low" method in which climbers do day hikes at high altitudes, then return to lower altitudes to sleep and recuperate.

Stay Hydrated: Forcing the body to adjust to altitude without proper hydration is a recipe for disaster. Drink lots of water.

No Depressants: This includes excessive alcohol and sleeping pills. These are respiratory depressants that can slow down the acclimation process.

Medical Options: There are a variety of medicines—everything from plant-based folk remedies to prescription drugs—that claim to prevent the onset of altitude sickness. However, such methods should always be cleared with a doctor and used with the utmost care. Certain drugs can simply mask the symptoms of altitude sickness, meaning a climber may feel relatively healthy when they're actually in danger. Many experts agree that acetazolamide (Diamox) is effective and safe in preventing altitude sickness, but all climbers should check with a doctor before beginning use.

Treatment: A key component of managing altitude sickness is the correct diagnosis of a climber's condition (see next page). Some form of acute mountain sickness (AMS) is experienced by over half of people

⌄⌄⌄ *continued* ⌄⌄⌄

who ascend to above 10,000 feet (3,048 meters) and generally goes away within 48 hours. HACE (high-altitude cerebral edema) and HAPE (high-altitude pulmonary edema) are serious medical emergencies and need to be dealt with as such. While there are some mildly effective innovations that can help an affected climber (such as supplemental oxygen or a hyperbaric chamber[1]) there is no substitute for descent.

Three Forms of Altitude Sickness

CONDITION	DESCRIPTION	SYMPTOMS	TREATMENT
Acute **M**ountain **S**ickness	Adverse symptoms commonly experienced at altitude	Headache, mild nausea, dizziness, shortness of breath, lethargy	Descent, symptom specific medication (such as ibuprofen for headache)
High-**A**ltitude **C**erebral **E**dema[2]	Buildup of fluid in the brain	Severe headache, vomiting, confusion, retinal bleeding, difficulty and unsteadiness in walking, lethargy, drowsiness	Descent, supplemental oxygen, dexamethasone,[4] several hours in hyperbaric chamber
High-**A**ltitude **P**ulmonary **E**dema[3]	Buildup of fluid in the lungs	Shortness of breath while at rest, shallow breathing, gurgling sound during coughing, coughing up white or pink spit, blue/gray lips, ears, or fingers	Descent, supplemental oxygen, nifedipine,[4] several hours in hyperbaric chamber[1]

1 ››› Also called a Gamow bag, a hyperbaric chamber is a portable pressure bag designed to simulate the air of lower altitudes. It weighs about 15 pounds (6.8 kilograms), is inflated by a foot pump, and can create an artificial atmosphere of 6,562 feet (2,000 meters) lower than current altitude.

2 ››› Symptoms usually begin to occur one to three days after ascending.

3 ››› Symptoms usually begin to occur two to four days after ascending.

4 ››› These are powerful prescription drugs that should be cleared with a doctor before use. These drugs only treat the symptoms of altitude sickness, as opposed to the root cause, and should therefore only ever be used as a temporary treatment.

Some Notable Altitudes

SOME NOTABLE ALTITUDES	METERS	FEET
Everest summit	8,848	29,029
K2 summit	8,611	28,251
Death zone: oxygen insufficient to sustain human life	8,000	26,247

SOME NOTABLE ALTITUDES	METERS	FEET
39% of oxygen available at sea level	7,600	24,934
Water boils at ~166°F(74°C)	7,200	23,622
Aconcagua summit	6,691	21,952
46% of oxygen available at sea level	6,400	20,997
No permanent human habitation above this altitude	6,000	19,685
Kilimanjaro summit	5,895	19,341
Considered extreme altitude	5,200	17,060
Most climbers need 1 week to acclimatize	5,000	16,404
57% of oxygen available at sea level	4,400	14,436
Highest altitude reached on Inca Trail	4,200	13,780
Altitude of La Paz, Bolivia	3,650	11,975
66% of oxygen available at sea level	3,200	10,499
.5–1% of people who ascend above get HACE	3,000	9,843
Altitude sickness symptoms may begin to appear	2,400	7,874

A DRINKER'S GUIDE TO CLIMBING SAFETY

Many describe AMS as feeling like a bad hangover: headache, nausea, and lethargy are commonly reported symptoms. On the other hand, someone suffering from HACE might act more like they're very drunk—confusion, vomiting, inability to walk in a straight line, and slurred speech are all indicators.

So, if a fellow climber is reporting the feeling of a hangover, that's bad. But if they suddenly start acting drunk, that's potentially a medical emergency that needs to be dealt with immediately.

THE GOLDEN RULES OF ALTITUDE SICKNESS

Credited to Dr. David Shlim

1. *If you feel unwell, you have altitude sickness until proven otherwise.*
2. *Do not ascend farther if you have symptoms of altitude sickness.*
3. *If you are getting worse then descend immediately.*

WILDLIFE MYTHS

Dispelling some common wildlife injury myths—and what you should actually do.

MYTH:
URINATE ON A JELLYFISH STING

WHAT TO DO

1. If you're swimming in a place known for dangerous jellyfish (such as box jellyfish), the affected area is unusually large, or the sting induces a severe allergic reaction, seek emergency medical help as soon as possible.
2. Remove any remaining tentacles by rinsing the affected area with salt water and using gloves, tweezers, or whatever tools are available.
3. Rinse the affected area with vinegar for 30 seconds. If vinegar is unavailable, baking soda or warm salt water can be used.
4. Soak in hot freshwater for 20 minutes. Applying cold packs to area can also be effective.
5. Apply hydrocortisone cream for itching. Take antihistamines for swelling or discomfort.

MYTH:
BURN OFF A LEECH

WHAT TO DO

1. Dry off your hands. The leech will continually try to reattach itself and excess moisture on the skin helps it do so.
2. Quickly slide a flat object or fingernail under the smaller, thinner end of the leech. This is the "head" and its where the sucker is located.
3. Do the same to the thicker end of the body.
4. Flick the leech away before it's able to reattach and check for other leeches—most leeches secrete some kind of anesthetic that numbs the area of attachment to prevent the host from noticing it.
5. Clean and cover wound as soon as possible. Excess bleeding is to be expected due to anticlotting enzymes in the leech's mouth. Do not scratch the healing wound.

WHAT TO DO

1. Remember the colorings and markings of the snake. It's important to be able to identify the type of snake so that the correct type of antivenom can be administered.
2. Seek emergency medical help as soon as possible. Though not all snakes are venomous, if you are unsure and wait before seeking help it may be too late.
3. Remove clothing or jewelry around the wound in anticipation of swelling.
4. Gently clean the area and apply a bandage about two inches (2.5 centimeters) above the wound. The bandage should be loose enough to easily fit a finger underneath. Too tight a bandage can cause permanent damage. Do not use a tourniquet.
5. Stay calm, stay hydrated, and keep the wound below the level of the heart.

STUCK IN THEIR WAYS

The only countries that have not officially adopted the metric system:

LIBERIA • MYANMAR • UNITED STATES

The only countries that measure temperature in Fahrenheit:

BAHAMAS • CANADA[1] • UNITED STATES • BELIZE • PALAU

The only countries that use the MM/DD/YYYY date format:

BELIZE • MICRONESIA • UNITED STATES

1 ››› Used in conjunction with Celsius.

THE DEAL WITH DEET

WHAT IS IT?

$$H_3C \overset{O}{\underset{}{\diagup}} N \overset{CH_3}{\underset{CH_3}{}}$$

Diethyltoluamide, commonly abbreviated as **DEET**, is a chemical compound that was first produced by the US Army in 1946. After encountering significant difficulties in jungle warfare during World War II, the military realized its soldiers needed an effective way to repel insects. This light yellow oil, originally thought to have further application as a farm pesticide, tested well and by 1957 the use of DEET had spread to the general public. Today it's the active ingredient in many popular insect repellents, in concentrations of anywhere from 4 to 100 percent.

HOW DOES IT WORK?

Scientists don't know exactly why DEET is so effective at repelling many different kinds of insects. There are two prevailing schools of thought: some researchers believe DEET "blinds" insects by negatively affecting the receptors they use to smell humans. Others think that the insect's receptors are unaffected but that they specifically don't like the smell of DEET and therefore stay away from humans wearing it. However it works, it is considered one of the most effective insect repellents on the market today.

IS IT SAFE?

The safety, or lack thereof, of using DEET has long been cause for debate. On the one hand, there are frightening reports of seizures and birth defects. On the other, there's the fact that an estimated 30 percent of Americans safely use DEET every year. This question of DEET safety is an important one to many travelers. In some parts of the world the use of effective insect repellent is absolutely critical, leading some to feel as if they're being forced to choose between two evils: either apply a potentially harmful pesticide to your skin or risk being bitten by disease-carrying mosquitoes.

The answer to whether DEET is safe to use is a basic matter of smart application and moderation. While it's true that in a very few cases DEET has led to medical complications and even death, in almost every one those instances DEET was used in a way specifically warned against by manufacturers. For instance, DEET should not be used on infants and should never be ingested—these are the types of situations in which DEET use has proven to be dangerous. All major American health organizations consider DEET safe to use for adults as long as all applicable directions are followed. Billions of people have used DEET without ill effects.

NOTES ON DEET USE AND CONCENTRATION

» DEET concentration is a measure of expected protection time, not effectiveness. That means 10 percent DEET protects just as well as 40 percent DEET; 40 percent DEET just lasts longer.

» Therefore, which DEET concentration is used should be based on how long protection is needed. 5 to 10 percent should keep a person covered for one to two hours, while anywhere from 30 percent to 50 percent is needed for all-day coverage. Protection times vary based on a variety of external factors, including environment and perspiration.

» The Centers for Disease Control and Prevention advises against the use of combination sunscreen-DEET repellent products because sunscreen will likely need to be reapplied more often than insect repellent.

» Many studies suggest that products containing over 50 percent DEET don't actually provide any increase in protection time. Furthermore, 30 to 50 percent DEET is almost always sufficient for all-day coverage. Therefore, use of repellents containing over 50 percent DEET is not recommended.

» A number of DEET alternatives such as icardin (also called picaridin) and permethrin (an insect repellent for use on clothing only) have gained popularity in recent years.

» Whatever insecticide and concentration you choose, always read and follow all instructions on the label.

WIDELY USED WRITING SYSTEMS

WRITING SYSTEM	TYPE	READING DIRECTION	"HELLO, NICE TO MEET YOU." (IN MOST POPULAR LANGUAGE)
Latin	Alphabet	→	*Hola, mucho gusto (Spanish)*
Chinese	Logography	→	你好，很高兴认识你 *(Chinese)*
Arabic	Abjad	←	انفرشت اب رحم *(Arabic)*
Devanagari	Abugida	→	नमस्कार, आपसे मलिकर अच्छा लगा *(Hindi)*
Cyrillic	Alphabet	→	Привет! Рад тебя видеть *(Russian)*
Bengali	Abugida	→	হ্যালো! তোমার সাথে সাক্ষাতে ভাল লাগছে *(Bengali)*
Kana	Syllabary	→	あなたに会えてこんにちは素敵な *(Japanese)*
Gurmukhi	Abugida	→	ਹੈਲੋ ਤੁਹਾਨੂੰ ਮਲਿਣ ਲਈ ਚੰਗੇ *(Punjabi)*
Hangul	Alphabet	→	당신을 만나서 안녕하세요 좋은 *(Korean)*
Telugu	Abugida	→	నిన్ను కలసినందుకు సంతోషం *(Telugu)*
Tamil	Abugida	→	ஹலோ உங்களை சந்திப்பதில் மகிழ்ச்சி *(Tamil)*
Malayalam	Abugida	→	നിങ്ങളെ കണ്ടതി സന്തോഷം ഹലോ *(Malayalam)*
Burmese	Abugida	→	မင်္ဂလာပါတွေ့ရတာဝမ်းသာပါတယ် *(Burmese)*
Thai	Abugida	→	สวัสดียินดีที่ได้รู้จัก *(Thai)*

» **Alphabet:** sounds of the language are assigned to symbols, which represent both consonants and vowels.

» **Syllabary:** each symbol represents a syllable instead of an individual sound of the language.

- » *Abugida:* also called an alphasyllabary, consonants and vowel sounds are represented together by a single symbol.

- » *Abjad:* a consonant-only system in which the vowel sounds of the language are not represented by symbols, but rather are determined by context or linguistic structures.

- » *Logography:* each symbol represents an entire word, phrase, or idea.

LONGEST AND SHORTEST FLIGHTS

A T THE TIME of this writing, the shortest and longest regularly scheduled, nonstop commercial flights in the world are:

SHORTEST

WESTRAY, ORKNEY ISLANDS, SCOTLAND ├───────┤ PAPA WESTRAY, ORKNEY ISLANDS, SCOTLAND

2 MINUTES[1] • 1.7 MILES *(2.7 KILOMETERS)* • LOGANAIR

LONGEST[2]

AUCKLAND, NEW ZEALAND ├───────┤ DUBAI, UNITED ARAB EMIRATES

17 HOURS, 25 MINUTES • 8,825 MILES *(14,203 KILOMETERS)* • EMIRATES

---

1 ››› This flight can be completed in 47 seconds in ideal wind conditions.

2 ››› The "holy grail" of the airline industry remains the 10,560 mile (16,995 kilometer) London to Sydney route. Though the flight is technically doable in a virtually empty aircraft, no airline has figured out a way to make the route commercially viable with passengers onboard. Boeing has announced preliminary plans to introduce a new version of their Boeing 777 in the year 2020 that can economically complete the trip.

LEST YOU BE JUDGED

Never make fun of people who speak broken English.
It means they know another language.

—H. JACKSON BROWN JR.,
American author, *Life's Little Instruction Book*, 1991

THE NORTH AND SOUTH POLES

NORTH
The Arctic

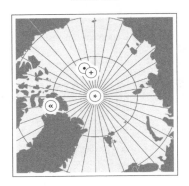

TERRAIN:	AVG. TEMPERATURES:	PROMINENT WILDLIFE:
Shifting sea ice	*32°F (0°C) / -40°F (-40°C)*	*Polar bears*

	GEOGRAPHIC NORTH POLE	
*	90°0'0" N	*The northernmost point on earth; the very "top" of the world*
	MAGNETIC NORTH POLE	
•	86°24'0" N, 166°18'0" W[1]	*The point at which the earth's magnetic field is directed vertically downward; where a compass points to*
	GEOMAGNETIC NORTH POLE	
«	80°22'12" N, 72°37'12" W[1]	*The northern focus of the magnetic field that surrounds the earth; considered one of the best places to view the aurora borealis ("northern lights") phenomenon*
	NORTHERN POLE OF INACCESSIBILITY	
+	85°48'0" N, 176°9'0" W	*The point in the Arctic Ocean that is farthest from any coastline*

SOUTH
The Antarctic

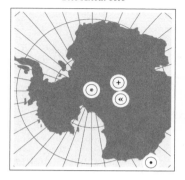

TERRAIN:
Desert covered in ice

AVG. TEMPERATURES:
-18°F (-28°C)/-76°F (-60°C)

PROMINENT WILDLIFE:
Penguins

		GEOGRAPHIC SOUTH POLE	
*	90°0'0" S	*The southernmost point on earth; the very "bottom" of the world*
		MAGNETIC SOUTH POLE	
•	64°16'48" S, 136°35'24" E[1]	*The point at which the earth's magnetic field is directed vertically upward*
		GEOMAGNETIC SOUTH POLE	
«	79°44'24" S, 108°13'12" E[1]	*The southern focus of the magnetic field that surrounds the earth; considered one of the best places to view the aurora australis ("southern lights") phenomenon*
		SOUTHERN POLE OF INACCESSIBILITY	
+	82°53'14" S, 55°4'30" E	*The point on the Antarctic continent that is farthest from the Southern Ocean*

1 ››› Position is not fixed, moves up 35 miles (56 kilometers) each year.

Uniquely Shaped[1]

NEPAL · SWITZERLAND · VATICAN CITY

Uniquely Sided[2]

PARAGUAY

1 ››› All other flags are oblong rectangles, with varying height-to-width ratios.

2 ››› While Paraguay is the only flag that has a different obverse (front) than reverse (back), there are other national flags which feature asymmetrical designs that need to appear exactly the same on both sides. For instance, the religiously important text on the flag of Saudi Arabia requires it be double-printed to appear exactly the same on both sides, as opposed to the "see-through" design of most national flags.

DIVING DETAILS

SCUBA

Self Contained Underwater Breathing Apparatus

SCUBA DIVING, ONE of the most popular activities in modern travel, requires certification to ensure divers have undergone appropriate safety training. The most popular recreational diving training and certification organizations include PADI (Professional Association of Diving Instructors), SSI (Scuba Schools International), NAUI (National Association of Underwater Instructors), and SDI (Scuba Diving International).

After completing training, divers are issued a certification card (sometimes called a C-card) that includes their photograph and the levels of instruction they've achieved. These cards are used when renting equipment and organizing diving trips as proof of a diver's experience.

Most dive shops will accept certification cards from any major training organization, regardless of whether or not the dive shop is affiliated with a particular organization. Thus, a dive shop offering PADI certification and courses will allow divers certified by SSI to rent equipment and join diving expeditions. However, note that advanced certifications are not directly comparable across all organizations and dive shops have the right to decline service to anyone they don't feel is qualified to dive safely.

In general, scuba certifications never expire, though some dive shops may insist a diver review training materials or basic techniques if they haven't dived in a number of years.

Details of PADI certifications, widely considered the most popular training organization among travelers, are provided below:

PADI SCUBA DIVER	A subset of Open Water Diver certification, this is a shorter course consisting of classroom instruction, 3 dives in a controlled environment, and 2 open water dives. The full course usually takes 2 to 3 days and is not considered a full certification: after completion you are only qualified to dive in the presence of an instructor.		
	↓		
OPEN WATER DIVER	As the first full certification, the Open Water Diver course usually takes 4 to 5 days and consist of classroom instruction, 5 dives in a controlled environment, and 4 open water dives. After completion, divers are qualified to a depth of 59 feet (18 meters), independent of professional supervision. Hours of instruction necessary for specialties and more advanced certifications vary greatly by dive shop.		
	SELECTED SPECIALTIES:		
	Altitude Diver	Dry Suit Diver	Peak Performance Buoyancy
	AWARE—Fish Identification	Emergency Oxygen Provider	Rebreather Diver
	Boat Diver	Enriched Air Diver	Sidemount Diver
	Digital Underwater Photographer	Equipment Specialist	Underwater Naturalist
	Diver Propulsion Vehicle Driver	Multilevel Diver	Underwater Navigator
	Drift Diver	Night Diver	Underwater Videographer
	↓		
ADVENTURE DIVER	Deep Diver		Wreck Diver
	↓		
ADVANCED OPEN WATER DIVER	Cavern Diver	Ice Diver	Search and Recovery Diver

↓
RESCUE DIVER
↓
MASTER SCUBA DIVER

DON'T BRING THAT IN HERE

THE DURIAN, A large spiky fruit native to Southeast Asia, has such a distinctive odor that these signs are often posted at hotels and restaurants reminding customers that the fruit is not welcome at the establishment.

DON'T FLY OCEANIC

WHILE IT'S PERFECTLY understandable that airlines don't want to have their company names associated with disaster, television and movies have featured plane crashes practically since the mediums began. As a result, it's been necessary to create fake airlines that can be freely hijacked, blown up, and crashed without real life brand reputation implications. And of these many fictional airlines, one has been more popular—and consequently more ill-fated—than all the rest.

Oceanic Airlines (sometimes Oceanic Airways) took its first fictional flight in a 1965 episode of the dolphin-starring series *Flipper*. In a two-part episode titled "The Ditching," Oceanic Flight 17 crashes into the Atlantic Ocean south of Miami. Thus began a series of very bad luck for the airline. Below are just some of the many recent tragedies that have befallen the cursed Oceanic.

FLIGHT NO.	YEAR	FILM, *TV SHOW*, or **VIDEO GAME**	DISASTER
343	1996	Executive Decision	*Hijacked by terrorists*
115	1996	Panic in the Skies!	*Majority of crew killed in lightning strike*
456	1997	*Diagnosis Murder*	*Copilot murdered, crew poisoned*
105	2000	*JAG*	*Hijacked by terrorists*
762	2000	Nowhere to Land	*Bomb with deadly nerve gas aboard*
815	2004	*Lost*	*Crashed on mysterious island*
1012	2011	**Dead Island**	*Crashed on zombie-infested island*

DELISTED

ONLY TWO SITES have ever had their UNESCO World Heritage Site[1] designation revoked.

ARABIAN ORYX SANCTUARY

Central Desert, Oman

DESIGNATION GRANTED: | DESIGNATION REVOKED:
1994 | 2007

REASONING:

A decision by the Omani government to reduce the area reserved for the oryx by 90 percent after oil reserves were discovered nearby.

DRESDEN ELBE VALLEY

Dresden, Germany

DESIGNATION GRANTED: | DESIGNATION REVOKED:
2004 | 2009

REASONING:

The building of the controversial Waldschlösschen Bridge across the valley, which opponents argued significantly reduced the integrity and appeal of the natural landscape.

1 ››› See page 62 for more information on World Heritage Sites.

A PERK OF THE JOB

THE LATE LORD Geoffrey Howe of Aberavon, a British politician who served as Margaret Thatcher's foreign secretary among other positions, had UK passport number 007. When the government began updating passports in the late 1980s, the number was offered to Prime Minister Thatcher, who declined. The mild-mannered Howe apparently surprised colleagues by immediately claiming the number made famous by James Bond for himself.

THE HERITAGE OF THE WORLD

T HE UNITED NATIONS Educational, Scientific, and Cultural Organization (UNESCO) maintains the following lists, aimed at identifying and protecting the world's most precious places and customs. Additions to the lists are determined by a rotating committee of UNESCO member states and benefits can include financial assistance, expert advice on preservation, and legal protection under the Geneva Conventions.

WORLD HERITAGE

Cultural or natural sites of exceptional significance, beauty, or historical relevance to humanity

1,052 SITES
814 cultural · 203 natural · 35 mixed properties

LEADING COUNTRIES
Italy (51) · China (50) · Spain (45)

EXAMPLES INCLUDE
Grand Canyon National Park, *United States*
Royal Hill of Ambohimanga, *Madagascar*
Prambanan Temple Compounds, *Indonesia*
Koutammakou, the Land of the Batammariba, *Togo*

WORLD HERITAGE IN DANGER

World Heritage sites threatened by war, pollution, poorly managed tourism, environmental concerns, or other dangers

55 SITES
37 cultural · 18 natural · 0 mixed properties

LEADING COUNTRIES
Syria (6) · Democratic Republic of Congo (5) · Libya (5)

EXAMPLES INCLUDE
Okapi Wildlife Reserve, *Democratic Republic of Congo*
Rainforests of the Atsinanana, *Madagascar*
Ancient City of Bosra, *Syria*
Tomb of Askia, *Mali*

INTANGIBLE CULTURAL HERITAGE OF HUMANITY

Treasured cultural traditions representative of the diversity of humanity

336 ELEMENTS

LEADING COUNTRIES
China (30) · Japan (22) · South Korea (18)

EXAMPLES INCLUDE
Zmijanje embroidery, *Bosnia and Herzegovina*
Georgian polyphonic singing, *Georgia*
Tinian marble craftsmanship, *Greece*
Smoke sauna tradition in Võromaa, *Estonia*

INTANGIBLE CULTURAL HERITAGE IN NEED OF URGENT SAFEGUARDING

Cultural traditions whose continued existence requires immediate assistance

47 ELEMENTS

LEADING COUNTRIES
China (7) · Mongolia (6) · Uganda (5)

EXAMPLES INCLUDE
Mongolian calligraphy, *Mongolia*
Secret society of the Kôrêdugaw (a rite of wisdom), *Mali*
Naqqāli (dramatic storytelling), *Iran*
Qiang New Year Festival, *China*

THE NATIONAL DIET

Items commonly found in the "American" section of foreign grocery stores:

Marshmallows	Barbeque sauce	Cake mix	Chocolate syrup	Children's breakfast cereals
Hot chocolate	Canned soup	Soda	Peanut butter	Assorted cookies and candies
Pancake mix	Maple syrup	Pretzels	Beef jerky	Instant macaroni and cheese

ALL IS NOT LOST

Follow these instructions if an electronic device gets wet:

POWER IT DOWN

Power down the device, disconnect any power cords, and take out any removable batteries immediately. Resist the urge to turn it on and check if the device still works. The liquid itself often isn't the root cause of damage—it's the short-circuiting triggered by electric current running through wet components that usually results in serious damage. Potentially salvageable devices are commonly destroyed by owners who attempt to turn them on too early and unknowingly ruin the interior circuitry of their devices.

TAKE IT APART

Remove all memory cards, SIM cards, cases, covers, and cords. This will not only protect those individual pieces from damage, it will help dry out the device.

SOAK IT UP

Using a towel or cloth to pat dry the device and soak up any moisture. Lightly shake the device to get out as much liquid as possible.

CLEAN IT UP

Before starting the drying process, it's important to clean any potentially damaging material from the device. Salt water and other liquids can leave behind impurities that will cause corrosion.

If your device falls into:

FRESH WATER	ANY OTHER LIQUID
Lightly clean with rubbing alcohol or distilled water, if available. If unavailable, do nothing—don't use any other materials to clean.	Lightly clean with rubbing alcohol or distilled water, if available. If unavailable, lightly clean with fresh water.

DRY IT OUT

Place the device, still disassembled, in a well-ventilated area. Turn it every few hours to ensure moisture in every area is evaporating or draining.

The following materials can help expedite the drying process but there is no substitute for patience. If you use a heat source to help dry the device, be sure to use low, consistent, indirect heat.

» **Rice:** An airtight container full of rice will absorb excess moisture

» **Device:** A vacuum cleaner or a fan can help remove liquid

» **Excess heat:** Refrigerators, cars, and televisions vent heat that can be used to dry wet devices

WAIT IT OUT

How long to wait depends on specifics of the device and drying techniques used but note that a large camera can take up to a week to properly dry. Remember that rushing the process can needlessly short-circuit an otherwise functional device. Don't attempt to reassemble and power on any device for at least 24 hours and wait longer if possible.

EXPECTED WATER SURVIVAL TIMES

NOTE THAT INTENSE physical activity can accelerate loss of body heat and decrease expected survival times.

°F	°C	EXHAUSTION	SURVIVAL
>80	>27	*Indefinitely*	*Indefinitely*
70–80	21–27	*3–12 hours*	*3 hours–indefinitely*
60–70	16–21	*2–7 hours*	*2–40 hours*
50–60	10–16	*1–2 hours*	*1–6 hours*
40–50	4–10	*30–60 minutes*	*1–3 hours*
32–40	0–4	*15–30 minutes*	*30–90 minutes*
<32	<0	*<15 minutes*	*<15–45 minutes*

I N 1939, IMPERIAL and Qantas Airways offered a London-to-Sydney itinerary that consisted of 30 layovers, took 11 days, and cost about £200 (the equivalent of $17,449 today).

Those who could afford a ticket traveled in the height of luxury. Empire-class flying boats were 88-foot (27-meter) metal seaplanes, capable of speeds of 200 miles (322 kilometers) per hour and accommodating a maximum of 24 passengers. In addition to lounging in the bar and smoking cabin, passengers were served oysters and fine cheeses while enjoying spectacular views from the promenade cabin, which featured reclining seats, 11-foot ceilings, drink service, and oversized windows. Miniature golf was offered inflight and passengers were provided with fishing poles to pass the time while in port.

MISDIRECTION

T HE CORIOLIS FORCE (also called the Coriolis effect) pertains to the movement of objects within a rotating entity. It is most easily observed on a large scale, for instance, the Coriolis force is what causes hurricanes to spin clockwise in the northern hemisphere and counterclockwise in the southern hemisphere.

While still theoretically present, the Coriolis force has a much lesser effect on smaller objects. The popular belief that water in toilets and sinks flows in different directions depending on the hemisphere is often attributed to the Coriolis force. This is nothing more than an urban myth; the direction water drains on such a small scale is determined by its prior motion and the shape of the container, not the Coriolis force.

Street hustlers in countries on the equator often exploit this common misconception by performing "tests" in which they show water draining clockwise into a basin in the northern hemisphere and then "walk across the equator" and show it draining counterclockwise in the southern hemisphere. This is a simple trick masquerading as science. Look carefully: the water is poured on different sides of the basin to achieve the desired effect.

WONDERFUL WORLD

ORIGINALLY DESCRIBED AS *themata* or "things to be seen" by ancient Greek scholars, **wonders of the world** have captured travelers' imaginations for millennia.

Throughout the centuries these lists have served as de facto global travel guides for explorers seeking the most impressive sights the world has to offer. Most sources agree that specifically *seven* wonders were originally selected because of the number's importance in Hellenic culture, it being a symbol of perfection and the number of prominent celestial objects in the sky.[1]

But as tempting as it is to think of "wonders of the world" as globally agreed-upon catalogs of man and nature's greatest achievements, this is decidedly not the case. Note that *The Seven Wonders of the Ancient World* below is the only list that can be considered at all definitive, and even it is flawed in that it focuses solely on wonders well known to early Greek civilization. Subsequent wonder lists were compiled by numerous entities, both public and private, each with wildly differing motivations as to what should be included. The publication of each successive list was met with harsh objection by advocates of the wonders not included and remain heavily disputed.

THE SEVEN WONDERS OF THE ANCIENT WORLD

REFERENCED BY MULTIPLE ANCIENT TRAVEL GUIDES AND HISTORICAL WORKS[2]

Colossus of Rhodes*	Pyramids of Giza
Hanging Gardens of Babylon*[3]	Statue of Zeus at Olympia*
Lighthouse of Alexandria*	Temple of Artemis at Ephesus*
Mausoleum at Halicarnassus*	

THE SEVEN WONDERS OF THE MIDDLE AGES

COMPILED FROM VARIOUS SOURCES [4]

Catacombs of Kom el Shoqafa	Leaning Tower of Pisa
Colosseum	Porcelain Tower of Nanjing
Great Wall of China	Stonehenge
Hagia Sophia	

THE SEVEN WONDERS OF THE MODERN WORLD

SELECTED BY THE AMERICAN SOCIETY OF CIVIL ENGINEERS IN 1994

CN Tower	Empire State Building
Channel Tunnel	Golden Gate Bridge
Delta and Zuiderzee Works	Itaipu Dam
	Panama Canal

THE SEVEN NATURAL WONDERS OF THE WORLD

SELECTED BY CNN IN 1997

Auroras borealis and australis	Harbor of Rio de Janeiro
Grand Canyon	Mount Everest
Great Barrier Reef	Parícutin volcano
	Victoria Falls

THE SEVEN NEW WONDERS OF THE WORLD

SELECTED BY SIX JUDGES IN ASSOCIATION WITH USA TODAY *AND* GOOD MORNING AMERICA

Great Migration of Serengeti & Masai Mara	Papahānaumokuākea Marine National Monument
Internet	Polar ice caps
Mayan ruins of the Yucatán Peninsula	Potala Palace
Old City of Jerusalem	

THE NEW SEVEN WONDERS
OF THE WORLD

*SELECTED BY A CONTROVERSIAL 2007 GLOBAL
POLL IN WHICH MORE THAN 100 MILLION
VOTES WERE CAST*

Chichen Itza	Petra
Machu Picchu	Colosseum
Christ the Redeemer in Rio de Janeiro, Brazil	Great Wall of China
	Taj Mahal

THE NEW SEVEN WONDERS
OF NATURE

*SELECTED BY A CONTROVERSIAL 2011 GLOBAL
POLL IN WHICH MORE THAN 100 MILLION
VOTES WERE CAST*

Halong Bay	Puerto Princesa Underground River
Iguazu Falls	Table Mountain
Jeju Island	Amazon Rainforest
Komodo Island	

---

* No longer in existence.

1 ››› Five discovered planets, in addition to the sun and the moon.

2 ››› Alternative sources include the Ishtar Gate as a wonder of the world.

3 ››› Due to a lack of evidence, the original location of the Hanging Gardens is heavily disputed and some historians have doubted whether they ever actually existed at all.

4 ››› Alternative sources include the Cairo Citadel, Cluny Abbey, Ely Cathedral, and the Taj Mahal as wonders of the world.

MAKE YOUR OWN PATH

*Most people who travel look only at what they are directed to look at.
Great is the power of the guidebook maker, however ignorant.*

—JOHN MUIR,

Scottish-American naturalist, author, environmental philosopher,
Travels in Alaska, 1915

ON PACKING

I N 1828, WILLIAM Hawes and Charles Fellows brought more than 30 bottles of wine and liquor with them on their summit of Mont Blanc. Russian cosmonauts carried double-barreled shotguns to ward off bear attacks in case their spacecraft crash-landed in the wilderness. In 1897, Prince Luigi Amedeo of Italy had his porters carry innumerable luxuries on his climb of Mount Saint Elias[1] including four iron beds, while a few years earlier Thomas Stevens bicycled around the entire world carrying only socks, an extra shirt, a raincoat, and a revolver. In short, every traveler and every journey is unique and thus there is no ideal packing list to prescribe.

Listening to a book about exactly what to pack is as absurd as blindly following a guidebook when deciding an itinerary. But there are some general tips that you might find useful.

DON'T WORRY SO MUCH

Many travelers tend to develop a pre-trip anxiety concerning the contents of their bag. Unless you'll be living for an extended period of time at remote wilderness outpost, remember that local people have been living there, often quite comfortably, for millennia.

Whatever you worry you might be forgetting, they probably have a local substitute for. Medical supplies and advanced electronic equipment should be carefully considered, but almost everything else can likely be purchased abroad.

DON'T PACK SO MUCH

Packing light may be simple in theory, but is an admittedly difficult concept to apply in practice. Many travelers consciously recognize before a trip that their bag is overfilled, but can't actually bring themselves to choose specific items to remove.

If you find yourself in such a situation, conceptualize things this way: most of what you bring, you'll be stuck with. Sending packages home is expensive[2] and, while you can often trade items,[3] you probably won't want to part with something of personal value. When you're deciding whether to bring that additional beloved T-shirt, recognize that even if you don't end up wearing it often, you will still be carrying it around wherever you go. That shirt will still take up space in your bag that could be occupied by some incredible memento found in a foreign market; it will still contribute to the weight regulations imposed by every airline. It will still need to be protected against damage or theft; it will still become wrinkled and worn from packing and repacking and the general wear and tear of the road. The cost, in effort, usage, and money, of every additional packed item is not insignificant and rarely used items quickly become burdens. Therefore, if an item is not going to provide you significant value, it's best to keep it safe at home.

ITEMS YOU MIGHT NOT HAVE CONSIDERED

The following unheralded but versatile items can be useful regardless of the specifics of your journey.

» Earplugs   » Zip ties   » Multiple pens and markers   » Dry bag

» Cheap waterproof watch: *Carrying an expensive smartphone everywhere can be more stressful than useful. Only carry a phone when necessary.*

» Small notebook: *Both for note taking and for the many important tickets, papers, forms, and maps you will accumulate.*

---

1 ››› After the porters had carried the beds halfway up the mountain, the prince decided he was more comfortable sleeping on the ground.
2 ››› See page 182 for more information on international shipping.
3 ››› See page 212 for more information on haggling and trading items.

A GOOD RULE

Decide your own life, don't let another person run or rule you.

—FIRST RULE IN THE HOBO CODE OF ETHICS

Created by Tourist Union #63
Voted on during the 1889 National Hobo Convention, St. Louis, Missouri.

THE "HOBO HIERARCHY":

HOBO : *Traveling worker*

TRAMP : *Works only when they have to*

BUM: *Refuses all work*

SMILING IN SELECTED COUNTRIES

How people of different nationalities cue their subjects to smile.

"Say_____"

Bulgaria	zele *("cabbage")*	Iran	بیس *("apple")*
China (Mandarin)	茄子 *("eggplant")*	South Korea	김치 *("kimchi")*
France	ouistit *("marmoset")*	Sweden	aplesin *("orange")*
Indonesia	buncis *("bean")*	Thailand	เป๊ปซี่ *("Pepsi")*

The Three Pillars of Photography

SETTING	APPLICABLE DEFINITION	MEASUREMENT AND EFFECT	
Aperture	Size of the opening in the lens	f/1.4	f/22
Shutter Speed	The amount of time the shutter is open	1/1000	1/2
ISO	The sensitivity of the sensor to incoming light	ISO 50	ISO 6400

KNOW YOUR FLASH

The maximum effective range of the built-in flash in most consumer cameras is about 15 feet (5 meters). Other settings can help lighten resulting images somewhat but relying on a flash to illuminate a dark, distant subject is often problematic.

MIX IT UP

*The sheer ease with which we can produce a superficial image
often leads to creative disaster.*

—ANSEL ADAMS,
"A Personal Credo," 1944

It is not unusual for a traveler to return home only to realize they've merely taken many versions of the exact same photo: a standard pose with a broad smile, the only distinguishing factor being the changing background. While there's certainly nothing wrong with a classic pose atop a mountain or in front of a pristine blue ocean, the best pictures from a trip often capture subtler or stranger moments. Encourage any travel companions to take candid photos and be sure to return the favor. Experiment with your camera's settings during downtime to learn its full range of capabilities. Take the kitschy photo with the typical pose, but be sure to use your camera unconventionally as well.

PHOTO ETIQUETTE

Be wary of taking pictures of local people. Many find it offensive, just as you might if someone came to where you live and started photographing you without asking. Ask permission first and be prepared to occasionally pay small amounts of money in exchange for taking a picture.

But it's not just local citizens that you should think twice about photographing. In many countries, there are a variety of things that are considered inappropriate or illegal to take pictures of. Punishments can range from a stern reprimand to immediate imprisonment. Regulations vary from place to place but as a general rule always be cautious of photographing the following people and locations:

• *Border crossings*	• *Security checkpoints*	• *Law enforcement*
• *Military bases or equipment*	• *Embassies*	• *Religious sites*
	• *Aircraft*	• *Bank interiors*

LET IT BE

Almost all travelers treasure their photos and videos as reminders of good times had in far-off locales. Yet some travelers develop an unhealthy obsession with recording their experience to such a degree that it significantly affects their trip. Exploration becomes a glorified photo shoot; the quality of an entire trip becomes defined by how many Facebook-worthy pictures are captured.

Take pictures while you're traveling but don't travel solely for the pictures. Enjoy experiences for what they are; don't ruin a genuine moment by insisting on somehow recording it. Take well-composed photos but don't manipulate the reality of a situation in pursuit of an impressive, but ultimately deceitful, picture. Reject the idea of travel as performance and in doing so you will reject the anxiety of trying to capture everything. Most of the best things in travel cannot be recorded anyway.

vvv *continued* vvv

GUIDE TO STORAGE

Lost and Found

The first picture you take on any new camera[1] or memory card should be of your relevant contact details. This will allow any good Samaritan who comes across the device to easily return it to its rightful owner.

If Found, Please Return to:

Full Name
Email Address
(Country Code) + Area Code + Phone Number

$$ Reward $$

THE TRIPLE BACKUP SYSTEM

Thanks to advancements in consumer camera technologies, the global reach of the Internet, and rapidly decreasing memory cards prices, it is now both practical and financially viable for most travelers to employ the triple backup system detailed below.

CARD

 In 2004, SanDisk released the world's first 1-gigabyte SD card with a suggested retail price of $500. Today the same company sells a 32-gigabyte SD card for about $10, a per GB price decrease of approximately 99.93 percent.

Memory cards have become so cheap it is now financially reasonable to suggest that they never be reused. At an estimated cost of only $.0020 to store a photo,[2] deleting a picture, no matter how boring or blurry it may be, simply to save money on digital storage no longer makes sense.

Note that memory cards can sometimes be more expensive, unreliable, or unavailable abroad. Stock up at home from a trusted vendor, and then hide fully used cards in a small waterproof bag somewhere safe in your luggage, separate from your camera and other electronics.

DRIVE

 Like memory cards, hard drives offer more space at lower prices every year. Whether this mode of digital storage is inside a laptop or tablet, or as an external hard drive, it is good practice to copy your photos from your memory cards onto a hard drive when you have some downtime. Waterproofness and shockproofness are two nice hard drive features to have for the adventurous traveler.

CLOUD

The latest in backup solutions uses the Internet to upload your photos to offsite storage, thus ensuring your images are secure no matter what happens to you or your equipment. The primary issue with this method is the availability of Internet access in some parts of the world. Frequent photographers would be unwise to assume they will regularly find Internet connections that are both fast and cheap enough to upload significant numbers of high resolution photos. It is therefore important to also back up photos using the previous two methods.

1››› While the large majority of images are stored on memory cards, most cameras also include a relatively small amount of storage within the camera itself. Be sure to also record contact details here, as it will allow for your camera to be identified even when there is no memory card in it.

2››› Assuming 20 megapixels per photo, 6 megabyte photo file size, $10 cost of 32 gigabyte SD card, 5 percent memory card capacity unavailability:

$(32,000-5\%)/6 = -5,066 photos$ $10/5,066 = \$.0020 per photo$

SHOULDER SEASONS

SHOULDER SEASONS ARE the months between "high" (or "peak") and "low" (or "off-peak") season when travel costs are lower but the weather is still pleasant enough for extensive travel. Great deals can be had on flights, accommodations, and activities and there are fewer tourists around. The timing of shoulder seasons varies around the world with local climates, holidays, and events but are often during spring or fall. Shoulder seasons are so-called because of the "shoulder" portion of the graph that they occupy.

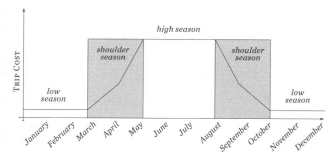

PAY THE PRICE

T RAVELERS SHOULD BE aware that selective pricing is a common practice throughout the world. Prices in many nations are not the same for all customers and, as much as some travelers consider the very concept an immoral insult to high-minded principles of global equality, tourist prices have and will always exist. Whether standardized, such as a historical site charging higher entry fees for foreigners, or informal, such as market vendors selling food to their fellow citizens at lower prices, almost all travelers will encounter selective pricing at some point in their journey, even if they don't realize it.

Though an admittedly imperfect system, tourist prices exist for many legitimate reasons including international income disparity and complex cultural traditions. Yet far more important than understanding why tourists may be charged different prices in a given area is accepting it as an inevitable reality and realizing the difference between paying a tourist price and being ripped off. Tourists' prices may be inevitable, but being ripped off is a choice. If you don't wish to pay a higher price based on your nationality, choose not to purchase the good. Haggle[1] as best you can, but never get upset a vendor for charging lowered prices to fellow locals. You are a temporary guest and shouldn't question how they choose to conduct their business.

1 ››› See page 212 for more information on haggling.

PARADISE LOST

I N 1516, THE English author Sir Thomas More invented perhaps the most enduring, and endearing, fictional country of all time. He describes the nation of Utopia as an island country near South America where the concept of private property doesn't exist and people are free to practice whatever religion they choose. Meals are eaten communally, doors have no locks, and only children wear jewelry, which they voluntarily surrender as they age. There is no unemployment, no poverty, and citizens devote themselves to learning new things after completing the standard six-hour workday.

More's *Utopia* became extremely popular in Europe, with sales no doubt helped by the interest generated from increasing exploration in the New World. Yet, despite it being so influential that it created a word still in use today, many readers may have missed the greater point. The philosophical lesson of *Utopia* can be found in its name alone: it is composed of Greek roots and literally means "nowhere." Scholars argue that what More was actually trying to tell people in the age of exploration is that there is no perfect society across the ocean, no paradise free from the immorality of conventional civilization. He may have been proposing that, as long as people are involved, such a place cannot exist.

ON VISAS

A VISA IS A document granting permission for a person to travel, work, study, or live in a foreign country. Some countries require visas for all foreign visitors, others do so only for visitors of certain nationalities.[1]

VARYING FORMATS

A visa may be awarded in the form of a small passport stamp, a large colorful passport sticker, a piece of paper stapled into a passport, a separate multipage document, or as a digital record.

NO STANDARDS

Visa application requirements vary greatly from country to country. Some are awarded **on arrival**: a traveler simply arrives at the border, shows their passport, and a free visa is automatically granted by officials. Others cost hundreds of dollars and require months of preparation, including letters of introduction and significant amounts of paperwork. Always confirm latest visa regulations before booking any transportation or accommodation.

GOING ON A RUN

A **visa or border run** refers to traveling outside of a country's borders specifically to be granted a new visa or an extension on a current visa. Be sure to check current regulations to ensure you will be readmitted into the country.

DO UNTO OTHERS

"Reciprocal" visa policies happen when a country alters their visa policies for travelers of a certain nationality in direct response to that

ᵛᵛᵛ *continued* ᵛᵛᵛ

country altering their own policies. For instance, after the United States raised their visa fee for Bolivian citizens to $160, the Bolivian government promptly raised their fee for American citizens to the same amount. Reciprocal visa policies also sometimes involve the length or intensity of visa applications and other factors that affect how difficult it is for a traveler of a certain nationality to enter a country.

Some experts argue that this is a shortsighted and emotional policy response that can have an adverse effect on lower classes. The example above assumes that tourism income is of equal importance to Bolivia and the United States when this is obviously not the case. Bolivia is much more heavily reliant on tourist spending than the United States is. So when higher visa fees deter some budget-minded tourists, Bolivian restaurant, hotel, and shop owners suffer much more than their American counterparts. Granted, additional money might be generated from higher fees—but those funds typically flow directly into the pockets of corrupt government officials, not to programs designed to benefit local citizens. In this way, raising a visa fee simply for reasons of national pride, or flat-out revenge, often only benefits the bureaucrats who control the border, not the millions of citizens behind it.

DENIED

Countries have the sovereign right to determine their own entry requirements and there is no international agreement on what constitutes fair or reasonable criteria. Entry requirements are the product of a country's cultural norms and no definitive proof is needed to deny entry. Among the limitless reasons a country may choose to deny a traveler entry are:

Accommodation	Border officials sometimes require proof of accommodation to ensure a traveler won't end up becoming a ward of the state.
Age	Some countries don't allow visitors under a certain age to travel alone; others issue certain types of visas depending on age.
Appearance	If the official thinks a traveler looks suspicious, poor, sick, or otherwise objectionable, they may deny entry.
Bribe	The paying of a bribe is a standard, expected, and necessary step in the bureaucracies of some countries in the world. Sometimes a bribe is the difference between approval and denial.[2]

Criminal History	Countries have all sorts of policies involving criminal records. For instance, Canada regularly denies visas of people who been convicted of driving under the influence.
Cultural Norms	Countries expect travelers to adhere to their cultural norms and will deny the visa of anyone they are not convinced will do so. For instance, border guards in conservative Muslim countries will not look kindly upon travelers dressed in revealing clothing.
Finances	A traveler who goes broke often becomes the responsibility of the state and countries want to avoid this at all costs. Border guards will deny entry if they think you don't have sufficient funds to travel within their country.
Gender	Saudi Arabia, among other countries, generally does not allow women to travel alone.
Health	This often concerns residency visas, rather than travel visas, but denials for health issues, obesity chief among them, are more common than many travelers think.
Letter of Endorsement or Invitation	In some countries this is a requirement, in others it will simply help to ensure entry.
Marital Status	Some conservative Muslim countries may take issue with unmarried couples traveling or staying in hotel rooms together.
Politics	Openly disagreeing with the policies of an authoritative government can result in a swift denial.
Prior Travel	Many Arab countries will deny entry to anyone with an Israeli stamp in their passport.[3]
Prior Violations	If you've overstayed or violated the terms of visas issued to you in the past, border officials may be wary to issue you a new visa.
Profession	Some jobs may cause an official to question a traveler's income level; unusual or unheard of jobs may arouse suspicion about motives for travel. Additionally, regardless of income level, it is best practice not to say you're self-employed. Come up with a creative alternative that is as professionally sounding as possible.

vvv *continued* vvv

Proof of Onward Travel	Lack of proof of onward travel is one most common reason visas are denied.[4]
Public Statements	This can involve anything from overheard conversations to Facebook posts to interviews.
Race	Some of the world is unequivocally racist. As absurd as it is in this day and age, the race of an applicant can affect visa approval.
Religion	Religion permeates every aspect of some cultures, and travelers can be denied for a whole host of religiously influenced reasons.
Security	Tourists being injured or killed can have serious geopolitical consequences for a government. Many countries will deny entry if they think a traveler will be in an unreasonable amount of danger.
Sexual Orientation	Homosexuality remains either officially illegal or culturally unacceptable in dozens of countries.
Suspicion	Remember that this isn't a court of law and that a border guard needs no proof to deny a visa application. Any thought that you might be a spy, drug smuggler, or just someone who may cause trouble can result in the denial of a visa.
Vaccinations	Lack of necessary vaccinations will always result in the denial of a visa.

PREPARE

Many facets of the modern travel experience may benefit from meticulous preparation but few require it. Visa issues are one such area. Not properly researching visa requirements can end a trip before it begins. Vaccinations, accommodation reservations, transportation tickets, and much more may all be necessary for a visa and many of these require advanced planning. Following a carefree, go-where-the-wind-takes-me travel philosophy is a good and admirable way to see the world, but visas are an area where one should briefly adopt a serious, detail-oriented mind-set.

PROTECT YOUR PEN

A simple but necessary reminder. Borders are notoriously understocked with pens with which to fill out visa applications. Having your own pens handy, in both blue and black ink, will expedite the process.

CHOOSE WISELY

All border crossings are not created equal. Some charge higher fees as a matter of national policy, and others simply develop a reputation for efficiency or ease of entry. As should be obvious from the previous list of potential reasons for visa denial, border officials have a large amount of leeway in deciding who is granted entry. Remember that any regulation is only as strict as the official tasked with enforcing it.

Some officials won't stamp your passport if you ask them not to, others will question you for hours for seemingly no reason. Some officials are unfailingly helpful and kind; others will only do their job if given a hefty bribe. Some officials will happily issue a multiple-entry three-month visa for the same price as single-entry one-month visa if you ask nicely; others will deny entry if a single line of a form is illegible.

This is a rapidly changing, fundamentally human process where a little research goes a long way. Ask fellow travelers who have recently crossed for the latest news and tips.

CONSIDER PAYMENT

Always expect that visa fees and entry/exit taxes will need to be paid in cash, to say nothing of bribes. This may require exchanging money at the border to pay in local currency.

KEEP EVERYTHING

Some countries require travelers to pay exit taxes or return a "tourist card" upon leaving a country. Always keep all paperwork and receipts given to you upon entering a country, it may be required on your way out.

....

1 ››› See page 46 for more information on how many countries holders of different passports can enter without a visa.
2 ››› See page 244 for more information on bribery.
3 ››› See page 172 for advice on avoiding unwanted passport stamps.
4 ››› See page 40 for more information on Proof of Onward Travel.

————— ◆ —————

FINDING POWER

CHECK WITH THE lost and found at airports, hotels, or car rental agencies: they often have dozens of chargers that have been left behind by absentminded travelers. Though some places will want to check that you're a paying customer, many are happy to give a forgotten charger away free to anyone who asks.

So I wander and wander along,
And forever before me gleams
The shining city of song,
In the beautiful land of dreams.

But when I would enter the gate
Of that golden atmosphere,
It is gone, and I wonder and wait
For the vision to reappear.

—HENRY WADSWORTH LONGFELLOW,
selected lines of the poem "Fata Morgana,"[1] 1873

A MIRAGE IS AN observable natural phenomenon in which bending rays of light produce distorted images. Though mirages can lead to confusion, they are distinct from hallucinations in that at least some of what the observer is seeing *does* actually exist, it is simply appearing out of place.

Below are the *definitions* and examples of the two general categorizations of mirages.

———

SUPERIOR MIRAGE: *The distorted image is seen above or higher than the actual object.*

An explorer in the arctic tundra sees what looks like an extraordinarily tall building in the distance and believes it be evidence of a large settlement. The structure is in fact an inverted image of a much smaller structure, appearing above its actual location.

INFERIOR MIRAGE: *The distorted image is seen below or under the actual object.*

A lost traveler in the desert sees a blue area among the sand in the distance and believes it to be a lifesaving oasis. The area is in fact an inverted image of the blue sky appearing below its actual location.

....

1 ››› Longfellow's poem actually describes an inferior mirage, not a fata morgana mirage. A fata morgana is a specific type of rapidly changing superior mirage named after the sorceress Morgan le Fay from the legend of King Arthur. A fata morgana mirage is often the scientific explanation behind nautical myths: the phenomenon can cause ships near the horizon to appear to be floating in the air, among many other strange visual effects.

JAMMED

T**HE LONGEST TRAFFIC** jam of all time is thought to have occurred between August 14 and August 25, 2010, on China National Highway 110. The 11-day traffic jam, partially caused by construction on the nearby Beijing–Tibet Expressway, stretched for 62 miles (100 kilometers) and involved thousands of motorists, many of whom averaged less than 1 mile (1.6 kilometers) per day. The prices charged by roadside vendors for instant noodles, bottles of water, and cigarettes increased by multiples of 3, 10, and 20, respectively, based solely on the traffic.

VALUE FOR MONEY

T**HE WORLD'S MOST** expensive city for expats is, surprisingly, Luanda, Angola. The country was once devastated by a 27-year-long civil war, which prevented most significant infrastructure projects, and today most Angolans still live on less than a dollar per day. However, since the fighting ended in 2002, foreign investment has flooded in at an incredible rate, which is rich in oil, among other natural resources. Prices for goods valued by expats[1] reflect this new economic reality.

OVERALL RANKING	CITY	MONTHLY RENT FOR A 2-BEDROOM UNFINISHED APARTMENT	PRICE OF A FAST-FOOD MEAL
1	Luanda	$6,800	$17.14
2	Hong Kong	$6,576	$4.75
12	London	$4,899	$6.72
16	New York City	$5,400	$7.93

Data provided by Mercer's 2015 Cost of Living Rankings.

1 ››› It's important to reiterate that these costs reflect the life of a typical expat, not a typical citizen. Rental rates quoted are for apartments in high-end neighborhoods and meal costs are for typical Western foods from chain restaurants.

ON THE TRYING OF NEW FOODS

They say that it is an "acquired taste" but what deprivations you have to undergo to acquire the taste they do not say.

—ALEC LE SUEUR,
British author, on Tibetan yak butter tea
The Hotel on the Roof of the World: Five Years in Tibet, 1988

THE MOST WIDELY UNDERSTOOD WORDS IN THE WORLD

NATIVE

These are the words that linguists believe arose organically from virtually every language on earth. Even though their spelling and exact pronunciation may vary slightly from culture to culture, their meaning remains the same in almost every language.

Huh? · Ha? · Ã? · E? · Aé? · Eh?

Recent studies have indicated that *Huh* may be the single most universal word in current usage. Almost every language seems to have a similar short, easily expressible, interrogative word said with rising intonation, used to express confusion or a need for clarification.

Mama · Madér · Ama · Majka · Maman · Mutter

Many experts believe the similarity of this word across cultures is caused by the fact that the "mmm" sound is one of the simplest for a newborn baby to produce, leading to it naturally being associated with motherhood.

Papa · Pai · Abba · Pare · Baba · Padre

Similar to *mama*, the universality of the word *papa* is thought to be the result of newborn babies naturally using easily pronounced sounds to refer to their main caregivers.

BORROWED

These words originated in only one language, but have spread across the globe and are now widely understood. There has been no definitive global study ranking the awareness of these words across every culture; instead this list simply represents an unofficial consensus among experts.

Okay · Coca-Cola · Taxi · No · Coffee · Hello

A CALL TO ADVENTURE

I must go down to the seas again, to the lonely sea and the sky,
And all I ask is a tall ship and a star to steer her by;
And the wheel's kick and the wind's song and the white sail's shaking,
And a grey mist on the sea's face, and a grey dawn breaking.

I must go down to the seas again, for the call of the running tide
Is a wild call and a clear call that may not be denied;
And all I ask is a windy day with the white clouds flying,
And the flung spray and the blown spume, and the sea-gulls crying.

I must go down to the seas again, to the vagrant gypsy life,
To the gull's way and the whale's way where the wind's like a whetted knife;
And all I ask is a merry yarn from a laughing fellow-rover,
And quiet sleep and a sweet dream when the long trick's over.

—JOHN MASEFIELD,
English poet and author, "Sea Fever," *Salt-Water Ballads*, 1902

WATER TO BED

No one knows the value of water until he is deprived of it . . .

—DR. DAVID LIVINGSTONE,
African explorer

ALWAYS BRING A bottle of clean water to bed. Tap water is often unsafe to drink and perpetually open convenience stores are largely a Western luxury. Any traveler who's laid awake on some foreign mattress so cotton-mouthed they can barely swallow, in plain sight of a faucet dripping water they know to be infected with dangerous bacteria, knows the importance of this tip.

NOTABLE TRAVEL CLUBS

Travel clubs, in varying forms, have existed for centuries. Over the years, they have provided a channel for travelers to swap stories and important information, helped to standardize regulations and best practices, promoted travel and exploration in all its many forms, and catered to evolving forms of traveler competition.

Furthermore, the specific motivation behind the founding of these clubs reflects the mentality of the travelers of the time. While all are fundamentally "travel" clubs, they are also a product of their era. Below is a list of some notable travel clubs, along with a brief summary of the main goals of travel during the eras in which they were created.

MAPPING THE WORLD

These clubs were founded on the idea that accurate geographical information should be a collective pursuit, mutually beneficial to anyone with a thirst for adventure. And though that may have been their official lofty credo, early members of these clubs were driven by the idea that if you can't be the first to discover a place then the next best thing is to be the first to map it.

The Royal Geographical Society

"Advancing geography and geographical learning."

FOUNDED: 1830, London | MEMBERSHIP: ~16,500

HOW TO GET IN:
Ordinary membership is open to the public
and costs ~$200 per year.

The Royal Geographical Society is one of the world's most respected travel-oriented clubs and has played an important role in the history of exploration. The support of the RGS was critical to explorers like Sir Richard Burton and Robert Falcon Scott, among many others, as both a source of funding and as a medium for organization and publicity. Today, the RGS preserves this history by maintaining a large collection and hosting exhibits, promoting travel through the publication of research and journals, and supporting the next generation of explorers through a variety of awards and grants.

National Geographic Society

"Inspire, illuminate, teach."

FOUNDED: 1888, Washington, DC | MEMBERSHIP: 6.8 million

HOW TO GET IN:
Membership in the society is now linked to
subscription to the magazine. Subscribing member status
is available for $19 per year.

The National Geographic Society has focused on not only promoting exploration, but also inspiring people to care about and protect the places they explore. As an innovator in travel photography and media, National Geographic provided the first glimpse of many distant countries to entire generations of the American public. In addition to helping popularize topics like archeology and biology, the society has funded a variety of conservation efforts and scientific expeditions. They continue this work today and are involved in the publication of multiple magazines, films, and television shows.

CONQUERING THE EXTREMES

After most of the inhabited world had been sufficiently mapped, the focus of brave travelers everywhere became the extreme reaches of earth. If the only unexplored places left were the frigid poles, the tops of the highest mountains, and the very bottom of the deepest oceans, then so be it. Exploring these inaccessible regions were the dreams these clubs were founded on.

The Explorers Club

"Dedicated to exploration of Earth, its oceans, and outer space."

FOUNDED: 1904, New York City | MEMBERSHIP: ~3,000

HOW TO GET IN:
Submit an application containing proof of an extensive
background in travel and specific contributions to the
general cause of exploration. Two sponsorships from
current members are also required.

That members of the Explorers Club were the first to reach the North Pole, the South Pole, the top of Mount Everest, the bottom of the Mariana Trench, and the surface of the moon may tell you all you need to

ᵛᵛᵛ *continued* ᵛᵛᵛ

know about this illustrious organization. The club continues their proud tradition through a series of lectures, grants, awards, and other events. The spirit of those famous adventurers lives on as current members continue to tell tales of past journeys and plan future expeditions in 30 chapters across the globe.

The Adventurers Club

"To provide a hearth and home for those who have left the beaten path and made for adventure."

FOUNDED:	MEMBERSHIP:
1912, New York City & Chicago	*Information not available*

HOW TO GET IN:
An application process regarding interest and experience in all types of adventurous travel needs to be approved by both the general membership and the board of directors.

The Adventurers Club nostalgically recalls the time of the classic American and British explorer, an era of khaki safari outfits, gin and tonics, and maps with country names like Rhodesia and Siam. The clubhouses have kept this tradition, often featuring rhino tusks on the wall and shrunken heads in the club museum. The organization has earned every bit of this vintage identity however. It counts Arctic explorer Roald Amundsen, Mount Everest summiteer Sir Edmund Hillary, and, perhaps the man who most embodies the club, President Theodore Roosevelt among its many notable alumni. Modern members belonging to chapters in Los Angeles and Honolulu carry on the tradition by engaging in activities like ice climbing, space exploration, and extended stays in remote areas around the world.

GOING EVERYWHERE

As the geographers were mapping the last unknown corners of the world and the adventurers were conquering the final earthly extremes, a new kind of travel club emerged.[1] With few "firsts" left to claim, and technology making travel accessible to more people than ever before, the new goal became to go everywhere.

The Travelers' Century Club

"World Travel: The passport to peace through understanding."

FOUNDED: 1954, Los Angeles | MEMBERSHIP: ~2,100

HOW TO GET IN:
An application detailing extensive world travel.
Membership is available only to those that have
traveled to 100 or more of the 325 official territories
designated by the club.

The Travelers' Century Club began as a social club for jet-setting Californians and has evolved into one the most popular organizations for frequent travelers. In 20 chapters throughout the United States, Canada, Germany, and the United Kingdom, globetrotters trade advice about how to get to some of the world's most remote places. Furthermore, the official TCC Countries & Territories list has become a leading comparison method for the world's most well-traveled people.

Most Traveled People

"On the road to everywhere . . . "

FOUNDED: 2005, online | MEMBERSHIP: 12,204

HOW TO GET IN:
MTP is open to the public and free to join using
a basic online application. Proof of travel is
required to be credited with places visited.

Five years after the *Guinness Book of World Records* decided it would no longer judge the Most Traveled Person category citing a lack of verifiable proof, Most Traveled People was created to satisfy some travelers' thirst for competition. Like TCC, MTP divides the world by areas, not countries, and the MTP Master List lists 871 areas for the extreme traveler to strive to visit. The leader at the time of this writing, Mr. Donald M. Parrish Jr. of Illinois has only 25 areas remaining.

1 ›› These types of travel clubs are not without their well-deserved controversies. Many travelers reject the idea of traveling simply for the sake of checking a place off a list.

THE COMPLICATED CUSTOM OF TIPPING

HOW MUCH TO tip when traveling is a common question without a simple answer. Tipping etiquette is so localized, rapidly evolving, and dependent on variable factors like the profession in question, level of service, and service charges that any definitive numerical advice would be so burdened with caveats as to be unusable. Check with other travelers to find out current local customs concerning who to tip, how much, and in what currency.

While specific tipping percentages vary greatly even within a single country, there is a defined, globally applicable protocol to giving money to those you do decide to tip:

» Do so subtly, in cash, out of view of the person's boss and coworkers.

» Do not ask for change.

» Putting bills in an envelope is appreciated, especially by hotel workers.

» Folding bills before offering them and disguising the handoff with a handshake is a tried-and-true method of tipping for good reason. It is always best to deliver a tip as discreetly as circumstances allow.

» If someone protests, claiming they cannot accept the generosity of additional payment, lightly insist.[1] If they protest further, withdraw the tip and thank them again for their service.

---

1 ››› In some cultures it is customary to humbly decline any gift the first time it is offered.

A DESTRUCTIVE SOUVENIR

IT COULD BE argued that the most critical duty of a customs official is not exposing drug smuggling or providing security, but stopping invasive species from crossing the border. There is almost nothing more damaging to an ecosystem than the introduction of a nonnative, rapidly reproducing species into a habitat with no natural predators. Throughout history, animals have hitched rides with travelers to new and highly favorable environments, often with disastrous results for local wildlife.

Regardless of whether it's a tiny exotic bug you want to show friends back home or a stray-dog-turned-beloved-pet, never travel internationally with animals without going through the proper channels.[1]

Rattus rattus
THE BLACK RAT

C. 100 AD
MULTIPLE LOCATIONS

The black rat was one of history's first invasive species and is undoubtedly one of the most destructive. Native to India and Pakistan, travelers have been unknowingly transporting rats around the world for millennia and they have thrived almost everywhere. Countless species of plants and animals have been decimated or completely destroyed by the black rat, to say nothing of the tragedy their disease-carrying has caused civilizations around the world. As humans have traveled to the far reaches of the earth, so too has the humble black rat, often leaving death and destruction in its wake.

Oryctolagus cuniculus
THE EUROPEAN RABBIT

1859
VICTORIA, AUSTRALIA

Settler Thomas Austin had two dozen gray rabbits brought over from England, stating "the introduction of a few rabbits could do little harm and might provide a touch of home, in addition to a spot of hunting." By 1920, the population had exploded to 10 billion and devastated many native Australian species of plants, among other negative effects.

Achatina fulica
THE GIANT AFRICAN LAND SNAIL

1966
FLORIDA, UNITED STATES

After a young boy smuggled three giant African land snails home from a trip to Hawaii, his grandmother released them into the garden of their Miami home. Within seven years, the area was overrun with more than 18,000 snails, causing significant damage to local property and wildlife.

1››› See page 168 for more information on properly traveling with pets.

To travel is to discover that everyone is wrong about other countries.

—ALDOUS HUXLEY,

English writer, novelist, and philosopher

MOST TRAVELERS ARE lucky enough to have the full power of their respective governments backing them when they go abroad. Governments maintain embassies that can assist travelers in foreign lands, protect travel routes from all manner of dangerous elements, coordinate expensive rescue operations when their citizens are in trouble, and are generally a much more valuable and useful resource than travelers usually give them credit for. That being said, when it comes to travel there are times that a government is not unlike an anxious parent who watches too much news.

With the issuing of travel advisories, governments around the world attempt to warn their citizens about areas that might be unsafe for them to explore. And many of these advisories are indeed the result of legitimate threats. Whether the cause is civil unrest, disease, weather, or country-specific animosity there are undoubtedly some places that would be extremely unsafe for citizens of certain countries. In issuing these advisories governments help to ensure that travelers have current information about conditions in every country around the world.[1]

Many governments also offer traveler registration or enrollment programs. These provide more detailed security information and advisories based on the specifics of your itinerary and easier access to embassy services, and can assist governments in locating citizens in the event of an emergency.

However, there are three significant issues that travelers should be aware of when it comes to interpreting any kind government-issued travel advisory. The first is that governments will always err on the side of safety and caution. Any type of incident, threat, or rumor is often enough for a government to issue a travel advisory, sometimes written in exaggerated language. Secondly, these travel advisories often imply that the entire country is enveloped in some kind of extreme crisis, when in reality the potential danger, if it exists at all, is often limited to one small geographical area. Lastly, travelers should realize that all governments are constantly engaged in a complex battle of geopolitics. Travel advisories are sometimes issued purely for the political effect of showing disapproval of a foreign government's actions. This means that a travel advisory might have nothing to do with safety concerns in a certain country, but merely that the ruling party of that country has done something to anger the ruling party of some other country.

Travelers should understand the realities and motivations behind travel advisories and interpret them accordingly. Never take a government's travel advisory at face value and always supplement the information provided with your own research when determining whether or not an area is safe for travel.

Below is a high-level summary and general comparison of four different country's system of travel advisories, which are similar to many of the systems used by governments around the world.

	AUSTRALIA[2]	CANADA[2]	U.K.[2]	U.S.[2,3]
CAUTIOUS →	Level 1: Exercise normal safety precautions	Exercise normal security precautions	No travel restrictions	No specific advisory issued
	Level 2: Exercise a high degree of caution	Exercise a high degree of caution	No specific advisory issued	Travel Alert: a short-term advisory concerning a specific, potentially dangerous event, like a controversial election that may result in riots
SERIOUS →	Level 3: Reconsider your need to travel	Avoid nonessential travel	Advise against all but essential travel	Travel Warning: a more serious, indefinite notice that advises against travel to a country because of consistent violence or danger
	Level 4: Do not travel	Avoid all travel	Advise against all travel	

1 ›› Travelers should be aware that some forms of travel insurance can be affected, and sometimes nullified, based on the issuing of travel advisories.

2 ›› These travel advisories are sometimes specifically issued only for certain areas of a country.

3 ›› The US government also issues Worldwide Travel Alerts (short-term) and Worldwide Cautions (indefinite) that warn citizens of global terrorist threats or situations in which Americans might be specifically targeted.

NATIVE CITIZENS POKE fun at tourists in a variety of ways, but one age-old tradition is the telling of urban myths about a terrifying and mysterious local beast. These creatures inevitably seem to only attack hapless travelers and stories about them serve to both ridicule the swarms of visitors and prove how gullible they are about the area they are exploring. Though some of these monsters have origins in ominous local legends, today most are thought of more as lighthearted, area-wide inside jokes and a way to sell souvenirs, rather than a serious attempt to discourage tourism.

Below are a few of the most notable creatures scaring tourists around the world today.

THE DROP BEAR
Australia

The **drop bear** is purportedly a vicious and carnivorous beast that resembles an extraordinarily large koala bear with vampirelike teeth. It is said to live mainly in the forests of southeast Australia, waiting to drop on an unsuspecting tourist from its hiding place high among the trees. The drop bear may be the most enthusiastically embraced tourist-scaring urban myth in the world today, with huge numbers of Australians committed to furthering the legend and even an official-looking page on the Australian Museum's website.

THE WILD HAGGIS
Scotland

The **wild haggis** is often depicted as a small furry animal with prominent ears and a cylindrical shape. Legend has it that there are two separate species of wild haggis, each with right and left legs of different lengths, which allows it to run around the mountains of the Scottish Highlands more quickly—though only in one direction.

The specific motivation behind the myth of the wild haggis is more based in proving tourist's naïveté, as opposed to actively trying to scare them. Its enduring legacy comes from the fact that few foreigners know what the classic Scottish dish of haggis is actually made from,[1] which leads to predictable common questions, which leads to a chance for Scots to perpetuate this urban myth.

THE JACKALOPE
United States

The **jackalope,** like Germany's *wolpertinger* and Sweden's *skvader,* is one of a surprising number of rabbit-based mythical creatures. This iteration is a mix of a jackrabbit and antelope, hence the name, and is said the roam the northwestern United States, especially Wyoming and South Dakota. Jackalopes apparently love whiskey, only mate during lightning storms, can mimic human speech, and use their horns to attack unsuspecting visitors to their woods. Tourists visiting certain towns can even buy jackalope milk, which is said to help cure a variety of ailments.

1 ›› Traditional haggis is sheep innards (such as heart, liver, and lungs), mixed with oatmeal, onion, and spices, encased in a sheep's stomach and boiled.

THE CANDY ECONOMY

FOR NATIONS WITH unstable economies, ensuring that enough hard currency is available can be a complex proposition. Wildly fluctuating forces of supply and demand mean that there is often not enough currency to go around—especially small change.

In these situations, it is common for vendors, ranging from small independent shops to large chain stores, to be unable to give small change. Though claiming "no change" is sometimes a tactic used to encourage customers to pay with smaller, more manageable bills, this is often the result of the economic reality of their country. And so a fascinating subeconomy emerges in which a variety of items are used to settle the small debts caused by the cash shortage. Lollipops, plastic bags, matches, soda, gum, and razor blades are all commonly used as substitutes for actual currency in these circumstances.

As bizarre as it may sound, this is a daily occurrence in some developing countries, such as Zimbabwe. So if you're given a handful of candy instead of your expected change, don't assume you're being ripped off. Simply enjoy this unexpected treat and move on with your shopping.

UNCONVENTIONAL TYPES OF TOURISM

TOURISM	TO VISIT, SEE, OR DO:	EXAMPLE DESTINATION
Agri-	Visiting or working on a farm	Tuscany, Italy
Atomic	Sites of early atomic testing	Nevada, United States
Dark	Places associated with tragedy	Chernobyl, Ukraine
Ghost	Famous haunted places	York, England
Medical	Traveling to get cheaper or better medical care	India
Romance	Traveling to find a spouse or significant other	Ukraine
Set-jetting	Popular movie filming locations	New Zealand
Sex	Places where prostitution is legal or culturally acceptable	Pattaya, Thailand
Slum	Impoverished areas	Brazilian favelas
Stuffed animal	Owners pay to have toys photographed in front of famous sites	Japan
Tombstone	The graves of famous people	Paris, France
Tornado	Tracking or chasing tornados and violent storms	Kansas, United States
Vino-	Famous vineyards and wine-making regions	Napa Valley, United States

---

THE RULES OF 3

THOUGH OBVIOUSLY DEPENDENT on fitness and health, this is a good, general guide to how long you can you survive.

3 {
minutes without **oxygen**

hours without **shelter** (*in extreme weather conditions*)

days without **water**

weeks without **food**
}

THE STARS ARE BORN

IN 1824, A playwright and author named Mariana Starke published a guidebook called *Information and Directions for Travellers on the Continent*. Along with travel advice for early Victorian travelers exploring France and Italy, she also included a rating system of exclamation points to help readers find the very best sights.

Starke's system ranged from a single exclamation point for notable works of art:

> *... torso of Jupiter, supposed to be an antique imitation, in marble, of the famous Jupiter Olympius of Phidas* !

To the rarely awarded five for truly magnificent sights:

> *The Cappella Sistina contains some of the finest frescos in the world, namely,* The Last Judgement, *by Buonarroti, immediately behind the alter, and on the ceiling, God dividing the light from the darkness, together with the Prophets and Sibyls, stupendous works by the same great Master* !!!!!

Since Starke's historic guidebook innovation, there have been all manner of stars, diamonds, rankings, and "best of" lists. However, travelers would be wise to remember that a professional rating is only as trustworthy as the organization bestowing it. There are, for instance, multiple hotels around the world that proudly display six or seven stars in their luxurious lobbies. Yet, careful examination often reveals that these stars were awarded by none other than the hotel itself, or by an organization closely related thereto. Without an unbiased third-party using precisely defined criteria, or a crowd-sourced ranking system with a clear methodology, such designations are essentially meaningless.[1]

....

1 ››› Or as a sign outside the Libertine Lindenberg in Frankfurt more bluntly puts it:

NEVER TRUST THESE
F ✳ ✳ ✳ ✳ ✳ G
HOTEL CLASSIFICATIONS

THE UNCONTACTED

UNCONTACTED TRIBES IS an all-encompassing term for groups of people currently living without any meaningful contact with modern civilization. Situations vary from isolated tribes with little understanding of the outside world to larger communities who are fully aware of the differences between their way of life and contemporary society. However, regardless of a specific uncontacted community's interpretation of their place in the greater world, in the overwhelming majority of cases these people have made a conscious choice to stay separate from conventional society. Whether that choice is the result of a negative interaction with outsiders long ago or a simple desire to live life in the way of their ancestors is generally not known. But in almost every case, these tribes have had ample opportunities to contact or join modern societies and have actively decided not to do so.

The morality of interacting with an uncontacted tribe is a complex and heavily debated issue. On one hand, forced contact can have all sorts of devastating cultural, physical, and societal consequences. From a purely biological perspective, many of these tribes lack natural immunities from modern diseases and therefore may be at risk of total extinction from just one germ-swapping interaction. On the other, some people feel that there is a moral obligation to improve the lives of less technologically advanced people through the introduction of modern medicine or to send aid during natural disasters.

There are a countless number of tourism activities, from village tours to jungle treks, that play on many travelers' desires to have an authentic interaction with an uncontacted tribe. As disheartening as this may be for some readers to realize, today it would be extraordinarily rare to encounter a truly uncontacted person in the course of normal tourism or travel.

Some local peoples may have never met a certain race of person or held a modern cell phone, but they are likely not *uncontacted* in the sense of the definition given above. This is not to say the "natives" trade their traditional clothing for T-shirts and tennis shoes the moment the tourists leave (though this is sometimes the case) but simply that, in some situations, local people may intentionally present an altered, more basic way of life or exaggerate their ignorance of the outside world, all for the benefit of the tourist.

Due to mining, deforestation, drug trafficking, as well as the general effects of globalization, the number of uncontacted people in the world is rapidly dwindling. Exact populations are difficult to estimate but most experts agree that only about a hundred uncontacted tribes still exist, many composed of only a few dozen individuals. Below are descriptions of some of these few remaining uncontacted tribes.

THE SENTINELESE[1]

BAY OF BENGAL, INDIA
50 to 500 Individuals

Very little is known about these inhabitants of the 28 square mile (72 square kilometer) North Sentinel Island, other than the fact that they clearly do not want to be bothered by outsiders. Marco Polo described them as "a most brutish and savage race . . . they are very cruel, and kill and eat every foreigner whom they can lay their hands upon" in 1290, and in the ensuing centuries their violent attitude toward outsiders seems to have remained unchanged. Almost every attempt to communicate with the Sentinelese has been met with a barrage of arrows and in 2006 two fishermen were killed for venturing too close to the island. One of the only attempts to not result in outright violence was in the late 1960s when anthropologists left the Sentinelese people a variety of food, livestock, and gifts on their beach in hopes of establishing friendly relations. Upon discovering these offerings, the Sentinelese quickly ate the coconuts, killed and buried the pigs without eating them, buried a children's doll, and gleefully took a group of red buckets into the forest, while rejecting a group of similar green buckets.

UNNAMED RONDÔNIA TRIBES

RONDÔNIA, BRAZIL
100 to 1,000 Individuals

The Jupaú, sometimes called the Urue-Wau-Wau, are a jungle-dwelling tribe who hunt tapir with poison arrows and wear large black facial tattoos in reverence to the macaw, a sacred animal among their tribe. They remain extremely isolated from contemporary society, but have been in sporadic contact with the outside world, mostly to broker uneasy truces or to protest loss of territory. In their brief interactions with anthropologists and government officials, they've indicated there are at least two additional, distinct tribes living deep in the Brazilian jungle.

Though aerial surveys have confirmed their existence, almost nothing is known about these unnamed tribes, other than the fact that they are hunter-gatherers and likely animist.[2] They've successfully remained apart for centuries, but it is highly unlikely they will be left alone for much longer.

ᵛᵛᵛ *continued* ᵛᵛᵛ

Disease, drug traffickers, and encroachment by mining and logging interests have decimated indigenous populations across South America to the point that some tribes have been forced to make unwanted contact simply to plead for assistance. Governments have been slow to act, even when presented with substantial evidence of the outright massacre of indigenous people by outsiders interested in controlling the area. Every new discovery of natural resources spells further doom and most experts predict the extinction of increasing numbers of tribes in the near future.

UNNAMED NEW GUINEA TRIBES

THROUGHOUT THE ISLAND
Unknown

The island of New Guinea is a place of extremely difficult terrain and home to at least a thousand languages. These isolating factors have helped the uncontacted tribes of the island remain separate from the outside world and many experts estimate that more than 40 distinct tribes may still exist. These tribes are believed to be a mix of farmers and hunter-gatherers and some may be in contact with one another, both for purposes of trade and warfare.

Indigenous tribes of New Guinea have a reputation for violence, partially because of the disappearance of Michael Rockefeller in 1961. Rockefeller, the son of an extraordinarily wealthy and powerful American family, disappeared while studying the Asmat tribe and collecting indigenous artwork. Some tribes in New Guinea have a history of cannibalism and he was rumored to have been captured and eaten, though this was never proven.

Contact has been made with a number of New Guinea's indigenous tribes with varying degrees of integration occurring. When the Korowai were first contacted in 1978, they communicated that they believed a mountain god would destroy the world with a great earthquake if they altered their customs and were therefore fearful of interacting with outsiders. Whether the still-uncontacted tribes follow similar belief systems is unknown but, because the unforgiving terrain naturally causes certain areas to be extremely isolated, some of the indigenous tribes of New Guinea haven't yet had to make a definitive choice on how to deal with outsiders.

....

1››› Because the tribe is uncontacted, it is not known how these people refer to themselves. This name has been arbitrarily assigned by outsiders.

2››› Animism is a belief system in which all animals, plants, and other elements of nature possess individual souls or spirits and therefore should be respected and, sometimes, worshipped accordingly.

THE RELATIVE SIZE OF THE VERY SMALL COUNTRIES

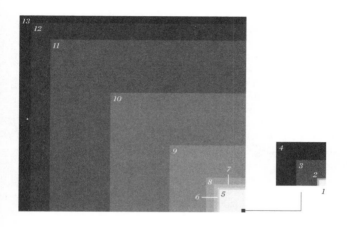

Key

	PLACE	MI^2	KM^2
1	VATICAN CITY	0.17	0.44
2	Augusta National Golf Course	0.22	0.57
3	MONACO	0.78	2.02
4	Central Park, New York City	1.32	3.42
5	NAURU	8.10	20.98
6	Penn State University Park Campus	8.78	22.73
7	TUVALU	10.00	25.90
8	Charles de Gaulle Airport	12.50	32.37
9	SAN MARINO	24.00	62.16
10	Walt Disney World	43.00	111.37
11	LIECHTENSTEIN	62.00	160.57
12	Washington, DC	68.30	176.89
13	MARSHALL ISLANDS	70.00	181.29

THE GREAT MAP DEBATE

If geography is prose, maps are iconography.

—LENNART MERI,
Estonian politician, writer, and film director

FOR MILLENNIA, THE practice of cartography has been plagued by a fundamental difficulty: how to accurately represent the spherical shape of the earth on the flat surface of a page. Despite the best efforts of countless mapmakers, this is a problem that will never truly be solved[1] and thus this central issue of cartography has become a matter of choosing which map projection is the least inaccurate.

Arguments surrounding map projections go far beyond geographical accuracy or navigational usefulness. For instance, a country's relative size and positioning on a world map can significantly influence how people understand that country. Therefore, which map projection is used can have far-reaching societal, political, and humanitarian implications. Below are brief summaries of the most popular map projections in use today, along with the inherent biases contained in each.[2]

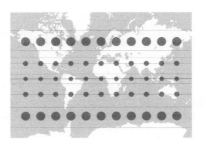

MERCATOR

CREATED BY: GERARDUS MERCATOR, 1569

Detriments: Only countries on or near the equator are at all accurately represented. Distortion greatly increases closer to the poles, to the point where Greenland appears larger than the entire continent of Africa, when it is in fact 14 times smaller.

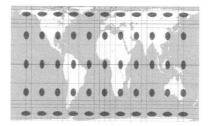

GALL–PETERS

CREATED BY[3]: JAMES GALL, 1855; ARNO PETERS, 1967

Detriments: Unlike Mercator, countries of equal size occupy equal amounts of space on a Gall–Peters projection. However, the shape of many countries is distorted. Most notably, regions near the equator are vertically stretched, while regions near the poles are horizontally stretched.

....

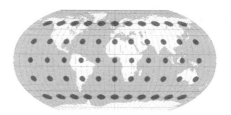

ROBINSON

CREATED BY: ARTHUR H. ROBINSON, 1963

Detriments: Many experts think of the Robinson projection as a compromise between Mercator and Gall–Peters. Where Mercator maintains the shape of countries but doesn't accurately represent the size of the area they occupy, and Gall–Peters ensures the area of countries is correct relative to one another but stretches their shapes, Robinson does a little of both. There is no one area on the Robinson projection, except for arguably the poles, with significant distortion. Rather, there is a minimal amount of distortion throughout.

....

1 ››› In 1828, Carl Friedrich Gauss published his *Theorema Egregium*, which mathematically proves that a sphere cannot be represented on a flat surface without some sort of distortion.
2 ››› The circles overlaid on the maps are called *Tissot's indicatrices* and are provided to help illustrate the effects of map distortion.
3 ››› Origin is disputed.

PHONE HOME

00 · 258 · 410 · 452-0315

International Dialing Prefix · Country Code · Area Code · Telephone Number

A N INTERNATIONAL DIALING prefix[1] is used when "dialing out" of a country's phone system to make an international call. This prevents the local system from interpreting the subsequent country code as a local number.

International dialing prefixes are represented by the "+" sign. If you see a "+" sign before a phone number, you'll need to begin the call by dialing the international dialing prefix of whatever country you're calling from. Many cell phones now provide this functionality automatically: simply press the "+" key and the appropriate international dialing prefix will be included.

The standard international dialing prefix is 00. All countries and territories use this code except the following[2]:

PREFIX	COUNTRY OR TERRITORY
0	Samoa
000	Kenya, Singapore, South Korea, Tanzania, Thailand, Uganda
001	Cambodia, Guyana, Hong Kong, Indonesia, Mongolia
005	Colombia
009	Nigeria
010	Japan
011	Anguilla, Antigua and Barbuda, Bahamas, Barbados, Bermuda, Canada, Dominica, Dominican Republic, Grenada, Honduras, Jamaica, Marshall Islands, Micronesia, Northern Mariana Islands, Palau, Saint Kitts and Nevis, Saint Lucia, Saint Vincent and the Grenadines, Sint Maarten, Trinidad and Tobago, Turks and Caicos Islands, United States
0111	Australia
0014	Brazil
119	Cuba
810	Belarus, Kazakhstan, Russia, Tajikistan, Turkmenistan, Uzbekistan

International calls can be extremely expensive when using a traditional telephone service. Many modern travelers instead prefer to use voice Internet protocol (VoIP) programs, such as Skype. Though call quality can be an issue, most VoIP programs are free and more convenient than traditional phone services. Note that VoIP calls still require inputting an international dialing prefix.

THE REMAINING MONARCHIES

BELOW IS A listing of the COUNTRIES that retain some form of royal ruling,[1] along with the current monarch's *official title,* ROYAL HOUSE, and *date of assumption* of the throne.

ABSOLUTE MONARCHIES

These rulers hold virtually absolute power over their lands and subjects.

BRUNEI

His Majesty Sultan Hassanal Bolkiah Mu'izzaddin Waddaulah

BOLKIAH . . . . October 4, 1967

SAUDI ARABIA

The Custodian of the Two Holy Mosques King Salman bin Abdulaziz Al Saud

AL SAUD . . . . January 23, 2015

OMAN

His Majesty Sultan Qaboos bin Said

AL SAID . . . . July 23, 1970

SWAZILAND

His Majesty King Mswati III

DLAMINI . . . . April 25, 1986

QATAR[2]

His Majesty Sultan Tamim bin Hamad Al Thani

AL THANI . . . . June 25, 2013

UNITED ARAB EMIRATES[3]

His Highness Sheikh Khalifa bin Zayed Al Nahyan

AL NAHYAN . . . . November 3, 2004

VATICAN CITY

His Holiness Pope Francis

N/A . . . . March 13, 2013

⌄⌄⌄ *continued* ⌄⌄⌄

CONSTITUTIONAL MONARCHIES

Situations range from dominating rulers who maintain significant power to purely ceremonial figureheads with no political influence.

ANDORRA[4]

His Excellency Archbishop Joan Enric Vives i Sicília and His Excellency President François Hollande

N/A. . . . . *May 12, 2003 & May 15, 2012*

BAHRAIN[5]

His Majesty King Hamad bin Isa Al Khalifa

AL KHALIFAH . . . . *March 6, 1999*

JORDAN

His Majesty King Abdullah II ibn Al Hussein

HASHIM. . . . . *February 7, 1999*

BELGIUM

His Majesty King Philippe

SAXE-COBURG & GOTHA . . . *July 21, 2013*

KUWAIT

His Highness Sheikh Sabah Al-Ahmad Al-Jaber Al-Sabah

AL-SABAH . . . . *January 29, 2006*

BHUTAN

His Majesty King Jigme Khesar Namgyel Wangchuck

WANGCHUCK . . . . . . *December 14, 2006*

LESOTHO

His Majesty King Letsie III

MOSHESH . . . . *February 7, 1996*

CAMBODIA

His Majesty Preah Bat Samdech Preah Boromneath Norodom Sihamoni

NORODOM . . . . *October 14, 2004*

LIECHTENSTEIN

His Serene Highness Prince Hans-Adam II von und zu Liechtenstein

LIECHTENSTEIN . . . *November 13, 1989*

DENMARK

Her Majesty Queen Margrethe II

GLÜCKSBURG . . . . *January 14, 1972*

LUXEMBOURG

His Royal Highness Le Grand-Duc Henri de Luxembourg

LUXEMBOURG-NASSAU . . *October 7, 2000*

JAPAN

His Majesty the Emperor of Japan

YAMATO . . . . *January 7, 1989*

MALAYSIA

His Majesty Almu'tasimu Billahi Muhibbuddin Tuanku Alhaj Abdul Halim Mu'adzam Shah ibni Almarhum Sultan Badlishah

KEDAH . . . . *December 13, 2011*

MONACO

His Serene Highness Prince Albert II

GRIMALDI . . . . April 6, 2005

MOROCCO

His Majesty Mohammed VI

ALAWI . . . . July 23, 1999

NETHERLANDS

His Majesty King Willem-Alexander of the Netherlands

ORANGE-NASSAU . . . . . . April 30, 2013

NORWAY

His Majesty King Harald V

GLÜCKSBURG . . . . January 17, 1991

SPAIN

His Majesty King Felipe VI

BOURBON . . . . June 19, 2014

SWEDEN

His Majesty King Carl XVI Gustaf

BERNADOTTE . . . . . . September 15, 1973

THAILAND

His Majesty King Maha Vajiralongkorn Bodindradebayavarangkun

CHAKRI . . . . October 13, 2016

TONGA

His Majesty King Tupou VI

TUPOU . . . . March 18, 2012

COMMONWEALTH REALMS

Commonwealth realms are unique in that they are independent countries that remain voluntarily associated with the British monarchy.

ANTIGUA *and* BARBUDA · AUSTRALIA · BAHAMAS
BARBADOS · BELIZE · CANADA · GRENADA · JAMAICA
NEW ZEALAND · PAPUA NEW GUINEA · SAINT KITTS *and* NEVIS
SAINT LUCIA · SAINT VINCENT *and the* GRENADINES
SOLOMON ISLANDS · TUVALU · UNITED KINGDOM

Her Majesty Queen Elizabeth II

WINDSOR . . . . Dates of assumption of throne vary among Commonwealth
realms, earliest being February 6, 1952.

1 ››› This section concerns only major, nationally recognized monarchies. Subnational, regional, and tribal forms of royalty also exist in many countries.

2 ››› Though the Qatari head of government and head of state are different people, most sources still consider the country to be an absolute monarchy.

3 ››› United Arab Emirates is technically a federation of seven absolute monarchies called emirates. One of these rulers, or emirs, is chosen as president of the federation and rules as head of state of the United Arab Emirates.

4 ››› Andorra is a coprincipality: the role of monarch is served jointly by the president of France and the bishop of Urgell in Spain.

5 ››› Hamad bin Isa Al Khalifa is so powerful that some sources consider Bahrain to be an absolute monarchy.

THE SLAVE

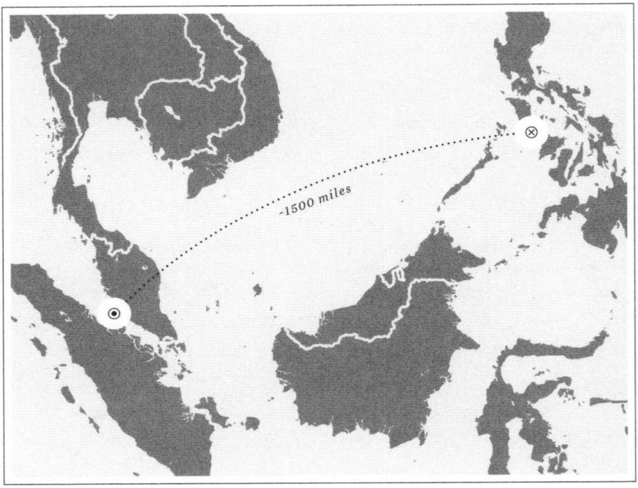

BIRTHPLACE OF ENRIQUE ⊙ ~1500 miles ⊗ BATTLE OF MACTAN

SOME HISTORIANS NOW believe that the first person to circumnavigate the earth was probably a slave by the name Enrique of Malacca. A native of the Malay Peninsula in Southeast Asia, Enrique became Portuguese navigator Ferdinand Magellan's personal valet in 1511 and returned with him to Europe. When Magellan's five ships left Spain in 1519 to investigate new spice trade routes, Enrique was on board acting as an interpreter.

After a disastrous journey filled with wrong turns, mutinies, and shipwrecks, the fleet landed in the Philippines in 1521, only about 1,500 miles (2,414 kilometers) east of Enrique's birthplace. Here, Magellan became distracted by local politics and obsessed with converting the indigenous population to Christianity. When an island king named Lapu-Lapu declined Magellan's religious advances, the Battle of Mactan broke out and the famed navigator was killed by poison arrows and bamboo spears.

Magellan's will explicitly stated that in the event of his death Enrique should be freed and given 10,000 Spanish coins for services rendered. However, Juan Serrano, the captain of the *Santiago* and the new leader of the fleet, insisted Enrique stay with the rapidly deteriorating expedition and remain a slave and interpreter.

According to the journal of one of the crewmen, this betrayal led a rightfully angry Enrique to secretly tell a local chief named Humabon that the Europeans were planning to enslave the native people, just as they had done to him. Humabon then allegedly arranged a surprise attack in which Serrano and dozens of others were killed. After this, Enrique disappears from the history books completely.

It's here that definitive history turns to informed speculation. Did Enrique ever make it home and circumnavigate the earth? And if he did, did he do so before the straggling remainder[1] of Magellan's crew returned to Europe? It's certainly possible. Traveling that relatively short distance in such a highly trafficked area would have been doable, and Enrique would have likely had a decent idea of where he was based solely on the languages being spoken. Some scholars are convinced, but whether Enrique actually completed history's first circumnavigation will likely never be known for sure. Regardless, today Enrique of Malacca is celebrated as a hero across Southeast Asia.

----

1 ››› One ship, the *Victoria*, eventually made it back to Spain more than a year later. Only 18 of the original 270-man crew survived the trip. They were not paid full wages.

SKYTRAX

S KYTRAX IS WIDELY considered to be a definitive authority on all aspects of air travel. It's well known for its airline rating system, which is based on 800 individual factors, incorporating everything from the design of an airline's website to the quality of its inflight meals. In 2016, 178 airlines were ranked, each receiving anywhere from one to five stars.

★ ★ ★ ★ ★

ALL NIPPON AIRWAYS
(Japan)

ASIANA AIRLINES
(South Korea)

CATHAY PACIFIC
(Hong Kong)

ETIHAD AIRWAYS
(UAE)

EVA AIR
(Taiwan)

GARUDA INDONESIA
(Indonesia)

HAINAN AIRLINES
(China)

QATAR AIRWAYS
(Qatar)

SINGAPORE AIRLINES[1]
(Singapore)

★

AIR KORYO
(North Korea)

REMAINING HEALTHY WHILE traveling is a matter of using the most current information available to prepare for and address medical issues in a timely fashion. Travelers need to be protected against a constantly evolving landscape of potential medical concerns, many of which appear and then are subsequently managed in rapid succession. It is critical that travelers always consult the latest available information before making medical decisions.

This section only concerns disease and health issues specifically related to travel. Travelers should continue to adhere to all typical health practices.

VACCINATION
Follow the Routine

The information provided below assumes an adult traveling who has already received the following routine vaccinations, many of which are normally administered during childhood. Note that some vaccinations, such as polio, may require an additional dose, commonly referred to as a "booster shot," before travel to ensure effectiveness.

Diphtheria	*Poliomyelitis (Polio)*
Haemophilus influenzae type b (Hib)	*Rotavirus*
Hepatitis B	*Rubella*
Human papillomavirus (HPV)	*Seasonal influenza (Flu)*
Measles	*Tetanus*
Mumps	*Tuberculosis (TB)*
Pertussis	*Varicella (Chickenpox)*
Pneumococcal	— — — — —

Though obviously dependent on the specifics of one's trip, it is often not possible to receive all necessary vaccinations in a single appointment. Further, many antimalarial medications require users to begin treatment before ever arriving in a malaria-infected area to ensure sufficient effectiveness. Thus, assuming a person planning on global travel who has only received routine vaccinations, it is recommended you visit a medical professional a minimum of **four weeks** before traveling.

Travel Vaccinations

On the next page is a list of common vaccinations that may be advisable, or required, for international travel, depending on one's itinerary. Note that receiving a vaccination should not be equated with having a lifelong immunity. Some vaccinations require booster shots to remain effective, and no vaccination provides license to neglect normal health concerns or engage in reckless behavior.

Some nations require that travelers be vaccinated against certain diseases before entering the country. Always remember that these entry requirements exist primarily to protect the citizens of the country, not travelers. For example, border guards are not concerned that you might catch yellow fever while traveling within their country, but rather that you are already infected and will spread the disease to their fellow citizens. Thus, vaccination requirements have little to do with risks to your personal health, and everything to do with defending others against a pandemic. For this reason, vaccinations are the single strictest type of entry requirements. Unless you can definitively prove you are not currently infected because you've been vaccinated, you will not be allowed in. Always check a country's latest regulations before booking travel and consult with a medical professional to determine which vaccinations you will need.

Further, remember that all countries have complete autonomy over who enters their sovereign territory. Yellow fever is almost always the only vaccination listed on the official entry requirements documentation of a country. However, if a traveler arrives at the border having come from a country besieged by a recent outbreak of a different infectious disease, and they are only vaccinated against yellow fever and nothing else, they may be denied entry. Countries are never beholden to any entry requirements, even their own stated regulations. **In the following chart, all vaccinations associated with travelers being denied entry to countries are noted in bold, rather than just official requirements.**

∨∨∨ *continued* ∨∨∨

VACCINATION[1] AGAINST:	NO. OF DOSES	TIME BETWEEN DOSES	FOLLOWING THE COMPLETE DOSAGE, PROTECTION BEGINS AFTER:
Yellow Fever	**1**	**N/A**	**10 days**
Cholera	**2**	**1–6 weeks**	**2 weeks**
Meningococcal (meningitis)	**1**	**N/A**	**2 weeks**
Polio booster shot[2]	**1**	**N/A**	**Immediately**
Hepatitis A	1	N/A	1 day
Typhoid	3	2 days, 2 days	1 week
Rabies	3	1 week, 3 weeks	1 week
Tick-borne encephalitis[3]	3	2–12 weeks, 5–12 months	Immediately
Japanese encephalitis	2	4 weeks	Immediately

1 ››› For some diseases, multiple types of vaccinations are available, dependent on where one is receiving medical care. In these instances, only information about the most globally common vaccination is provided.

2 ››› Though polio is routinely vaccinated against in most countries, many sources recommend adults receive a booster shot before extended travel.

3 ››› The first two doses provide some protection and is sufficient for most travelers.

Get Carded

The **International Certificate of Vaccination or Prophylaxis** (ICVP), also known as the carte jaune or yellow card, is an official vaccination record created by the World Health Organization. It can be thought of as a personal "medical passport" and is required for entry into many countries. Due to the yellow color of the document, and the fact that yellow fever is a commonly required vaccination for travel, many travelers mistakenly believe that the ICVP only pertains to yellow fever. In reality, the card is internationally accepted as proof of the bearer having received a variety of vaccinations and booster shots, not just for yellow fever.

For an ICVP to be considered valid, it needs to be signed and stamped by an authorized medical professional for each vaccination received. Medical professionals should be aware that the card will be used internationally and complete the card accordingly. Dates should be written in DD/MM/YYYY format, vaccination details should be clear and globally comprehensible,[1] and all relevant contact information should include country codes.

An ICVP also includes a section on personal health information, such as blood type and allergic reactions, that is not directly related to vaccinations. While this is not required for travel, travelers would be wise to fill out this section as it can greatly assist foreign medical personnel in the event of an emergency.

1››› For instance, an ICVP should clearly reference what disease is being vaccinated against, rather than specific brand names of vaccines being used.

Notable Infectious Diseases Without Vaccinations

Below is a listing of infectious diseases associated with travel that cannot currently be vaccinated against. The geographic distribution of these diseases is highly variable and many do not show symptoms in all infected individuals. If you suspect you may be infected, seek medical help immediately.

COMMON NAME	TRANSMISSION	CONTAGIOUS THROUGH	TYPICAL INCUBATION PERIOD	COMMON SYMPTOMS
Amoebic dysentery	Contagious; contaminated food or water	Casual contact	2 days–4 weeks	Diarrhea, cramps, weight loss, fatigue
Dengue	Mosquito	N/A	3–10 days	Fever, rash, joint pain, headache
Giardiasis	Contagious; contaminated food or water	Casual contact	1–3 weeks	Diarrhea, fatigue, cramps, bloating
Hepatitis C	Contagious	Shared needles or syringes	6–10 weeks	Abdominal pain, nausea, fatigue, dark urine
Hepatitis E[1]	Contagious; contaminated food or water	Casual contact	3–8 weeks	Fever, loss of appetite, lethargy, jaundice
Norovirus	Contagious; contaminated food or water	Casual contact	12–48 hours	Vomiting, diarrhea, cramps, fever
Zika[1]	Contagious; mosquito	Sexual contact; pregnancy	3–7 days[2]	Fever, rash, red eyes, muscle pain

1››› While there are reports that an effective vaccine may be in development, is not widely available at the time of this writing.
2››› Estimated, has not been definitively proven.

▾▾▾ *continued* ▾▾▾

MALARIA

Transmission

Malaria is transmitted to humans through female *Anopheles* mosquitoes infected with a parasite called *Plasmodium*. There are four species of *Plasmodium* known to infect humans:

P. falciparum	Most lethal, can cause "cerebral" malaria
P. malariae	If untreated can cause lasting infection
P. ovale	Rare, thought to cause less than 5% of infections in humans
P. vivax	Most globally prevalent

Contagious Through

Malaria is not contagious through casual or sexual contact, though in rare cases can be spread through the sharing of infected needles.

Malarial Areas of the World

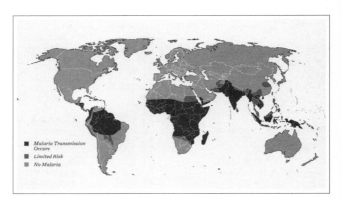

■ Malaria Transmission Occurs
■ Limited Risk
■ No Malaria

Typical Incubation Period

The incubation period of malaria is dependent on the species of *Plasmodium* in question, but usually ranges from 7 to 30 days. However, in rare cases incubation may take much longer. If you experience malaria-like symptoms within one year of traveling it is best to advise medical professionals that you have recently traveled in malarial areas.[1]

Common Symptoms

One of the many reasons malaria is so dangerous is the extensive range of effects it has on people. Some contract *P. vivax* malaria multiple times throughout their life with little more than mild flu symptoms, while severe cases of *P. falciparum* malaria can be fatal within 24 hours after incubation. Therefore, it's important to treat all signs of malaria seriously. What form you may be infected with cannot be known without medical intervention and potential consequences can be dire.

Early symptoms of malaria may include: fever, chills, headache, sweating, nausea, vomiting, body aches, general malaise, and shivering. If you experience these symptoms while traveling in a malarial area seek help immediately. Though forms of malaria other than *P. falciparum* are rarely life threatening, always err on the side of caution. Testing for malaria becomes more widely available, cheaper, and faster with each passing year.

Prevention

BEHAVIORAL

Preventing mosquito bites is the most important thing a traveler can do to avoid malaria. Protecting oneself at night is of particular importance: *Anopheles* mosquitoes almost only bite humans between dusk and dawn. Apply insect repellent, wear long sleeves, and sleep under mosquito nets when traveling in malarial areas.

MEDICAL

There are a variety of antimalarial drugs on the market that can help reduce a traveler's chance of contracting malaria. However, no antimalarial provides complete protection and antimalarials are only effective when taken with strict regularity. Also note that many antimalarials need to be taken both before and after traveling in malarial areas to be effective.

Work with a medical professional to determine which antimalarial drug is right for you. Though some can have significant side effects, the protection they provide is well worth the inconvenience.

Never base your medical decisions on the habits of local citizens. Locals may develop immunities and therefore not require the same protection as travelers.

1›› In very rare cases, *P. vivax* and *P. ovale* parasites can remain dormant in humans for up to four years.

ⱽⱽⱽ *continued* ⱽⱽⱽ

GENERAL HEALTH

Cleanliness when travelling is doubly necessary;
to sponge the body every morning with tepid water, and then rub it
dry with a rough towel, will greatly contribute to preserve Health.

— DR. WILLIAM KITCHINER,
The Traveller's Oracle, 1827

In addition to protecting oneself from infectious disease, it is critical for travelers to maintain their personal hygiene and properly address injuries when they occur. Traveling through changing climates, irregular diet and sleep schedules, and general travel exhaustion can all contribute to a weakened immune system. Below is advice on how to remain healthy out on the road.

DRINKING PROBLEMS

The cleanliness of drinking water varies greatly around the world. Many travelers elect to only use bottled water, others carry purification systems, and some longer-term travelers or expats choose to adjust to the use of local water sources. Whichever you choose, be sure to consider all ramifications of that choice. If you aren't using local water, remember to brush your teeth with bottled water, avoid ice cubes of unknown origin, and reclean any raw produce or beverage containers that may have been washed using potentially contaminated water.

PHARMACEUTICAL PACKING

Despite the effects of globalization, the practice of medicine remains fairly culturally specific. Terminology and brand names are often difficult to translate, medical techniques and standards differ greatly from country to country, and some cultures practice traditional healing methods that may be unfamiliar to travelers. For this reason, if you'll be traveling in relatively remote areas, it is best to bring whatever specific medical supplies you think you may require. A small first-aid kit containing the following is suitable for most traveler's needs.

Antibiotic medication	Bandages (various sizes)	Pain relief medication	Thermometer
Antihistamine medication	Antidiarrheal medication	Hydrocortisone cream	Tweezers
Eye drops	Cough drops	Scissors	Rehydration packets

If you will be traveling with prescription medication be sure to carry all necessary documentation to avoid issues when crossing borders.

FINANCIAL PROTECTIONS

Travel insurance can help to offset potential medical costs and is purchased by many travelers. Be sure to read all terms and conditions when considering travel insurance and note that certain high-risk activities and areas can affect coverage.

QUICKLY COVER CUTS

Infected cuts, especially on the feet, cause far more medical issues for travelers than almost any highly publicized disease. Remember that your immune system is already at a distinct disadvantage—don't put further strain on your body by neglecting to properly bandage wounds.

RIDE SAFE

Motorbike, scooter, and motorcycle accidents are an extremely common cause of injury among independent travelers. Regardless of instruction provided, be sure you are completely comfortable on a bike before riding on public roads, the traffic on which may be dictated by laws and customs far different than what you're used to. Wear a helmet, don't ride with passengers or at night until you're experienced, and never ride when you've had too much to drink.

SIGN OF THE TIMES

. . . for us Fucking is Fucking—and it's going to stay Fucking.

—Municipality mayor Siegfried Höppl after the citizens of Fucking, Austria, voted not to change the name of their village, which is thought to be at least 800 years old. The vote was proposed primarily because of tourists repeatedly stealing street signs, at great cost to local taxpayers. The signs have since been modified to be theft-resistant and closed-circuit cameras have been installed to deter tourists from having sex in front of them, which has also been a recurrent issue.

WHERE EVERYONE IS

GLOBAL POPULATION:
7.4 billion

POPULATION DENSITY:[1]
129 per mi^2/50 per km^2

Population Density Ranking

COUNTRY	POPULATION PER MI^2	POPULATION PER KM^2
Monaco	49,236	19,010
Singapore	20,194	7,797
Bahrain	5,038	1,945
~		
Australia	8.2	3.2
Namibia	7.6	2.9
Mongolia	4.9	1.9

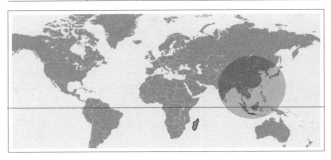

Key

More than half the global population lives within the circled region.

89% of the global population lives in the northern hemisphere.

More than 1 in 5 people who live in the southern hemisphere
live on the island of Java in Indonesia.

The most densely populated city in the world is Dhaka, Bangladesh
(114,300 per mi^2/44,100 per km^2). At that population density,
more than triple the current global population
would fit on the island of Madagascar.

1 ››› All population density statistics are calculating using only land area, not total area.

STEEP ENTRY FEE

IN SOME EARLY zoos, admissions fees were waived for visitors who brought live animals to feed to the large carnivores. During the 1700s, the Royal Menagerie in the Tower of London charged each guest either three halfpence, or one dog or cat to be fed to the lions.

TOO MUCH HEAT

IF YOU'VE TAKEN a bite of an unexpectedly spicy dish and are seeking relief, avoid drinking water and try the following:

*Milk or other dairy products · Bread, rice, or other starches
Sugar · Salt · Chocolate · Honey*

NAVIGATING THE SOUND BARRIER

*Our ability to fly faster is actually limited more
by the law than by the law of physics.*

—EDWARD BURNETT

An engineer at Skunk Works (Lockheed Martin's advanced development division), working on the challenges faced in modern commercial airline design. Overland supersonic flight[1] has been banned in the US and parts of Europe due to the resulting sonic boom, so engineers are attempting to design planes that can travel faster than the speed of sound without producing such a deafening sound effect.

---

1 ››› In excess of the speed of sound, commonly referred to as Mach 1. The speed of sound varies based on temperature and other factors, but is roughly 768 mph (1,235 km/h) at 68°F (20°C).

SLOW EVEN FURTHER DOWN

HISTORIANS BELIEVE THE world's first speeding violation was issued to Walter Arnold of East Peckham, a small village in Kent, England, on January 2, 1896. Peckham was allegedly going 8 miles (13 kilometers) per hour in a 2 miles (3 kilometers) per hour zone, and failed to have someone walking in front of his vehicle waving a large red flag to warn people of an approaching car, which was the law of the time. A police officer on a bicycle pulled him over and issued a one-shilling fine.

DON'T GET BURNED

THE BEGINNING OF MODERN SUN PROTECTION

IN 1938, A chemistry student named Franz Greiter suffered a severe sunburn while climbing and decided to do something about it. Within a decade, he had developed a product called Gletscher Crème ("Glacier Cream") and begun selling it through the company Piz Buin, named after the very mountain on which he'd gotten the idea-inspiring sunburn. Most sources consider this the first modern and effective sunscreen ever created.

WHAT NEEDS TO BE PROTECTED AGAINST

The are two[1] types of rays in sunlight that are harmful to humans:

	ULTRAVIOLET A (UVA)	ULTRAVIOLET B (UVB)
% of total UV rays reaching earth	95%	5%
Commonly known as	"Aging rays"	"Burning rays"
May cause	Spots and wrinkles	Tan and sunburn
Seasonality	Approximately equal year round	More intense in summer
Glass	Can pass through	Cannot pass through

Excessive exposure to either UVA or UVB rays can cause skin cancer.

SERIOUSLY PROBLEMATIC FORMULA

Along with the first modern sunscreen, Franz Greiter also developed the **sun protection factor** (SPF) rating system, which remains the most commonly used standard for sunscreen effectiveness. Though revolutionary for its time, many experts now consider SPF to be a deeply flawed metric for describing sunscreen effectiveness, if only because the general public continues to be misinformed about its meaning. Note that this formula assumes an even application of 2 mg per .16 in^2 (1 cm^2):

1/SPF Rating = % of UVB rays reaching skin

This means that, with an SPF of 10, about 90 percent of UVB rays will be blocked. The problem is that these ratings only measure what fraction of UVB rays will reach the skin. It doesn't account for UVA rays, which can also be very harmful. Further, SPF ratings are not an accurate measurement of how long sunscreen will be effective. The length of a sunscreen's effectiveness can vary greatly by person, and is significantly affected by exposure to sweat and water.

HIGHER MAY NOT BE BETTER

As a result of the misplaced importance customers often place on SPF ratings, companies have been steadily introducing increasingly higher SPF-rated sunscreens in recent years. This can have the dangerous effect of customers believing themselves to be especially well protected, or to be protected for a long periods of time, solely because they're using a high-SPF sunscreen. In reality this is almost never the case.

Lack of protection against UVA rays notwithstanding, higher SPF products only provide marginally more protection against UVB rays. While most customers assume a 60 SPF sunscreen provides twice the protection of a 30 SPF sunscreen, the equation stated above shows there is actually only a very small difference between the two products:

30 SPF Rating = Blocks 96.6% UVB Rays

60 SPF Rating = Blocks 98.3% UVB Rays

To mitigate some of the confusion surrounding these issues, the American Food and Drug Administration (FDA) has declared advertising sunscreen above SPF 50 to be "inherently misleading" and many countries have disallowed companies from labeling sunscreens higher than SPF 50.

ᵛᵛᵛ *continued* ᵛᵛᵛ

When considering sun protection, travelers should remember that potential exposure to UV rays can vary greatly dependent on specific conditions.

Effect of UV Rays[2]

DETERMINING FACTORS	
Location	Exposure to UV rays increases the closer you are to the equator
Time	60% of UV ray exposure occurs between 10 a.m. and 2 p.m.
Altitude	Every 3,281 ft (1,000 m) increase in altitude increases exposure to UV rays by 10%
Ozone	Increasing depletion of the ozone layer means that certain geographical areas, like parts of Australia, are being more heavily exposed to UV rays

UV RAY REFLECTION[2]		UV RAY PENETRATION[2]	
Grass and soil	>10%	Dry white cotton T-shirt	20%
Water	10–25%	Wet white cotton T-shirt	25–30%
Sand	15–25%	Heavy cloud cover	30%
Sea foam	25%	5 ft (1.5 m) deep water	40%
Snow	50–80%	Shade	1–50%

STAY PROTECTED

Suit Yourself

The fairness of a person's skin is not the only factor to consider when it comes to sun protection. Medications, such as the pills many travelers take to guard against malaria, can increase sensitivity to sun and strenuous activity will decrease the effectiveness of sunscreen. Age is also a factor and younger children are particularly vulnerable to UV rays. Lastly, note that already being tan will not protect against further skin damage.

Dress to Protect

Eyes are extremely susceptible to UV ray damage and sunglasses are strongly recommended for prolonged exposure. Also remember that not all clothing is created equal when it comes to sun protection. Darker colors and heavier fabrics provide better protection, though may be uncomfortable to wear in hot climates.

A rating system for apparel called **ultraviolet protection factor** (UPF) was developed to help consumers easily determine the amount of sun protection provided by clothing. UPF is similar to SPF but accounts for both UVA and UVB rays, not just UVB rays. It is calculated using the following formula:

$$1/UPF\ Rating = \%\ of\ UV\ rays\ reaching\ skin$$

This means that, with an UPF of 40, about 97.5 percent of UV rays will be blocked. Specially designed sun-protective clothing with high UPF ratings is available from a variety of retailers.

Plan Ahead

The **ultraviolet index** (UV index or UVI) is an internationally recognized system of determining the intensity of UV rays and their effect on humans. The scale measures the risk of UV ray damage to an average adult using color-coded warning signs. If possible, consult the day's predicted UV Index when planning sun protection.

UV INDEX										
UVI	1	2	3	4	5	6	7	8	9	10	11
Risk of UV Damage	Low		Moderate			High		Very High			Extreme
Associated color	Green		Yellow			Orange		Red			Purple
Recommendation	No protection required. Sunglasses suggested for bright days.		Protection required. Cover up, use sunscreen, seek shade during midday.					Extra protection required. Take all possible precautions, severely limit exposure to sun, especially during midday.			

vvv continued vvv

Choose Properly

Many dermatologists recommend choosing a sunscreen that is:

» **Broad-spectrum:** Meaning it protects against both UVA and UVB rays.

» **Water-resistant[3]:** These products are specially formulated to continue to provide protection while in the water, but should still be regularly reapplied, as detailed below.

» **SPF 30:** The best SPF to use depends on a person's skin and other factors, but this is a good rule of thumb. Remember that higher SPF products do not provide significantly more protection.

» **Only sunscreen:** Combination insect repellent and sunscreen is not recommended because sunscreen will need to be reapplied more frequently.[4]

Apply Always

Remember not to equate a day's brightness with potential UV exposure. Sunscreen should be applied any time you expect prolonged exposure to UV rays.

Apply Early

Plan to put on your first application of sunscreen about 20 minutes before exposure to sun.

Apply Enough

Studies have shown most people only apply 25 to 50 percent of the sunscreen needed for protection. Sources recommend that the average-sized adult apply one ounce (25.6 ml) of sunscreen, which is about a palm full, the size of a golf ball, or enough to fill a shot glass.

Apply Everywhere

Ears, lips, back of the neck, back of the hands, and top of the feet are just some of the places people often forget to apply sunscreen.

Apply Often

Reapply every two hours, or after swimming or sweating excessively.

1 ››› A third type, UVC, is absorbed by the ozone layer.
2 ››› This chart shows the maximum possible effect of these conditions.
3 ››› Most countries no longer allow companies to label sunscreens "waterproof" or "sweat-proof," arguing this is an incorrect and misleading description.
4 ››› See page 52 for more information on insect repellent.

SHOCKED BY CULTURE

Some notable psychological symptoms involving travel include:

PARIS SYNDROME

Paris, arguably the most romanticized city on earth, is the namesake of this condition that purportedly affects a small number of tourists visiting European cities every year. Often described as "extreme culture shock," **Paris syndrome** is characterized by a variety of psychological symptoms, including but not limited to anxiety, hallucinations, depression, and dizziness. This condition is said to be caused by standard traveling issues—such as jet lag, exhaustion, and language difficulties—mixed with the disappointment some visitors feel when a destination doesn't live up to the idealized version they might expect. Japanese tourists are the most commonly diagnosed sufferers of this syndrome and the Japanese embassy in Paris now maintains a 24-hour hotline for affected citizens.

JERUSALEM SYNDROME

Jerusalem syndrome describes travelers so overcome with religious mania that they become mentally unbalanced. A visit to Jerusalem, a revered city in the eyes of Christian, Muslim, and Jewish people alike, is apparently the cause of such religious fever and an average of a hundred tourists per year are said to be affected. Reported symptoms include brief psychosis, anxiety, obsessions with religious imagery, and religiously oriented forms of egomania.

MEAN WORLD SYNDROME

Pioneered by Dr. George Gerbner, **Mean World syndrome** is based on the idea that media, especially television, can cause some people to believe the world is far more threatening than it actually is. By proving a direct correlation between the amount of media people consume and the amount of fear people feel about the outside world, researchers investigating this syndrome have helped illustrate the negative influence that danger and violence shown in media can have on a person's perception of people and places outside their own insulated ethnic or socioeconomic group. It is important to note that researchers made no claims about television violence leading to an actual increase in violent acts being committed, only to an increase in people's irrational fear of harm, due to exposure to violence in television and other media.

ON SPECIFICITY

I had not yet got accustomed to the idea that time, as a measured and recorded period, had been left behind on the coast.

— GRAHAM GREENE,
Journey Without Maps, 1936

TRAVELERS SHOULD BE aware that many parts of the world are far less specific than they may be used to at home. In most industrialized nations, the details of life are highly definitive. Prices of things are exact, clearly printed on the packaging, and the same for every consumer. Store hours are shown on the front window and strictly adhered to. Public utilities are reliable, traffic laws are regularly enforced, exact change is always given. In short, these cultures demand specificity in all that they do. However, travelers who subconsciously impose this mind-set when exploring certain countries will do so with problematic results.

AHORITA.
—A Spanish word that can mean anything from
"right now" to "a few days from now"

Many travelers hail from Western cities with highly reliable transportation systems that run on unfailingly precise schedules. Therefore, when they first buy a bus ticket in a distant country, they naturally assign a high value to the stated departure time. They begin blocking out units of time until departure and arrive at the station early to ensure they don't miss their ride. They essentially do what they would do in their home country. This line of detailed-orientated thinking is certainly understandable, but not necessarily advisable.

It is critical to realize that, in many countries, a departure time is nothing more than a general guidepost and an appeasement for tourists.[1] For instance, "4 p.m." often does not refer to a specific hour, but rather a window of time in the late afternoon. A planned two-hour ride taking five hours is not an embarrassing mistake worthy of a refund, it is just how long the journey happened to be that day. Long-term travelers should realize that adjusting to this unspecific form of timekeeping early on in a trip is highly useful in effectively, and calmly, traveling through a developing country.

POLE-POLE.
—*A popular Swahili phrase that colloquially translates
to "slow down" or "relax"*

When deciding where to eat, many travelers naturally assume from prior experience that a restaurant's menu details exactly what's available. Travelers should note that in many countries a menu is often simply a broad advertisement of what type of food the restaurant specializes in, not a definitive listing of what dishes are currently available. It is not at all unusual for the majority of menu items to be unavailable on any given day.

It is important to recognize the fundamental difference in philosophy at work in some countries around the world. Many cultures prefer a far less exacting approach toward these types of details and do not value specificity in the same way as highly industrialized nations.

JUST NOW.
—*A South African idiom used to indicate an
unspecified time in the future*

Phrases that exemplify this slower, more relaxed approach to life can be found in cultures across the globe.[2] All are distinct in meaning, to be sure, but all also contain an element of conscious decision that needless exactitude, whatever the context, is simply not worth becoming stressed about. These phrases are not muttered apologetically, but instead said proudly, often like a national motto of sorts. These people are not lazy, they just refuse to sweat the small stuff. Indeed, these cultures' disdain for minutia lends itself to a natural optimism that things will eventually all work out anyway. To them, it is the people from highly industrialized nations, who always seem to be rushing from place to place and worried about every little thing, who are living life unconventionally.

In time, travelers may find their own sense of detail slowly fading away as they begin to adjust to this refreshing new lack of specificity. It is up to you whether you adopt this easygoing mind-set or simply travel through areas dictated by it. But know that this far more relaxed philosophy exists out in the world and that rebelling against it will result only in your own frustration.

----

1 ››› After studies showed that widespread lateness was costing the country's economy billions every year, Ecuador began a national campaign in 2003 to make the country more punctual. Unfortunately, the television announcement for the initiative was delayed because a government spokesman was late in arriving to the studio.

2 ››› See page 178 for more information on the Thai concept of *mai pen rai.*

IN A SURVEY of 500 commercial airline pilots by the British Airline Pilots Association, more than half admitted they've fallen asleep while flying. More than one in four of those who admitted to falling asleep reported waking up only to find that the other pilot was also asleep. Worry not, however, technology has improved air travel safety to such a degree that your chances of dying in a plane crash on a UK airline are roughly 287 million to 1.

DRINK UP

How to phonetically pronounce the word or phrase for
Cheers! in 54 languages.

Afrikaans	ge-SUND-hate	Farsi	beh sala-ma-TI
Albanian	geh-ZOO-ah	Finnish	kee-PIS
Azerbaijani	NUSH ohl-sun	French	ah VO-tre sahn-TAY
Basque	TO-pa	German	prohst
Bengali	joy	Greek	YA-mas
Bosnian	ZHEE-ve-lee	Greenlandic	gas-UD-da
Bulgarian	naz-DRA-vey	Hebrew	l'HI-yem
Burmese	au-ng my-in par say	Hungarian	EGG-esh ay-ged-reh
Catalan	sah-LUT	Icelandic	skoll
Croatian	ZHEE-ve-lee	Irish Gaelic	SLAWN-che
Czech	naz-DRA-vey	Italian	sa-LOO-tay
Danish	skoll	Japanese	kahn-PIE
Dutch	prohst	Khmer	CHUL moi
Estonian	TER-vih-sex	Korean	gun-BEH

Latvian	*PREE-eh-ka*	Serbian	*ZHEE-ve-lee*
Lithuanian	*EE-sweh-kata*	Slovenian	*naz-DRA-vey*
Macedonian	*naz-DRA-vey*	Spanish	*sah-LUD*
Maltese	*SAHh-ha*	Swahili	*AF-ya*
Mandarin	*gan BAY*	Swedish	*skoll*
Mongolian	*Er-UHL men-diin toloo*	Tagalog	*mah-BOO-hai*
Nepali	*sub-HA-ka-mana*	Thai	*CHOK dee*
Norwegian	*skoll*	Turkish	*sher-i-FEH*
Polish	*naz-DROH-vee-ay*	Ukrainian	*BOOD-mo*
Portuguese	*sa-OO-d*	Uzbek	*OL-dick*
Romanian	*no-ROCK*	Vietnamese	*mote hi bah, yo*
Russian	*naz-da-ROVH-yeh*	Welsh	*YEH-chid-dah*
Samoan	*mah-NU-ia*	Zulu	*OO-gy WA-wa*

SETTING OUT

. . . my mother had got up early and cooked me a heavy breakfast, had stood wordlessly while I ate it, her hand on my chair, and had then helped me pack up my few belongings. There had been no fuss; there had been no attempt to persuade me to stay; she just gave me a long and searching look. Then, with my bags on my back, I'd gone out into the early sunshine and climbed through the long wet grass to the road.

It was 1934. I was nineteen years old, still soft at the edges, but with a confident belief in good fortune. I carried a small rolled-up tent, a violin in a blanket, a change of clothes, a tin of biscuits, and some cheese. I was excited, full of self-confidence, knowing I had far to go; but not, as yet, how far. I left home that morning and walked away from the sleeping village. It never crossed my mind that others had done this before me.

—LAURIE LEE,
English poet, novelist, and screenwriter
As I Walked Out One Midsummer Morning, 1969

THE FALLACY OF RECOLLECTION

Like all great travelers, I have seen more than I remember,
and remember more than I have seen.

—BENJAMIN DISRAELI,
British writer and politician

———————— ◆ ————————

FRIENDLY NEIGHBORS

T HE SCHENGEN AREA is composed of countries that have less-
ened border restrictions for international travel. This means that
travelers within the area can move about freely without repeatedly
showing identification at every border. These countries adhere to a
common visa policy and, though the Schengen area is closely associated
with the European Union, not all EU countries participate and some
countries not in the EU are members. Further, while the Schengen Area
simplifies international travel in Europe, all countries involved are still
sovereign nations. All can, and many do, reintroduce border restrictions
in response to security and/or geopolitical concerns. Thus, while the
Schengen Area can save travelers time and money, it does not necessarily mean one will never need to show their passport. Lastly, note that the
Schengen Area only applies to continental Europe, not distant territories or dependencies of European countries.

MEMBERS OF THE SCHENGEN AREA

Austria · Belgium · Czechia · Denmark · Estonia · Finland · France
Germany · Greece · Hungary · Iceland[1] · Italy · Latvia · Liechtenstein[1]
Lithuania · Luxembourg · Malta · Netherlands · Norway[1] · Poland
Portugal · Slovakia · Slovenia · Spain · Sweden · Switzerland[1]

DE FACTO MEMBERS OF THE SCHENGEN AREA[2]

Monaco · San Marino · Vatican City

EU MEMBERS NOT IN THE SCHENGEN AREA

Opt Outs: United Kingdom · Ireland
Prospective Members: Bulgaria · Croatia · Cyprus · Romania

---

1 ››› Not a member of the EU.

2 ››› These small countries are not officially members of the Schengen Area, but maintain
open borders.

SELECTED BISLAMA

V ANUATU IS THE world's most language dense country, with at least 112 indigenous languages actively spoken in a nation of only 272,000 people spread across 4,707 square miles (12,190 square kilometers). The most popular common language among citizens is Bislama, a creole[1] language incorporating words from English, French, and local dialects, that developed as a means for the linguistically diverse population to communicate.

Airport	*epot*
Bad	*nogud*
Beach	*sanbij*
Helicopter	*mixmaster blong Jesus Christ*
Prince Charles	*nambawan pikinini blong Missus Kwin*
Refrigerator	*aisbokis*
Sea	*solwota*
Spiderweb	*bed blong spaeda*
Unconscious	*haf ded*

1 ››› A **pidgin** language is a simplified language with no native speakers, used between two adults who don't share a common tongue. A **creole** language is a stable language that developed from a **pidgin** language, but now has a fully functional vocabulary and grammatical structure and is being taught to children as a native language.

━━━━◆━━━━

GRINNING GLOBALLY

A smile without reason is a sign of idiocy.
—A popular Russian proverb

W HILE SMILING AT strangers is thought of as friendly in many Western countries, in other cultures doing so is sometimes considered odd or impolite. In Russia, China, and Japan, among other places, less emotion is shown in public and smiles are considered a more intimate gesture, to be reserved only for those one knows personally. Smiling at someone you don't know might make you seem insincere, or as if you're ridiculing them. Don't be offended if someone doesn't return your smile—they may be interpreting the expression quite differently than you're used to.

SEASICKNESS

At first you are so sick you are afraid you will die, and then you are so sick you are afraid you won't die.

—MARK TWAIN,
American author

DISCORDANCE

Most experts agree that **motion sickness,** be it sea-, air-, or car sickness, is caused by conflicting signals being sent to the brain simultaneously. The eyes perceive movement while the body remains still and the brain interprets this contradiction as a hallucination caused by the ingestion of poison. The brain then attempts to expel the assumed toxin by inducing vomiting.

TREATMENT

Motion sickness is such an age-old[1] and common problem that all manner of "cures" exist—from misguided folk remedies[2] to cutting-edge scientific devices.[3]

Below is a collection of some of the most popular and effective treatments.

NONMEDICINAL

» Sit facing forward in a window seat near the front of cars and trains (drive the car if possible), near the wings of planes, and in lower level center cabins (to sleep) or the upper decks (for fresh air) of ships.

» Don't smoke, drink alcohol, or eat greasy or high-fat foods.

» Focus on the horizon or a fixed point in the distance.

» Chew gum, preferably peppermint.

» Stay hydrated and well-rested.

» Eat dry crackers and toast.

» Press your thumb onto your inner forearm about two inches (five centimeters) down from your wrist. Hold until symptoms subside.

» Minimize head movements. Close eyes and attempt to sleep.

MEDICINAL[4]

» Gingerroot supplement.

» Over-the-counter antihistamines such as meclizine (Bonine), diphenhydramine (Benadryl), dimenhydrinate (Dramamine), and cinnarizine[5] (Stugeron).

» Prescription scopolamine (Transderm Scop) patches.

1 ››› The very word *nausea* comes from the Ancient Greek *naus*, meaning "ship."
2 ››› A medical journal from 1838 suggests *"large doses of ammonia with opium."*
3 ››› NASA is testing a type of LCD strobe glasses designed to reduce nausea of astronauts during space flight.
4 ››› Always check with a medical professional before beginning use. Many of the medicines listed can have severe side effects.
5 ››› Not available in the US or Canada.

THE SEVEN SEAS, OLD AND NEW

SEAS (MODERN)[1]	SEAS (ANCIENT)[2]
Arctic	Adriatic
Antarctic	Aegean
North Atlantic	Black
South Atlantic	Caspian
Indian	Mediterranean
North Pacific	Persian Gulf
South Pacific	Red

1 ››› Though colloquially referred to as seas this list is technically composed of oceans or, depending on interpretation, the different areas of the world's one interconnected ocean.
2 ››› Alternate ancient listings of the seven seas sometimes included the Indian Ocean and the Arabian Sea, which it contains.

THE SEVEN SUMMITS

CONTINENTS	SUMMITS	PEAKS
Africa	Kilimanjaro	19,341 ft (5,895 m)
Antarctica	Vinson	16,050 ft (4,892 m)
Asia	Everest	29,029 ft (8,848 m)
Australia	Puncak Jaya[1]	16,024 ft (4,884 m)
Europe	Elbrus	18,510 ft (5,642 m)
North America	Denali	20,322 ft (6,194 m)
South America	Aconcagua	22,838 ft (6,961 m)

1 ››› Also known as Carstensz Pyramid, this mountain is on the Indonesian side of the island of New Guinea, not the Australian mainland.

OUT THERE

ON EARTH, THE maximum distance a person can be from the place of their birth is about 12,450 miles (20,036 kilometers).[1]

In space however, the possibilities are literally endless. At 7:21 p.m. EST on April 14, 1970, the Apollo 13 astronauts were traveling around the far side of the moon, using its gravitational pull to propel them back toward earth. At that moment, Jim Lovell, Jack Swigert, and Fred Haise were 248,655 miles (400,171 kilometers) away, the farthest distance from home that anyone has ever been.

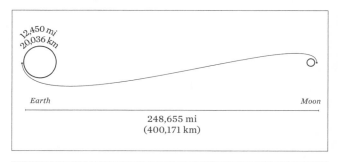

12,450 mi
20,036 km

Earth
Moon

248,655 mi
(400,171 km)

1 ››› This is assuming a calculation of surface area. The maximum "straight line" distance would be two points on opposite sides of the equator: 7,926 miles (12,756 kilometers).

THE INEXPRESSIBLE CALL OF MOVEMENT

> *"Sal, we gotta go and never stop going 'till we get there."*
> *"Where we going, man?"*
> *"I don't know but we gotta go."*
>
> —JACK KEROUAC,
> American author, *On the Road*, 1957

THE WRONG SIDE OF THE ROAD

Left-side driving countries:

Antigua and Barbuda · Australia · Bahamas · Bangladesh · Barbados
Bhutan · Botswana · Brunei · Cyprus · Dominica · Fiji · Grenada
Guyana · India · Indonesia · Ireland · Jamaica · Japan · Kenya
Kiribati · Lesotho · Malawi · Malaysia · Maldives · Malta · Mauritius
Mozambique · Namibia · Nauru · Nepal · New Zealand · Pakistan
Papua New Guinea · Saint Kitts and Nevis · Saint Lucia
Saint Vincent and the Grenadines · Samoa · Seychelles · Singapore
Solomon Islands · South Africa · Sri Lanka · Suriname · Swaziland
Tanzania · Thailand · Timor-Leste · Tonga · Trinidad and Tobago
Tuvalu · Uganda · United Kingdom · Zambia · Zimbabwe

	LEFT	RIGHT
Country ratio	28%	72%
Rule(s) of thumb	Former British colonies .... Island nations	Everywhere else

THE BIG FIVE

T HE TERM *BIG FIVE* was coined by big-game hunters and refers to the five African animals that are most difficult to hunt on foot. Inclusion in this grouping had nothing to do with the actual size or abundance of the animal, rather it was solely based on the degree of hunting difficulty and danger, specifically the likelihood of the animal to attack, rather than flee, if shot at.

The term is now more commonly used by safari operators for advertising purposes. With an experienced tour guide and a bit of luck, the entire Big Five can be seen in a single day on safari throughout East and Southern Africa. Many tour guides use the Big Five as a default wish list of what their visitors are most interested in seeing. However, safari participants should consider beforehand whether, for all its fame, seeing the Big Five is their personal definition of a successful safari. Some might consider animals like the cheetah, crocodile, giraffe, hippo, hyena, or zebra to be far more interesting and exotic than, for instance, the cape buffalo, and should inform their guides accordingly.

↑ *Most Commonly Seen*		**CAPE BUFFALO** *SYNCERUS CAFFER*
		AFRICAN ELEPHANT *LOXODONTA*
		AFRICAN LION *PANTHERA LEO*
		AFRICAN RHINO *DICEROS BICORNIS/ CERATOTHERIUM SIMUM*
Least Commonly Seen ↓		**AFRICAN LEOPARD** *PANTHERA PARDUS PARDUS*

IT'S A TRAP

TRAP STREETS IS a collective term for secret nonexistent roads, topographical features, and even complete towns that mapmakers include in their work to prevent plagiarism. By intentionally including what are essentially random mistakes, mapmakers can provide definitive evidence to "trap" anyone who tries to copy their maps without permission.

In one such situation, cartographer Otto G. Lindberg and his assistant Ernest Alpers of the General Drafting Corporation accused map publisher Rand McNally of stealing their work. Their proof was the fact that a fictitious New York "trap" town they created called Agloe (an anagram of their initials) appeared on a Rand McNally map. But in what was surely a mind-bending surprise for the two cartographers, researchers sent to the area found that there actually *was* a place called Agloe, right where the two men had pretended that there would be, complete with an Agloe General Store.

It was then discovered that the oil conglomerate Esso, a client of the General Drafting Company, had used one of their maps when researching a new location. Seeing the name Agloe on the map, they assumed that was what locals called the area and named their new gas station Agloe General Store. This is thought to be the only time in history a "trap" location has led to the actual development of an area.

MONEY TROUBLES

THE UNITED STATES is the only country in the world whose paper currency is all the exact same size, of a generally similar color, and without tactile features to distinguish between bills. This has drawn criticism from advocacy groups who claim the currency is discriminatory against the visually impaired and, after a lawsuit was filed by the American Council of the Blind, a federal judge agreed and ordered the United States Treasury to begin developing possible solutions. The new American $20 bill set to be introduced in 2020 will reportedly have tactile distinguishing features, as well as feature the abolitionist Harriet Tubman, the first woman to appear on American paper currency in more than a century.[1]

---

1 ››› Martha Washington, wife of first US president George, appeared on a dollar silver certificate from 1891 to 1896.

TYPES OF SHIPWRECK

MARITIME LAW SEPARATES shipwrecks into the following four categories, which are significant in that they may determine ownership over wreckage or cargo found at sea.

FLOTSAM	JETSAM
Floating wreckage or cargo.	*Floating wreckage or cargo that was intentionally discarded by the crew, often to lighten the ship in a time of distress or emergency.*

DERELICT	LAGAN
Sunken wreckage or cargo that has been abandoned and will not or cannot be recovered; a floating ship that has been abandoned by its owner.	*Sunken wreckage or cargo that was intentionally discarded by the crew, that has been marked so that it can later be reclaimed.*

THE BEST ADVICE

DON'T PANIC

—DOUGLAS ADAMS,

English author, *The Hitchhiker's Guide to the Galaxy*, 1979

THINGS TO LEAVE AT HOME

» *Meat of frogs*

» *Christmas trees*

» *All types of fireworks*

» *Cameras which permit viewing the body without clothes (naked)*

» *Annoying horns*

» *Entertainment devices with hysterical laughters*

» *Pencils in the shape of syringes*

» *Commodities which have names & photos of celebrities*

» *Greeting cards with small musical devices which work automatically when the card is moved*

» *Old newspapers*

—SELECTED ITEMS FROM SAUDI ARABIA'S LIST OF "BANNED PRODUCTS"

ROUGH RIDE

ON JULY 26, 1959, Lieutenant Colonel William Rankin was flying at 47,000 feet (14,326 meters) when the engine of his F-8 Crusader failed and he was forced to eject. Lacking a pressurized suit, he immediately suffered severe decompression and frostbite, only to then fall directly into a massive thunderstorm. After freefalling for an estimated five minutes, the intense storm conditions caused his malfunctioning parachute to deploy, which resulted in him spending the next 35 minutes caught in storm updrafts thousands of feet in the air, some of which were so powerful he was thrown into the fabric of his own parachute. In the almost complete darkness of the storm clouds, he was surrounded by hail and described "feeling thunder" and witnessing lightning from within the cloud as "blue blades several feet thick." He was eventually thrown clear of the storm and landed in a tree. Though badly injured at the time, he suffered no long-term medical damage and eventually returned to flying. He is thought to be the only person in history who has survived parachuting through a major thunderstorm.

ON TRAVEL SCAMS AND PICKPOCKETING

BE AWARE

Many of the tales of robbers which one hears abroad are invented by guides who resent that a man should go about alone; and a traveller soon finds out that a peasant with every mark of being a brigand may be a very peaceable person.

—REVEREND FRANK TATCHELL,
The Happy Traveller, 1923

BEING AWARE, BOTH of one's immediate surroundings and of known criminal elements in the area, is the traveler's greatest defense against being the victim of a crime. One reason travelers are targeted by criminals is that many are already somewhat overwhelmed just by virtue of being in a hectic, foreign place. Travel scams exploit this inherent disadvantage by forcing travelers into unfamiliar situations and then increasing their levels of stress and confusion in any way possible.

While you needn't walk the streets constantly fearful, eyeing every local as a bandit in disguise, you should be cognizant of what is happening around you. If a total stranger seems intent on monopolizing your focus remain wary of their true motives. Recognize that listening to loud music through headphones in a dangerous neighborhood or getting exceptionally drunk far from where you're staying can significantly lower your level of alertness and make it far easier for unsavory characters to rob you. Be fully engaged in the things you are seeing and doing, but don't allow yourself to be taken advantage of by being needlessly distracted or reckless.

Further, arm yourself with information. Many travel scams have defined life cycles: local thieves start employing some new scheme, it works well for a few weeks, travelers begin warning each other, and then that particular tactic falls out of favor with the criminal community as potential victims become too well informed. Talk to other travelers to find out the latest prevalent local scams. Check with hostel or hotel staff about any neighborhoods you should particularly avoid. Never allow your itinerary to be dictated by fear but always remember that travel scams are only successful when the victim doesn't have enough information to accurately recognize what's going on.

BE UNQUALIFIED

Take every precaution and abandon all fear.

—MARY HALL,
Victorian world traveler

All con artists, consciously or subconsciously, use an informal set of criteria called **prequalifiers** to select targets. Prequalifiers help identify the people most likely to fall for a scam, so the scammer doesn't need to take unnecessary risks or spend time on targets that probably won't yield a successful result.

The prequalifiers commonly used by street criminals include people who are:

» *Angry or distracted*

» *Disrespectful or mean-spirited*

» *Drunk or exhausted*

» *Doing something illegal*

» *Obviously carrying expensive equipment or large sums of cash*

» *Unaware of their surroundings*

» *Who seem lost, nervous, overwhelmed, or excitable*

Avoid projecting these characteristics and you are far less likely to be targeted by thieves.

BE CALM

Keep cool—but do not freeze.

—Listed instructions on how to properly store
Hellmann's Mayonnaise

The most important thing a traveler can do if they suspect they are the target of a scam is to remain calm. Your only goal is to extract yourself from the situation as cleanly as possible and walk away. No street justice will be had when you're a foreigner in the middle of a crowded market.

Remember that the people who engage in these types of scams often do so as a result of extreme poverty or drug addiction. Truly desperate people can be unpredictable. Getting overly upset or confrontational can turn a merely inconvenient situation into a dangerous one.

Pity aside however, remember that your distraction is often the very objective of many of these scams. They want to get you so upset that you won't notice an accomplice slipping a hand into your pocket or to lash out so you won't feel your backpack being lifted. Any outburst or physical contact is to their benefit, not yours. Keep a level head.

▾▾▾ *continued* ▾▾▾

WANDER WITH PURPOSE

For every walk is a sort of crusade, preached by some
Peter the Hermit in us, to go forth and reconquer this
Holy Land from the hands of infidels.

—HENRY DAVID THOREAU,
Walking, 1862

When exploring a foreign city known for its criminal elements, travelers should try to disguise their unfamiliarity in any way possible. While there may be undisguisable physical features that easily distinguish travelers from locals, and there is no need to purchase an entire locally appropriate wardrobe, travelers should consciously work to avoid displaying any of the prequalifiers detailed in the previous section. Simply being cognizant of one's body language when walking the streets can go a surprisingly long way in achieving that camouflage.

Walk decisively, as if you know precisely where you're going, even if you're utterly lost. Try not to display outward signs of confusion, like opening a large folded map in a public place. Stand up straight and explore with confidence as if you're a local or a long-term expat well versed in the madness the city has to offer. If you're upset or stressed, try to maintain a neutral expression. Recognize that wearing outrageous or out-of-place clothing will immediately mark you as a foreigner. If you're approached by a stranger you don't wish to interact with, remain calm, keep moving, and firmly but politely rebuff them. In short, personally enjoy the city at your own leisure but maintain the outward appearance of being just another resident, hastily running errands in their hometown.

THE SCAMS

These traps are not made to catch the legs, but to ruin the
fortunes and break the hearts of those who unfortunately
step into them. Their baits are artful, designing, wicked men
and profligate, abandoned, and prostitute women.

—PHILIP THICKNESSE,
from a letter advising a friend about travel scams in France, 1777

There are 27 common scams the traveler should be aware of. They are listed on the following pages, along with information about how to evade them.

Every one of these scams is designed to rob travelers of either their money or their possessions. They are frustrating and immoral, to be sure, but their successful execution results in nothing more than the loss of things both insurable and replaceable.

Though incidents are increasingly rare and paranoia is artificially high, there is another, worse breed of criminal whose intentions are far more sinister than relieving naïve travelers of relatively small amounts of money. Recognizing the moment a situation turns from annoyingly troublesome to legitimately dangerous is a critical skill for any traveler.

If you ever feel you are in physical danger, abandon any thoughts of protecting your valuables or outwitting a criminal whose tricks you think you know, and immediately call for help. Remove yourself from situation as swiftly as possible, through whatever means necessary, and get to a public place.

Transportation

THE CUT BAG

Someone sitting next to you on a long bus or train journey secretly cuts into your bag and robs you.

Keep your valuable items within arm's reach and remember that thieves can easily cut new openings into most kinds of luggage. Be especially cautious if you are sitting next to someone whose hands you cannot see.

THE DAMAGED RENTAL

You rent a vehicle and, upon returning it, are informed that it's damaged and that you need to pay for repairs.

Always take multiple photographs of the vehicle, with an employee present, before leaving the rental location. Point out any prior damages to the employee and insist they be noted.

THE RIP-OFF

A vendor or taxi driver uses sleight of hand to switch out a large-denomination bill with a smaller one, then belligerently claims that you are trying to cheat them.

This scam, like so many others, relies on the use of unexpected aggression to intimidate travelers into quickly complying with demands before they have time to fully process the situation. Remain calm; always count bills out one by one, and never hand over folded wads of cash.

∨∨∨ *continued* ∨∨∨

A taxi driver takes an unnecessarily long route, doesn't use a meter, insists on driving you to a store or business you have no interest in visiting, or demands to be paid an unfair price at the end of the ride.

As difficult as it is to follow exactly where you are in a hectic foreign city, if you feel unsafe in a taxi be insistent with the driver about being taken to your desired location. Try to determine or estimate the expected driving time before getting in and, if you're unfamiliar with the area or if the taxi doesn't have a meter, always agree on a price beforehand.

Shopping and Accomodation

THE DREAM RENTAL

You book an apartment or house online, only to arrive and find it doesn't exist.

As private rental websites have greatly expanded one's options for accommodation in foreign cities, scammers have been quick to prey on naïve travelers unfamiliar with the area. Remember that if a rental rate seems to good to be true it usually is; compare rental properties across multiple sites, insist on verifying ownership of the property, and never send payment through untraceable methods.

THE UNLOCKABLE LOCKER

You lock your things in a seemingly secure locker, not realizing it's been fitted with a false backing that allows access through the other side.

Remember that your security is your personal responsibility and no one else's. Thoroughly test the security of anywhere you plan on leaving your possessions, regardless of what anyone promises you.

THE BIG BILL

After a meal in a restaurant you are given a bill that is much higher than you expected.

Local customs surrounding dining, like tipping etiquette and whether water is provided free of charge, vary greatly around the world. Further, it is not always common practice for restaurants to provide itemized bills listing the cost of each item that was ordered. However, you should be able to generally understand how the final price was determined. If you believe the bill to be incorrect, kindly ask to see the menu and add the prices yourself. Be sure the menu you are given is the same one you were shown when you first arrived, not a duplicate listing higher prices.

THE CURRENCY CONVERSION

You're considering a purchase by credit card when a vendor offers to convert the local price to your home currency. Though they claim this is to make things easier for you to understand, they use an unfair exchange rate and you end up paying a higher price for the item.

This is not so much a scam as it is an unfair type of electronic payment that invariably favors vendors and banks. Always carefully review credit card transactions before your card is charged: in addition to unfavorable exchange rates, a variety of fees might be charged.

THE FAKE DEMO

A vendor offers an electronic device or accessory, such as a memory card, at a drastically reduced price. Sensing that you're skeptical, the vendor then insists on "proving" its worth by testing it right in front of you. You buy it and it never works again.

Be aware that there are many different ways—from basic sleight of hand to specialized computer software—to make something appear functional. Be extremely wary of buying complex electronics in open markets of developing countries at heavily reduced prices. At worst, they'll never work again; at best they're stolen property.

THE EARLY CHECKOUT

The "hotel manager" calls your room and explains that their computer system has crashed and the line at the front desk is very long. They ask that you check out over the phone, and ask you to provide credit card information to pay for your room.

Insist on checking out in person and never give out credit card information over the phone if you feel suspicious or can't confirm the identity of the employee.

ᵛᵛᵛ *continued* ᵛᵛᵛ

THE LIGHT SCALE

A vendor uses a rigged scale to make an item appear to be heavier and thus more expensive.

A vendor should take no issue with you examining their scale, especially if large amounts of money are at stake.

THE CARD, TRICKED

These types of scams can be especially hazardous in that you often don't even know you're being robbed. Credit card skimmers (small devices used to quickly steal credit card information), fake ATMs, and a variety of other devices used to steal digital payment information are becoming increasingly commonplace and are usually not immediately recognizable as scams.

Be cautious when using credit cards while abroad and regularly check statements. As annoying as it can be to have your credit card frozen, banks can be helpful in recognizing this type of fraud.

THE FORCED PURCHASE

This scam can start a lot of different ways: an old woman grabs your hand and starts reading your fortune, a shoe-shine man drops his brush and starts shining your shoes to "thank" you for helping him pick it up, a vendor begins tying a personalized bracelet onto your wrist while claiming they created it "just for you," a food merchant offers a sample of a local delicacy, an aspiring musician hands you his CD just to look at—but they all end the same way: an aggressive demand for payment.

These scams use quick, unexpected aggression to force someone into agreeing to a demand without fully processing the situation. To be publicly admonished, or accused of theft, can be so uncomfortable that many travelers agree to pay simply to be rid of the embarrassment caused by the interaction. Whether through the use of stress or guilt, proprietors of these scams go to great lengths to antagonize travelers into paying for something they never actually wanted. Prevent this by remaining calm and asking at the beginning of the interaction whether something is free or not. Be forceful, but composed, if someone doesn't listen to your repeated declinations of their offer of services.

THE HIDDEN CHARGES

You go to check out, when you're given a bill listing multiple charges you weren't aware of: standard usage claimed as "damages," charges for using included amenities like a television or refrigerator, forced upgrades to a room with higher rates, per person charges (as opposed to charging by the room), and much more.

As with dining, customs surrounding accommodation vary from country to country. Always confirm rates and additional charges upon arrival to avoid angry interactions with management upon checking out.

THE SLOW SERVICE

A cashier, currency trader, or vendor uses an extremely slow or irregular cadence when counting out bills. Con artists know that travelers are generally anxious when their money is out in the open, so they use these tactics to either confuse the already distracted traveler or to simply goad them into grabbing the remaining money and declaring the transaction to be complete.

Remain calm and aware of your surroundings. If you suspect someone of intentionally wasting time or trying to cause confusion, stop the transaction immediately and insist on recounting the bills yourself.

THE FAKE TICKET AGENT

A person approaches offering to sell you tickets directly to save you time or money.

This scam can occur anywhere from a train station to a sporting event. One variant of this scam involves scammers selling very cheap entrance "tickets" to places that don't even charge admission, like public historical monuments.

While legitimate ticket scalpers do exist, the intricacies (and legality) of buying tickets in a secondary market varies greatly from country to country and the potential of being ripped off is unquestionably high. The only way you can be sure to receive legitimate tickets is to buy them from authorized sellers.

ᵛᵛᵛ *continued* ᵛᵛᵛ

THE BROKEN GLASS

You're walking through a crowded city when someone bumps into you and drops their bag. You hear glass shatter and they begin loudly accusing you of breaking their expensive prescription glasses or other glass items and demand you reimburse them.

The bag is filled glass bottles or already broken items to achieve the correct sound effect. Don't respond to their aggression with aggressive behavior of your own, but also don't submit to their demands. Walk away, and head toward a public area if they begin following you.

THE CURRENCY CONFUSION

A currency trader gives counterfeit notes, uses a different than agreed-upon exchange rate, or proposes a fair rate and then underpays through the use of sleight of hand.

Insist on recounting the money you receive. Advanced currency exchange scams can be prevented with proper preparation.[1]

1 ››› See page 254 for more information on currency exchanges.

THE DRUG DEALER

A stranger offers to sell you drugs. While you're in the process of either declining or accepting, a policeman arrives and arrests you.

It is common for corrupt policeman to work with drug dealers to entrap travelers and extract bribes.[1] If someone you don't know begins openly discussing illegal drugs, walk away immediately.

1 ››› See page 244 for more information on bribery.

THE STREET GAME

A crowd is gathered, watching people bet on a seemingly simple and fair street game like three-card monte. Other tourists seem to be winning large sums of money but when you put down your cash, you lose immediately.

What most people don't realize about this popular scam is that everyone —from the proprietor to the other players to people in the crowd—is in on it. The point is to make the game appear legitimate; no one is actually competing before you put your money in, they're simply acting for your benefit. Also beware that pickpockets may be lurking in the crowd.

THE FRIENDLY TOUR GUIDE

A gregarious local approaches you on the street under the guise of wanting to practice English or meet a foreigner. After a few hours of walking around, they demand payment for their service as a tour guide.

As soon as you suspect someone might expect payment for their time, address the issue calmly and directly.

THE FIRST DATE

A seemingly friendly (and often attractive) local strikes up a conversation, possibly under the guise of wanting to practice their English. They suggest a coffee shop, restaurant, or nightclub where you can continue your conversation. A few hours later, the exorbitantly high bill arrives and they are nowhere to be seen.

While most locals will have absolutely no ulterior motives when meeting foreigners, be wary if someone you've only just met insists on going to a particular place for seemingly no reason. The establishment is almost always involved in this scam and will charge unusually high prices for basic items. Further, it's always best to ask for a menu with prices on it before ordering anything.

THE SUDDEN CLOSURE

A taxi driver or seemingly helpful local regretfully informs you the restaurant or hostel you are looking for has recently closed. Luckily, they know of a different place and insist on taking you there.

Restaurants and hotels regularly pay kickbacks to locals who send tourists to their establishments. Insist that you want to go to your intended destination, regardless of whether it is open or not.

▾▾▾ *continued* ▾▾▾

THE GOLD RING

A seemingly honest good Samaritan picks up a ring off the ground near you and asks if you dropped it. When you say no, they pretend to examine it and then claim that it's real gold, and then offer it to you in exchange for a surprisingly low amount of money.

Kindly decline their offer and walk away.

THE TOURIST POLICE

A group of men approach you claiming to be "tourist police" and want to see your passport, or search you for drugs or counterfeit currency.

This is a difficult situation as they may be legitimate policemen, corrupt policemen, or outright thieves. If they are uniformed, be aware this very well may be a disguised robbery. Ask to see identification, do not hand over your important documents or wallet, and do not agree to follow them. If they appear to be actual policeman, they may be aiming to extract a bribe.[1]

1 ››› See page 244 for more information on bribery.

THE VICTIM

Someone hysterically rushes up to you claiming they've just been robbed, or are the victim of some other calamity. They ask for money to contact their families or to pay for a ride home.

Explain that they should contact the local police if they've been the victim of a crime.

THE WINDFALL

You notice a bag of cash on the ground or wallet on the ground. You pick it up and are immediately accosted by someone loudly claiming the money is theirs and that you've pocketed some of it. They demand you replace the money you "stole."

Always be wary of seemingly unattended wallets or bags of money lying around in public areas. Calmly explain you haven't stolen anything and offer to get the authorities involved. Remember to remain cognizant of your valuables as the entire interaction may merely be a distraction for a hidden pickpocket.

Pickpocketing Techniques

In addition to standard travel scams, there are also a variety of common pickpocketing methods the traveler should be informed about. For all their variations, each of these techniques is the same in their ultimate goal of using deceit or distraction to momentarily interrupt a traveler's focus on their personal possessions.

If you're in a public place, be initially wary of anything that seems designed to draw your eye. Pause and momentarily assess the situation before devoting your attention toward the unexpected occurrence happening nearby. A belligerent drunk, a commotion in the crowd, a fast-talking stranger—these are the tools a lurking pickpocket uses to create a brief moment of distraction that can disguise a swift robbery.

THE SWARM

A large group of children surround you, making a lot of noise or pressing against you; while you are distracted, someone picks your pocket.

THE INK

Ink (or some other liquid) is thrown on your clothes or bags. In the ensuing confusion, as you try to clean yourself off, you are robbed.

THE SUDDEN STOP

Someone in front of you on a crowded street stops suddenly, causing you to bump into them. A pickpocket behind you goes to work.

THE MAP

A seemingly lost person asks you to draw them a map, or holds out a map and asks for directions. This provides an excuse to get physically close, ensures your focus will be on giving directions, and provides a convenient sight barrier.

THE BABY

A woman approaches you carrying a baby and either unexpectedly thrusts it at you or pretends to lose her balance. As you are occupied trying to hold the infant or help the woman regain her footing, you are pickpocketed. The "baby" is nothing more than a doll.

▾▾▾ continued ▾▾▾

THE FIGHT

A fight breaks out right in front of you, usually a one-sided affair in which one person appears to be at risk of serious physical harm. As you try to help, or in the ensuing commotion, you are robbed.

THE OLD WOMAN

An old woman falls down in the middle of a crowded public place, spilling her possessions everywhere and requiring help to get up. As you move to assist her, a pickpocket robs you.

THE PETITION

An enthusiastic group of young people ask you to sign a petition for a noble cause. While your focus is on the clipboard, you are robbed.

THE PICTURE

Someone approaches you asking you to take a photo. They monopolize your focus by explaining some obscure setting on the camera, as an accomplice robs you.

THE CLUMSY THIEF

Someone makes a poor attempt at pickpocketing you and then immediately runs off, naturally causing you to check that none of your possessions have been stolen. This allows an accomplice, who is a much more competent thief, to see exactly where your valuables are hidden.

THE UNZIP AND GRAB

Someone behind you or passing by you unzips your backpack. As you turn to confront them, an accomplice reaches and in grabs whatever they can.

THE TOUR GROUP TRAITOR

You're on a walking tour and, unbeknownst to you, a pickpocket seamlessly integrates themselves with the large group. After walking around for a while you become familiar and comfortable around your fellow tour group members and are then pickpocketed by someone you assumed was a fellow traveler.

THE HERO

You're standing with a few bags of luggage, when a thief suddenly appears and attempts to rob someone near you. You put down your bags to fight or chase the thief, when an accomplice sneaks up and steals one of your bags.

THE WARNING

Whether a posted sign, an announcement from a loudspeaker, or words of caution spoken by a seemingly friendly stranger, "beware of pickpockets" warnings often cause people to immediately check their valuables, which has the ironic effect of showing lurking thieves exactly which pockets to target. Be wary of who might be watching when checking on personal possessions.

THE INSTANT ESCAPE

A thief waits near the doors of a crowded bus or train, then forcefully grabs your bag and jumps out right as the door closes. Be especially aware of your surroundings when standing near the exit of any form of transportation.

THE SHOW

This can take many forms—a thrilling street performance, a loud public argument, an impromptu street dance—all of which aim to monopolize your attention. You can and should participate in all of these things; just be aware the thief may be in the crowd, hoping to take advantage of the commotion.

DIGITAL DEFENSE

There is no more rapidly evolving area for scammers than cyberspace. Digital attacks become more sophisticated every year and the equipment necessary to execute all manner of complex hacks is now very cheap and available globally. Hackers usually focus on stealing credit card information, other more complex forms of identity theft, or stealing a person's files and holding them "hostage" until a ransom is paid.

⌄⌄⌄ *continued* ⌄⌄⌄

To avoid being hacked while traveling, be sure to keep all operating systems and antivirus programs up to date. But, as important as having current software is, even the strongest forms of digital security can become obsolete within a short time. Just as critical as ensuring your software is current is developing habits that ensure your data stays protected.

Understand the Process

Remember that hacking doesn't require physical contact with a device. Any time you allow *digital* access to your electronics, whether through an unfamiliar Wi-Fi connection, plugging in a USB at an Internet café, or other means, you run the risk of being hacked.

Streamline Your System

Take stock of your files before traveling. Traveling with a laptop containing the only copies of important files not necessary for travel is a recipe for disaster.

Know Who You're Talking To

The world is online—and that includes the criminals. The many technological innovations that benefit travelers, from social media platforms that allow people to stay in touch to dating and accommodation apps that help people connect, can also be used for harm. Be wary of revealing too much information about yourself or detailing your exact travel plans to people you've never met in person.

Understand "Unsecured"

While it's certainly advisable to avoid unsecured Internet connections, it's also not overly realistic. Many of the Internet connections found in coffee shops and hotels around the world are unsecured and there are often few other options for travelers. Choose a secure connection if available, but if you do use an unsecured connection[1] remain cognizant of what that means. Avoid inputting sensitive information, make sure any file sharing options in your system are off, log out of websites when not actively using them, regularly clear your cookies and Internet history, log out of and turn off Wi-Fi after using, and never download files or programs you're not familiar with. For extra security, consider using a virtual private network (VPN).[2]

---

1 ››› Usually noted by "this connection is unsecured and others may see your information" appearing on your screen.
2 ››› See page 181 for more information on VPNs.

NICE SOUVENIRS

A FTER SPENDING 340 days on the International Space Station, NASA astronaut Scott Kelly returned two inches (five centimeters) taller (the near-complete lack of gravity caused his spinal column to stretch, he will eventually return to his normal height) and eight milliseconds younger (due to a phenomenon called time dilation) than he would been had he stayed on earth.

THE NEW HOLLYWOOD(S)

I NDIA IS THE world's most prolific maker of films, producing close to 2,000 movies nationally every year.[1] Just some of the regional film production industries include:

INDUSTRY	CITY OR REGION
Bollywood	Mumbai
Jollywood	Assam
Kollywood	Chennai
Mollywood	Kerala
Ollywood	Odisha
Pollywood	Punjab
Sandalwood	Karnataka
Tollywood	West Bengal

It is not unheard of for Indian film productions to recruit traveling foreigners to appear in movies as background actors to help make scenes set in Western cities seem more authentic. Travelers are usually paid a small fee, in addition to meals, for appearing in nonspeaking parts.

1 ››› By way of comparison, the United States produces around 700 films each year.

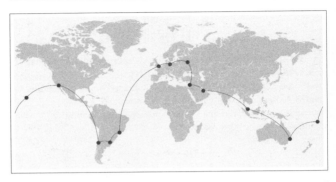

A ROUND-THE-WORLD TICKET (or RTW ticket) is a type of multiuse plane ticket that allows the purchaser to take multiple flights from multiple locations on an airline or participating alliance of airlines.[1] The basic idea behind RTW tickets is that travelers can simplify their trip planning and save money by buying plane tickets in bulk and in advance, for use over multiple months. RTW tickets are typically valid for one year from the date of the first flight.

While the concept may seem appealing, RTW tickets have become notorious for their fine print. Specific restrictions vary but often include significant fees for any alterations to flights, limitations on travel in certain areas, the ability to only travel in one direction, and much more. Any travelers considering an RTW ticket should extensively research all terms and conditions before purchasing. The bottom line is that buying an RTW ticket often means sacrificing a substantial amount of flexibility to potentially save a relatively small amount of money. And even the critical loss of travel flexibility notwithstanding, the simplicity of online travel booking, increasingly competitive fares, and the advent of ultra-budget airlines have made it easier and cheaper than ever for travelers to simply book necessary flights along the way.

Many experts consider RTW tickets to be a relic from a travel era gone by, when booking flights under short notice was so expensive and complicated that arranging all of one's travel beforehand made much more sense. Considering the cost of and regulations imposed on standard RTW tickets currently offered by major airlines, there are now only three specific sets of circumstances in which it is advisable to purchase one.

ONLY BUY AN RTW TICKET IF:

You are embarking on a precisely defined international trip through major cities and have absolutely no need or want of travel flexibility. RTW tickets can still save travelers money, provided they know exactly where and when they are traveling, long in advance of their trip.

OR

You have a flexible schedule and an unchangeable final destination that is only reachable by way of an expensive, lengthy flight. In this case, an RTW ticket may only cost a little more, but allow for much more extensive travel.

OR

A significant portion of your flight costs are being paid for through the use of frequent flier miles or some other type of airline membership system. With enough credit built up in a given loyalty program, the cost of an RTW ticket within that program may be less than buying separate flights on other airlines.

1 ››› Major airline alliances:
Star Alliance: 28 airlines totaling 4,657 planes serving 1,330 destinations in 192 countries.
SkyTeam: 20 airlines totaling 3,946 planes serving 1,062 destinations in 177 countries.
Oneworld: 15 airlines totaling 3,560 planes serving 1,016 destinations in 161 countries.

RELIGIOUS DIRECTION

A QIBLA POINTER IS an arrow indicating the direction of the Kaaba, in Mecca, Saudi Arabia, considered Islam's most holy place. Qibla pointers are often painted onto hotel room ceilings and public places to assist Muslims, who face in the direction of the Kabaa during their five daily salat prayers.

FLYOVER JOKE

WELCOME TO CLEVELAND.

—Written on the roof of a building directly in the flight path of Mitchell International Airport in Milwaukee, Wisconsin. Photographer Mark Gubin painted the massive sign as a joke in 1978 and it's still startling absentminded travelers to this day.

PROTECTING PARADISE

o·mertà (oh-MER-tuh)

noun. An agreed-upon code of silence; a refusal to discuss certain subjects.

From the Spanish *hombredad* ("manliness") and the Sicilian *omu* ("man")[1]

---

*It is almost axiomatic that as soon as a place
gets a reputation for being paradise it goes to hell.*

—PAUL THEROUX,
The Happy Isles of Oceania, 1992

In a world that can sometimes feels thoroughly discovered, there is a particular kind of joy in encountering a place that still seems somewhat under the radar. Whether that hidden paradise is as large as a newly accessible country blissfully free of a developed tourist trade, or as small as an empty stretch of a pristine beach, the joy of discovery remains the same.

When you arrive in that travel oasis and giddily realize that no guidebook points the masses this way, no popular film is advertising this paradise, no magazine features its glossy picture on a cover, it's as if you've earned a wonderful secret, available only to those courageous enough to wander off the beaten path. It is especially bittersweet, then, to wonder how long this secrecy could possibly last.

The word *omertà* encapsulates the symbolic attempt at preserving that bubble of secrecy for just a little while longer. A Sisyphean task, to be sure, but one that some travelers and expats attempt wholeheartedly. There are wonderful little hostels that actively campaign to keep their names out of guidebooks, sleepy mountain outposts that discourage any sort of short-term tourism, paradises whose occupants are wary to speak of. Whether it is morally valid for outsiders to try and preserve some distant utopia all for themselves is up for debate. But when you discover such a place, and feel the thrill that accompanies discovering somewhere wonderfully unknown, it's hard not to want to try.

....

1 ››› This etymology is disputed: some sources consider the original source of omertà to be the Latin *humilitas* ("humility") which led to the southern Italian *umiltà* ("humility").

A WITNESS TO HISTORY

When Columbus discovered America he did not know what the outcome would be, and no one at that time knew; and I doubt if the wildest enthusiast caught a glimpse of what really did come from his discovery. In a like manner these two brothers have probably not even a faint glimpse of what their discovery is going to bring to the children of men.

—AMOS IVES ROOT,
Gleanings in Bee Culture, 1905

FROM THE FIRST article ever published about Orville and Wilbur Wright's invention of the world's first successful airplane. *Gleanings in Bee Culture* was a magazine Root founded in which he occasionally discussed gardening, science, and religion but mostly focused on his interest in beekeeping. Why the notoriously secretive Wright brothers allowed the eccentric Root to observe and report on their experiments is unknown. Root also sent the article to *Scientific American*, where his writing had been published in the past, but editors rejected it, believing heavier-than-air human flight to be impossible.

ONE GOOD KNOT

THE BOWLINE (USUALLY pronounced "bow-lin") is a simple, safe, and versatile knot that can be used for everything from tying a backpack to the top of a jeep to securing a ship to a dock. It can be tied with one hand and untied easily after use.

"The rabbit comes out of the hole, / around the tree, / and then back down the hole."

King (deceased).

—Occupation listed on the Egyptian passport of Ramses II when his mummified body was sent to Paris for examination in 1974. Though the pharaoh had been dead for approximately 3,187 years, French law requires that the body of any deceased person entering the country must have some official form of identification.

THERE'S NO ESCAPING CUSTOMS

UPON RETURNING FROM the moon, the Apollo 11 astronauts were greeted as national heroes and then promptly forced to go through customs. Highlights from astronaut Edwin "Buzz" Aldrin's[1] paperwork are included below. Though the forms themselves may have been done partially as a tongue-in-cheek joke about military bureaucracy, the astronauts reentry into the United States, like all customs matters, was treated with the utmost seriousness. Due to the fear that they may be infected with some sort of unknown lunar disease, Aldrin and fellow astronauts Neil Armstrong and Michael Collins were forced to spend 21 days in quarantine when they returned. They passed the time playing Ping-Pong, watching television, and talking to their families on the phone, among other activities.

CUSTOMS

Date	July 24, 1969
Flight No.	Apollo 11
Departure from	Moon
Arrival at [2]	Honolulu, Hawaii, USA
Cargo	Moon Rock and Moon Dust Samples
Any other condition on board which may lead to spread of disease	To Be Determined

Aldrin also claimed $33.31 in travel expenses. He was reimbursed
for gas mileage driving his car in the days leading up to the launch, as well
as given per diems for his time spent on the mission.

NATURE OF EXPENSES	1969 $	2016 $
8 miles in privately owned vehicle at authorized mileage rate of $.07 per mile:	$.56	$3.63
Privately owned vehicle authorized for official vicinity travel at Cape Kennedy, Fla. in lieu of rental car	$10.00	$64.89
1 day per d @ $8.00	$8.00	$51.91
19¼ days per d @ $1.00	$19.25	$124.91
Less $2.25 for meals (2)	($4.50)	($29.20)
Grand total reimbursement	**$33.31**	**$216.14**

1 ››› Aldrin's mother's maiden name was Moon.
2 ››› The Apollo 11 command module actually landed in the Pacific Ocean about 926 miles (1,491 kilometers) southwest of Honolulu but recovery ship the USS *Hornet* brought them to Hawaii two days later.

A GOOD PRESCRIPTION

This is to certify that the post-accident convalescence of the Hon.
Winston S. Churchill necessitates the use of alcoholic spirits
especially at meal times. The quantity is naturally indefinite but the
minimum requirements would be 250 cubic centimeters.

—OTTO C. PICKHARDT, MD

A note from Winston Churchill's doctor authorizing him to consume alcohol while abroad in 1932, after he'd been hit by a car in New York City. Alcohol was banned in the United States at the time due to Prohibition.

Two roads diverged in a yellow wood,
And sorry I could not travel both
And be one traveler, long I stood
And looked down one as far as I could
To where it bent in the undergrowth;

Then took the other, as just as fair
And having perhaps the better claim,
Because it was grassy and wanted wear;
Though as for that the passing there
Had worn them really about the same,

And both that morning equally lay
In leaves no step had trodden black.
Oh, I kept the first for another day!
Yet knowing how way leads on to way,
I doubted if I should ever come back.

I shall be telling this with a sigh
Somewhere ages and ages hence:
Two roads diverged in a wood, and I—
I took the one less traveled by,
And that has made all the difference.

—ROBERT FROST,
"The Road Not Taken," *Mountain Interval*, 1920

PERHAPS THE MOST well-known of the traveler poems, Robert Frost's "The Road Not Taken" elegantly describes the inevitable crossroads every traveler knows all too well. In just a few dozen words, the poet captures the sorrow at having to leave one path unexplored, the paralyzing terror of making a wrong choice, the desire for any type of guidance in the face of decision, the false self-promise of return, the implications of a seemingly simple choice, and more. It's no surprise that these universal themes often particularly resonate with travelers, who deal with the literal manifestation of this very subject and all its implications on a near constant basis.

"The Road Not Taken" is a powerful distillation of choice and everything that comes with it. The traveler, who has already in some sense made a significant choice by deciding to travel at all, lives at this crossroads and embraces the fear and doubt inherent in doing so. To describe this complicated emotion in such an effective but simple way is a feat in itself—and is accomplished by the end of the third stanza. The poem could end here and still be a meaningful work on destiny.

Yet, it's the often quoted fourth stanza—Frost's discussion of *"the one less traveled by"* —that makes this poem both famous and possibly misunderstood. Some interpret this portion as an endorsement of unconventionality and therefore claim "The Road Not Taken" as an unofficial slogan for all things nonconformist. However, as alluring as this interpretation sounds to the traveler, that may not have been what the author intended.

It may come as a shock to the legions of rebels who use Frost's work as justification for their latest risky pursuit that many literary scholars consider "The Road Not Taken" to be one of the most famously misunderstood works in all of poetry. After all, careful reading reveals Frost actually repeatedly describes the two paths to be of basically equal condition (*"the other, as just as fair"* and *"Had worn them really about the same"*). The path the speaker chooses is no riskier than the other and is only described as *"less traveled"* in the speaker's own expected future retelling. Furthermore, the very last words—*"all the difference"*—do not necessarily refer to some fulfilling reward given to those with the courage to diverge from the mainstream, readers only assume the *"difference"* to be positive. Frost himself often described the poem as *"very tricky."* Indeed, instead of endorsing adventures into the unknown, the fourth stanza very well might be Frost describing what he thinks to be final effect of any choice: that *"ages and ages hence"* a person will inevitably describe their decision as bold or significant, even if that truly wasn't the case.

Whether Frost meant for "The Road Not Taken" to be an encouraging call to risk-takers everywhere or a complex analysis of the embellishment that naturally accompanies any choice, cannot be known. Regardless, the value of any poem is in control of the reader alone. Frost may have never intended to inspire countless readers toward the riskier, more adventurous choices life has to offer but that hardly matters. In fact, it might be the noblest unintended consequence in the history of poetry.

LOVE OF THE ROAD

A nomad I was even when I was very small and would stare at the road . . .
A nomad I will remain for life, in love with distant and uncharted places.

—ISABELLE EBERHARDT,
Swiss explorer and writer, Diary, 1903

A GUIDE TO THE STARS

UNLIKE CROWD-SOURCED REVIEW systems that are designed for ease of use, some professional restaurant rating methodologies can be more difficult to decipher. Below is a guide to the most prominent professional restaurant review systems currently in widespread use.

LOWEST	ORGANIZATION	HIGHEST
✿	MICHELIN	✿ ✿ ✿
"Very good restaurant in its category"	Began in 1900 as a driving guide for French motorists, is now considered the premier restaurant review system for high-end cuisine.	*"Exceptional cuisine, worthy of a special journey"*

Europe, United States, and Japan

LOWEST	ORGANIZATION	HIGHEST
★	FORBES	★ ★ ★ ★ ★
"Provides a distinctive experience through culinary specialty, local flair, or individual atmosphere"	Began in 1958 as Mobil Travel Guide, is now an increasingly global ranking system focusing on luxury travel.	*"Delivers a truly unique and distinctive dining experience"*

Europe, North America, the Caribbean, Latin America, Asia

LOWEST	ORGANIZATION	HIGHEST
♙ 13/20[1]	GAULT & MILLAU	♙ ♙ ♙ ♙ ♙ 19.5/20
"Very good kitchen with more than conventional cuisine"	Began in 1961 as a series on progressive restaurants in Paris, is now a highly influential guide to upscale cuisine.	*"Awarded for ground-breaking and outstanding cuisine"*

Europe

LOWEST	ORGANIZATION	HIGHEST
♦	AAA	♦ ♦ ♦ ♦ ♦
"Simple, economical food, often quick-serve, in a functional environment"	Began in 1902 as a car club, now a large not-for-profit organization specializing in automotive services and travel information.	*"Leading-edge cuisine of the finest ingredients, uniquely prepared by an acclaimed chef"*

North America

LOWEST	ORGANIZATION	HIGHEST
0–10	ZAGAT[2]	26–30
"Poor to fair"	Began in 1979 as a restaurant guide to New York City, now a Google-owned review system covering multiple industries.	*"Extraordinary to perfection"*

United States (as well as Toronto, Vancouver, and London)

1 ›› Though restaurants are graded on a full 1 to 20 point scale, low-ranking restaurants are generally not listed in the guide and only high-ranking restaurants are awarded toques (traditional white chef hats), using the following system:

| 1–12 | — | 15–16 | 🎩 🎩 | 19 | 🎩 🎩 🎩 🎩 |
| 13–14 | 🎩 | 17–18 | 🎩 🎩 🎩 | 19.5 | 🎩 🎩 🎩 🎩 🎩 |

2 ›› Uses crowd-sourced reviews in addition to professional reviews.

————◆————

DRAWN TO THE ROAD

The untented Kosmos my abode,
I pass, a wilful stranger:
My mistress still the open road
And the bright eyes of danger.

—ROBERT LOUIS STEVENSON,
Scottish novelist and poet, "Youth and Love: I",
Songs of Travel and Other Verses, 1896

A QUICK GUIDE TO RAPIDS

ORIGINALLY DEVELOPED BY the American Whitewater association, the following scale is now the internationally recognized standard for grading the technical difficulty of safely navigating a section of river. Note that this scale is intended only as a general guide to the potential dangers posed by fast-moving rapids, not an exact description of a river's current conditions. Further, fluctuating water levels can quickly and significantly change the safety level of any body of water.

International Scale of River Difficulty

	CLASS[1]	DESCRIPTION
I	Easy	*Fast-moving water with riffles and small waves. Few obstructions, all obvious and easily missed with little training.*
II	Novice	*Straightforward rapids with wide, clear channels which are evident without scouting. Occasional maneuvering may be required.*
III	Intermediate	*Rapids with moderate, irregular waves which may be difficult to avoid. Complex maneuvers in fast current and good boat control in tight passages or around ledges are often required.*
IV	Advanced	*Intense, powerful but predictable rapids requiring precise boat handling in turbulent water. Water conditions may make self-rescue difficult.*
V	Expert	*Extremely long, obstructed, or very violent rapids which expose a paddler to added risk. Rapids may continue for long distances between pools, demanding a high level of fitness. Rescue is often difficult even for experts.*
VI	Extreme and Exploratory Rapids	*These runs have almost never been attempted and often exemplify the extremes of difficulty, unpredictability and danger. The consequences of errors are very severe and rescue may be impossible. For teams of experts only.*

+/- may be used to further specify level of difficulty within a given class

---

1 ››› Sometimes referred to as *grades*.

BABY ON BOARD

MANY AIRLINES HAVE policies concerning whether or not near-term pregnant women can fly. These policies have little to do with potential health complications, and are instead motivated by the fact that airline personnel are not equipped to assist a passenger who unexpectedly goes into labor. Details vary by airline, but many require written authorization from a medical professional for any woman more than 28 weeks pregnant, and some do not allow women more than 36 weeks pregnant to fly as standard policy. It is recommended that all pregnant women check with a doctor before flying, regardless of stage of pregnancy.

PLEASE FASTEN YOUR SEATBELT

TURBULENCE, WITHIN THE context of plane travel, is essentially the irregular, unanticipated movement of air. Invisible to the naked eye and difficult to predict, turbulence can cause a plane to shake and wobble, but poses no real threat to the actual integrity of the aircraft. Thanks to advances in aircraft technology and irritating but necessary seatbelt regulations, injuries caused by turbulence are extraordinarily rare. In the United States, the chances of a passenger being injured by turbulence are roughly 1 in 30 million. Particularly concerned passengers should avoid the rear of the plane, which most experts agree experiences the most extreme effects of turbulence.

The real consequence of turbulence is psychological: it causes already-frighthened[1] passengers to wonder why they left home at all. They have nothing to worry about: though turbulence can cause a briefly bumpy ride, flying remains by far the safest way to travel.

---

1 ››› An estimated one in six American adults suffer from some sort of fear of flying.

PET PASSPORT

No road is long with good company.
—Turkish proverb

THERE IS CURRENTLY no globally accepted "pet passport," so always extensively research a country's animal entry requirements before traveling internationally with a pet. However, in an attempt at standardization, several EU countries introduced the **Pet Travel Scheme (PETS)** in late 2001. This set of guidelines aims to help simplify traveling with pets while minimizing the amount of time animals spend in quarantine. PETS has now been adopted in a total of 51 countries around the world.

The noble idea behind PETS is that animals from countries that utilize the program can freely travel among other member countries provided they have been checked for certain diseases and issued the required documentation. In practice, however, so many countries enforce additional regulations that the idea of a single, standard "pet passport" that grants an animal entry into a large number of countries remains the eventual goal, rather than the current reality.

But while there's no universal "pet passport," the basics of PETS does provide insight into the modern regulations of animal travel. This can be thought of as the minimum requirement for significant international travel with animals. Note that the following policies apply only to domestic dogs, cats, and ferrets. Traveling with other species of animal can be significantly more complicated.

YOUR PET MUST:

» Be at least 12 weeks old.

» Be fitted with a microchip.

» Have been vaccinated against rabies at least 21 days ago.

» Have documentation detailing their vaccination record and confirming they are healthy enough for travel.

Again, most countries determine which pets can enter based on a whole host of additional criteria involving the animal's travel history, vaccinations, specific breed, and much more. Further, many airline, rail, and shipping companies may use an entirely different set of criteria to determine which animals are allowed on board.

Clearly, traveling with a pet can be a complicated endeavor. But these regulations are in place for valid reasons: animal-specific diseases can have devastating effects on entire species, and animal smuggling remains a concerning issue in many parts of the world.

OLD PEOPLES' HOME

BLUE ZONES IS a term coined by researchers Gianni Pes and Michel Poulain for areas in which local citizens live especially long lives. These regions have some of highest concentrations of 100-plus-year-old people anywhere on earth.

Okinawa, Japan · Sardinia, Italy · Loma Linda, California, USA
Nicoya, Costa Rica · Icaria, Greece

The researchers attributed the longevity of these people to factors including moderate but constant physical activity, social and familial engagement, and a largely plant-based diet.

ANCIENT ACCOMMODATION

THE OLDEST HOTEL in the world is thought to be Nisiyama Onsen Keiunkan, located near a popular hot spring in Yamanashi, Japan. The 35-room establishment was founded in 705 AD and has been operated by 52 successive generations of the same family.[1]

---

1 ››› While all are members of the same family, not every generation is comprised of blood relatives. Adult adoption for the purpose of continuing a family name or maintaining a business is a common practice in Japan. In a typical year, more than 95 percent of adoptees are men between the ages of 20 and 40.

DRIVEN

Inveniam viam aut facium.
(I shall find a way or make one.)

—Originally attributed to the philosopher Seneca the Elder, the phrase was written by polar explorer Robert Peary in 1899 on the wall of a hut on Ellesmere Island after his severely frostbitten toes began falling off. He eventually had seven of them amputated and continued exploring for years afterward wearing stuffed shoes. Whether he ever reached the geographic North Pole, as he claimed to have done in 1909, is disputed.

* * *

ON PASSPORTS

ADDITIONAL REQUIREMENTS

Many countries impose at least two additional conditions on passports:

Number of blank pages: 2 | *Time to expiration:* 6 months

This is to ensure that a traveler's passport remains valid through the entire length of their stay. Always check a country's latest passport requirements to ensure entry.

PASSPORT PHOTO

A passport, as I'm sure you know, is a document that one
shows to government officials whenever one reaches a border
between countries, so the officials can learn who you are,
where you were born, and how you look when
photographed unflatteringly.

— DANIEL HANDLER (AKA LEMONY SNICKET),
American author

Passport photos are generally needed for two reasons: when applying for (or renewing) a passport or to satisfy the entry requirements of a country. In most situations, either size passport photo listed on the following page will be considered satisfactory.

Many countries require two passport photos to be submitted with a visa application so it is recommended you travel with multiple pre-printed passport photos. Though it is usually possible to find places that will print passport photos in most parts of the world, simply printing a large amount before departing can save time, money, and hassle. Note that the guidelines below apply to almost everywhere in the world, but the only way to be completely sure is to double-check a given country's current requirements.

U.S. Standard Passport Photo

E.U. Standard Passport Photo

U. S. photo dimensions: 2" x 2" (50.8mm x 50.8mm)

E.U. photo dimensions: 1.38" x 1.77" (35mm x 45mm)

YOUR PASSPORT PHOTO SHOULD BE:

» *In color*

» *In sharp, clear focus with normal light and contrast*

» *Printed on photo-quality paper*

» *Taken within the past 6 months to show accurate appearance[1]*

» *Of the full face, directly facing the camera*

» *Taken with a neutral expression with both eyes open*

» *Taken without wearing any hats or dark tinted glasses*

» *Taken in front of a plain white or off-white background with no shadows*

» *If preferred, taken wearing any prescription glasses, wigs, or hearing devices normally worn in daily life[2]*

» *Taken wearing normal street clothes; no uniforms*

» *Taken without hair obscuring or casting shadow on any part of the face*

1 ››› Though this is technically a requirement of some countries, it is rarely enforced unless a person's appearance has significantly changed.

2 ››› Due to the fact that there can be absolutely no glare reflecting off of glasses, most sources recommend removing glasses as best practice.

ᴠᴠᴠ *continued* ᴠᴠᴠ

Travelers may be interested to know that it is sometimes possible to avoid having your passport stamped. This is generally done for one of three reasons:

Save Space

While most travelers view passport stamps as colorful reminders of past adventures, frequent travelers may be annoyed at the speed in which they run out of usable passport pages.

Trouble Abroad

As a public display of deep hostility toward another nation, some countries do not allow travelers who have visited certain other countries to cross their borders.

The constantly evolving realm of geopolitics means these policies are always in flux, but the Israeli passport stamp remains the most notable and consistent example. At the time of this writing, travelers who have visited Israel may be prevented from entering Iran, Iraq, Kuwait, Lebanon, Libya, Pakistan, Saudi Arabia, Sudan, Syria, or Yemen.[1]

In these situations, a border guard may be amendable to not stamping a passport or stamping a piece of paper instead and then stapling that into the passport, which can later be removed and thus help prevent issues down the road. Note however that this is not a foolproof plan: vigilant border guards sometimes closely examine entry-exit points and travel dates to determine an exact itinerary.

Trouble at Home

Some governments require their citizens to have special licenses, permits, or visas to travel to certain countries, or restrict travel to certain countries altogether. Though the destination country might not have a problem with the visit, travelers may land in hot water when they return home. Explaining this to a border guard may persuade them to leave your passport unstamped, or stamp a piece of paper instead. But this also is not guaranteed to be effective, as your government may have other ways of discovering your specific travel history.

As always, these policies are subject to change without warning and are only as strict as the border guard tasked with enforcing them. Some of these rules are rarely adhered to, others can be avoided with a well-placed bribe,[2] and still others are the result of decades of internation hostility and will undoubtedly be strictly enforced. Research current conditions and talk to other travelers to find out the best way to avoid an unwanted passport stamp.

1 ››› Though less frequent, travelers also may encounter issues in Algeria, Bangladesh, Brunei, Indonesia, Malaysia, Oman, and United Arab Emirates. These countries, in addition to the list on the previous page, do not allow Israeli passport holders. Unlike the
previous list, however, they generally accept travelers of other nationalities who have
visited Israel.
2 ››› See page 244 for more information on bribery.

DOUBLING UP

While diplomats, international aid workers, and government officials
regularly travel using multiple passports,[1] the use of a secondary passport is not limited solely to those with certain itinerant professions.
Normal travelers also regularly obtain secondary passports, using the
following methods:

Dual Citizenship

Regulations vary from country to country: some do not recognize any
form of dual citizenship; others will swiftly issue you a passport if any of
your parents or grandparents were born in the country.

Application

Some governments will issue citizens a secondary passport if they can
provide a compelling reason for requiring one. For instance, the US government issues secondary passports, unrenewable and valid only for
two years, to frequent travelers who:

Have a current passport that contains passport stamps or visa information that may result in them being denied entry to other countries.[2]

or

Cannot access their current passport because it is in possession of a foreign government for the purposes of a visa application.

If you travel using two passports, it is best practice not to inform
border officials unless absolutely necessary as this may result in confusion or suspicion. Additionally, remember to always use the same passport to enter and exit a country.

1 ››› High-ranking diplomatic officials are issued *diplomatic passports*; many aid workers
travel internationally using a *United Nations Laissez-Passer* which is commonly called
a "UN Passport"; and government officials often carry *service passports* (sometimes
called *official passports*).
2 ››› See page 77 for more information on country entry requirements.

PROTECT YOUR PASSPORT

A passport is arguably the single most important item in a traveler's
bag. Here are some tips on protecting this key item.

⌄⌄⌄ *continued* ⌄⌄⌄

Giving Out Your Number

Passport numbers are unique to the passport itself, not the person, and will therefore be completely different on every new or updated passport issued.

Unlike your social security number or credit card information, it is generally accepted that there is little risk in giving out passport information. It is common practice, and in some countries a legal requirement, for hotels and hostels to request passport numbers, expiration dates, and possibly a photocopy of the actual passport when reserving or checking into a room. This allows the establishment to check your identity and confirm that you are in the country legally. Though you should never give out any personal information if you feel uncomfortable or suspicious, most security experts agree that there is almost nothing an identity thief can do solely with the information found on a passport.

If you are traveling for an extended period of time, it is advisable to memorize your passport number and expiration date early on in the trip, to avoid repeatedly retrieving your passport during self check-ins or when filling out visa forms.

Leaving It with the Desk

Some hotels or hostels may request that travelers leave their passport with the front desk, either for a few hours or for the entire length of their stay. Whether this is done for the sake of convenience (so they can record the necessary information at a less busy time of day) or collateral (to ensure a traveler doesn't leave without paying their bill), this policy makes many travelers understandably nervous.

Just as you wouldn't normally get into a car with a stranger but regularly take taxis, leaving your passport with the desk is a basic matter of trusting the establishment. If a hotel or hostel has a good reputation and seems trustworthy and secure, you should feel safe in leaving your passport with them. If not, other arrangements can often be made.

Back It Up

Hide multiple color copies throughout your luggage, email digital scans of your passport to yourself and a trusted friend, and upload all relevant passport information to a cloud service. If the worst happens and your passport is stolen, it is critical you have this information readily available.

Lock It Up

If you trust the security of where you're staying (whether that security is provided by your own locks on a personal locker, a hidden spot in a locked room, a hotel safe, or other means) always lock up your passport.

Travel is about freedom, and carrying something as critical as a passport on your person for every trip to the beach or visit to the market may cause unnecessary daily anxiety. Though obviously dependent on specific circumstances, public robberies and in-person muggings are generally much more common than burglaries of a hostel or hotel.

If the official regulations of the country state that foreigners must have their passports on them at all times, be sure to carry a color copy. While lacking your actual passport may result in the rare disgruntled official, or give a corrupt police officer a good chance to extract a small bribe, travelers rarely, if ever, incur any sort of serious punishment for disobeying this law.

If the Worst Happens

If your passport is lost or stolen, find a backup copy of your passport and immediately get in contact with your local embassy.[1] If you were robbed, contact the local police and be sure to get some type of official report as embassy officials will ask for documentation when issuing an emergency passport.

1››› See page 260 for more information on embassies, or for what to do if your country doesn't have an embassy within the country.

REAL JET LAG

T HE FIRST-NIGHT EFFECT (FNE) is a term neuroscientists use to describe the fact that, after accounting for extraneous factors such as bed comfort and level of exhaustion, almost all people wake up feeling groggy simply by virtue of sleeping somewhere new. Though this physiological occurrence has been recognized for decades, only recently developed neuroimaging techniques have allowed scientists to try and identify the root cause.

A 2016 study from Brown University has indicated that the left hemisphere of the brain naturally remains almost fully alert the first night a person sleeps in an unfamiliar place, likely the result of an evolutionary trait protecting humans from predators. Researchers have shown that a brain in this "half-awake" state is far more reactive to unusual sounds, with the left hemisphere functioning as a kind of night watchman. Subjects studied returned to typical sleep on the second night and researchers speculated that the brains of people who travel often are likely able to subconsciously decrease this effect when desired.

BARRIER TO ENTRY

*The entry of "hippies" and men with long hair
and flared trousers is forbidden.*

—A Malawi visa entry requirement put into effect during the rule of
President Hastings Kamuzu Banda. Male travelers with long hair were
offered haircuts by border guards and if refused they were denied entry.

OVERBOOKED

EVERY AIRLINE, HOTEL, tour operator, and car rental company shares a common and obvious goal: 100 percent occupancy.
Yet, empowered by increasingly lenient refund and cancelation policies,
the general public has become notoriously unreliable.

Depending on specific circumstances, anywhere from 10 percent
to 50 percent of customers usually don't show up for their reservations and the majority of these absent customers receive some type of
refund. Therefore, to account for the revenue lost by these anticipated
no-shows, companies engage in overbooking.

Overbooking is the practice in which companies intentionally
oversell their product to precisely account for the number of expected
refund-seeking customers. Statistical models based on historical data
determine the exact amount these companies overbook and they are
often astonishingly accurate.[1]

As frustrating as overbooking may be to someone who has paid and
reserved far in advance only to be "bumped," this is a completely legal
practice that most experts agree is beneficial to the consumer. Without
overbooking, refund policies would either be far more restrictive or
most companies would have to raise prices.

To avoid being bumped, confirm your reservation and show up early.
But if you are that unlucky traveler whose plane seat or hotel room is
threatened by overbooking, here are a few things to keep in mind:

» Depending on travel flexibility, being bumped may be a good thing.
  Companies offer all kind of incentives, from flight vouchers to meal
  coupons, to convince travelers to be bumped voluntarily. If you're

not on a tight schedule, investigate what type of perks you might be able to negotiate if you offer to change your plans.

» The laws of some countries entitle you to even more if you're bumped involuntarily. In the US, travelers bumped from flights involuntarily can receive up to $1,300 in compensation, in addition to a rescheduled flight.

» As annoyed as you may be, try to remain civil when interacting with employees. If you're going to complain, complain intelligently: calmly describe your situation and clearly outline what you want. A person who gets bumped involuntarily is a victim of statistics, nothing more. But once that process is initiated, employees often have a large amount of discretion in making other travel or accommodation arrangements and compensating customers. If you are unnecessarily cruel, they will ensure you receive the very minimum that the law or company policy requires. But if you're pleasant and understanding, even under these trying circumstances, they very well may repay you with additional perks.

....

1››› In 2014, less than a tenth of a tenth of one percent of passengers were bumped from flights on major US airlines. Only .0091 percent, or roughly 1 in every 10,000, were bumped involuntarily.

———————————◆———————————

A MATTER OF PERSPECTIVE

» *Citizens could be bothered or questioned without motive at any moment.*

» *It is comparatively easy to obtain possession of guns. If you are the victim of an armed attack, do not try to fight back!*

» *Within large metropolitan areas, violent crime more commonly occurs in economically disadvantaged neighborhoods, particularly from dusk to dawn. Verify official neighborhood crime statistics before planning an outing.*

» *Tap water—while not very tasty (it's chlorinated)—is usually considered safe to drink.*

—Travel warnings issued about the United States by the governments of Mexico, Germany, Canada, and Austria, respectively

mai pen rai (my-pen-RYE) *Thai*

idiom. A versatile phrase that can mean everything from "you're welcome" to "no worries."
From the Thai *mai* ("no"), *pen* ("is"), and *rai* ("water bug")

This popular Thai idiom might be said while waiting on a late bus or staring at a broken motorbike. It is an indicator of contented acceptance; a commitment to not getting upset over life's unavoidable misfortunes.

Mai pen rai captures the essence of a friendly and relaxed attitude toward life, embodied by the Thai people and found in cultures around the world. Similar phrases are popular in many languages, from Swahili's *hakuna matata* to the Spanish phrase *que sera, sera,* and, while each has its unique attributes, all speak to the same philosophy of accepting what one cannot change and maintaining a composed mind-set regardless of outside circumstances.[1]

Understanding and embodying the *mai pen rai* attitude is essential for the independent traveler. Travel rarely goes according to plan, that is indeed one of its strongest attributes, and being able to adapt to rapidly changing conditions is a critical skill. Lost luggage, delayed flights, broken ATMs, and a thousand other issues can suddenly coalesce to cause a traveler to wonder why they left home at all. In these moments, it's important to take a deep breath and consider that you're on a great adventure on the other side of the world, in a place so foreign you can't even understand the language being spoken, much less control the forces at work. Travel problems are frustrating, to be sure, but a worthwhile inconvenience. Whisper a phrase like *mai pen rai* to yourself, release that stress, and keep exploring.

1 ››› Both popularized by song:
"Hakuna Matata" was featured in Disney's 1994 film *The Lion King*. The phrase literally translates to "there are no troubles here" and, though it's gained popularity because of the film, most native Swahili speakers use *hamna shida* or other phrases to express a similar sentiment.
Que sera, sera means "what will be, will be" and was the title of a hit song from 1956, notably performed by Doris Day, among others. Like "Hakuna Matata," its relevance in pop culture has led to an increase in common usage.

KEEP IT CLEAN

T RAVELERS SHOULD BE aware that in some parts of the world it is standard practice for vendors to accept only pristine foreign currencies. Widespread counterfeiting, a history of economic instability, or general unfamiliarity with different currencies may all contribute to the deep distrust of foreign money common in many countries. Contrary to popular belief, merchants are not legally obligated to accept certain forms of currency and are well within their rights to refuse service. Expect to encounter intense scrutiny and make sure your money is in mint condition—otherwise you may have trouble getting fair value for it.

YOUR MONEY MAY BE REJECTED IF IT'S:

Creased · Dirty · Faded · Folded · Old · Ripped · Written On

THE GREAT LOUNGE WAR

I N THE EARLY 1970s, major American airlines suddenly found themselves with massive new jumbo jets, like the Boeing 747, and a distinct lack of passengers. An economic downturn meant fewer people were flying and it wasn't unusual for large aircraft to take off with less than half of their seats filled. When American Airlines decided to remove 40 of 270 coach seats from a plane and install a bar to attract new customers, what would become known as the Great Lounge War began.

In response to American Airlines, Trans World Airlines (TWA) offered living room–style lounges full of cocktail tables. American Airlines then put pianos on 16 of their planes and encouraged passengers to enjoy martinis from the stand-up bar and join sing-alongs. Stevie Wonder performed during a United Flight, which also regularly featured wine tastings and caricature artists. Continental hired a duo called the Pineapple Splits to sing "folk rock pop" songs on its four daily Los Angeles to Honolulu flights. And then, almost as suddenly as it had begun, the Great Lounge War was over.

As the recession eased and passengers returned to flying, airlines came to an informal truce, realizing that trying to outdo one another with increasingly expensive promotions would result in lower profits for all. Global oil shortages in 1973 increased fuel prices and began to redefine the profitability margins of air travel. In essence, airlines began focusing on maximizing the quantity, not quality, of the air travel experience, a trend that continues to this day.

As ACCESS TO the Internet becomes increasingly integral to the modern travel experience, it's important to note that many countries heavily censor what type of information can be viewed online. Some governments deny access to specific sites (such as social media platforms), others block any web page containing certain keywords (such as references to political opposition), and certain totalitarian regimes have been known to intentionally disable entire networks to stop the spread of information. Though more and more people have access to the Internet, global Internet freedom is arguably on the decline as governments realize how powerful a tool it can be.

Not only is widespread Internet censorship standard practice in many countries, arrests associated with government Internet monitoring are becoming increasingly common. Recently, citizens and travelers alike have been detained and arrested for everything from blog posts to Facebook status updates. Many of those prosecuted have not been fervent political organizers or radicals calling for revolution—these are students and common people, who have done nothing more than retweet a vaguely satirical cartoon or comment on the picture of a powerful royal family. Travelers from developed countries tend to value the Internet as a place of total anonymity, and can scarcely imagine online actions having such significant real-life consequences. Remember that you must follow all the rules of the nation in which you're traveling, even if those regulations only exist digitally. Always be wary of posting anything critical, especially using an identifiable user name, of those in power in countries where censorship laws exist.[1]

In a very basic sense, every Internet-enabled device, be it a watch, phone, or laptop, transmits identifying information about itself when online. Censoring governments use this information to see what sites are being accessed and, in some cases, track the identity of the person using the device. To counter these efforts, it's necessary to disguise the source of the data, which is commonly done through one the following two methods.

	PROXY	VIRTUAL PRIVATE NETWORK (VPN)
Applicable definition	Acts as an intermediary between your device and the Internet, which makes your Internet traffic appear to be originating from a different device.	Acts as an intermediary to disguise the origin of Internet traffic, but also encrypts all information being sent or received.
Common analogy	A public bridge	A private tunnel
Cost	Free, paid options available	Paid, usually via monthly fee
Commonly accessed through	An Internet browser	A dedicated program running on your device
Security	Very low, data is easily intercepted, never enter a password or access sensitive information via proxy	High
Stability	Low, crashes common	High
Average speed	Slow—often many users sharing limited bandwidth	Fast—options vary, but because a VPN is a dedicated connection to a single user, it is usually faster than a public proxy
Commonly used for	Briefly accessing nonsensitive sites blocked by censorship. For instance, watching a YouTube video at an Internet café in China.	Both circumventing censorship and protecting one's identity. Some travelers use VPNs for all online activity.

Reporters Without Borders publishes the following list, highlighting the countries who engage in the most severe Internet censorship and surveillance:

ENEMIES OF THE INTERNET

Bahrain	North Korea	United Arab Emirates
Belarus	Pakistan	
China	Russia	United Kingdom
Cuba	Saudi Arabia	United States of America
Ethiopia	Sudan	
India	Syria	Uzbekistan
Iran	Turkmenistan	Vietnam

1 ››› See page 38 for more information about laws surrounding insulting royalty or government officials.

SHIPPERS BEWARE

TRAVELERS SHOULD BE aware that sending things home in the midst of a trip can be a very tricky proposition. It is unwise to mindlessly fill your bag with heavy souvenirs under the vague rationalization that you can send your collected treasures home whenever your luggage becomes unmanageable. This concept is only simple and comforting in theory, not in practice. In many countries a frustrating dilemma exists: the national postal system is relatively cheap but notoriously unsecure or slow, while private delivery companies are more trustworthy but prohibitively expensive. This leaves travelers understandably stressed about the prospect of either having their possessions lost in the mail or paying far more than those possessions are actually worth simply to ensure they reach their destination within a reasonable amount of time. Plan ahead, try to be objective about the actual value of the items, consider trading things you probably won't use again,[1] and be sure to research all applicable customs regulations in both the sending and receiving countries.

If you do decide to send a package home, be aware that almost all international shipping charges are now calculated using the volumetric weight[2] formula to more accurately account for transportation requirements. Below are volumetric weight formulas with the international dimensional shipping factors currently used by major carriers such as FedEx, UPS, and DHL.

	Imperial Volumetric weight lb =	$$\frac{(\text{length in} \times \text{width in} \times \text{height in})}{(139)}$$
	Metric Volumetric weight kg =	$$\frac{(\text{length cm} \times \text{width cm} \times \text{height cm})}{(5,000)}$$

The resulting volumetric weight is then compared to the actual weight of the package, and whichever is greater is used to calculate shipping costs. This means that a large, light box may now cost just as much, if not more, to ship than a small but heavy box. Note that other costs and regulations often apply and dimensional factors are subject to change.

---

1 ››› See page 212 for more information on trading.
2 ››› Also known as the *dimensional weight* or *cubed weight*.

THE GRAND TOUR

According to the law of custom, and perhaps of reason, foreign travel completes the education of an English gentleman.

—EDWARD GIBBON,
Memoirs of My Life and Writings, 1796

WIDELY CONSIDERED THE birth of modern tourism, the grand tour was a tradition begun in 17th-century Europe. Wealthy families would send their newly graduated sons on trips through the major cities of the continent, hoping this rite of passage would educate them in the ways of art, music, philosophy, and diplomacy. These young men were expected to collect artwork, keep detailed journals, and associate with the heirs of other aristocratic families, in hopes of strengthening relationships. The custom eventually spread across the Atlantic, where North and South American families would send their sons, and eventually daughters, to learn about classic European culture and etiquette.

In practice, grand tours were not always the sophisticated, intellectually stimulating expeditions they were intended to be. Participants were often more interested in visiting foreign brothels than perusing art collections and many devoted large portions of their family fortunes to gambling and wine. Still, the tradition helped spread and normalize the concept of traveling without a specific military, commercial, or religious reason for doing so.

The 19th century arrived and brought with it railroads and steamships, helping end the exclusivity of travel in Europe. Suddenly international travel was no longer reserved for the wealthy elite and the popularity of a defined grand tour faded, replaced by the beginnings of mass tourism.

A TYPICAL TOUR

» **Important luggage:** Letters of introduction and credit, notebooks and sketching materials, sword and pistol for dueling, sundial, multiple formal outfits for dining with royalty

» **Travel companions:** A cicerone or "bear-leader" (who filled the role of both tutor and chaperone), coachman, cook, porter, personal servant

» **Itinerary:** London → Calais → Paris → Geneva → Turin → Milan → Florence → Rome → Naples → Venice → Munich → Vienna → Berlin → Brussels → London

FAST FRIENDS

ichigo ichie (each-ee-go each-EH)   *Japanese*

idiom. A proverb used to remind people that every interaction is fundamentally fleeting and therefore should be treasured.
From the Japanese ichigo ("time") and ichie ("meeting")

Ichigo ichie, which literally means "one time, one meeting," emphasizes the idea that spending time with someone is a gift that should never be taken for granted. It encourages people to cherish others in the moment, rather than in retrospect, by reminding them that regardless of circumstance no future meetings are ever guaranteed.

Travel is full of inherently brief relationships; it's one of the sacrifices that continual movement requires. Yet, many of those relationships, perhaps because of the very fact of their brevity, become surprisingly intense. Bonds are formed quickly on the road, through the repetition of meals, searching for accommodation, and exploring the wonders of a new place together. You find teammates to help navigate these intimidating, foreign lands and begin instantly relying on one another for far more than watching your bag or taking your picture. These fellow travelers help fill the emotional void magnified by the thousands of miles between you and everyone you know. And then, all too suddenly, you're headed north and they're headed south.

Today's travelers should feel lucky that staying in touch now requires nothing more than the exchanging of social media handles. But the addition of a new international Facebook friend isn't necessarily the point. Value the relationship for what is was: you spent time together in a strange place on the other side of the world and it was wonderful. Even if you never see them again, if you follow the lesson of *ichigo ichie* and cherish that meeting, that's enough.

———————————— ◆ ————————————

EXPERIENCE THE WORLD

Live in the sunshine, swim the sea, drink the wild air's salubrity.

—RALPH WALDO EMERSON,
American poet and essayist, *The Conduct of Life*, 1860

TALK LIKE A LOCAL

AN ENDONYM IS what a native person calls the place they are from while an **exonym** is the name assigned to that place by outsiders. When it comes to names of countries, these two designations are usually one and the same, or at least recognizably similar, but in rare cases may be very different. Below is a list of countries whose endonym and exonym are notably dissimilar.

Note that in countries with multiple official languages, several endonyms may exist, each different dependent upon the language in question. This list only concerns endonyms commonly used when speaking the country's most widely used language. Further, note that spelling and pronunciation may vary.

COUNTRY	ENDONYM
Albania	*Shqipri*
Armenia	*Hayasdan*
Austria	*Österreich*
Bhutan	*Druk-yul*
Cambodia	*Kampuchea*
China	*Zhong Guo*
Croatia	*Hrvatska*
Egypt	*Misr*
Estonia	*Eesti*
Finland	*Suomi*
Georgia	*Sakartvelo*
Germany	*Deutschland*
Greece	*Hellas*
Hungary	*Magyarország*
India	*Bharat*
Japan	*Nippon*
Jordan	*Al-Urdunn*
Maldives	*Dhivehi Raajje*
Montenegro	*Crna Gora*
Morocco	*Al Maghribiyah*
North Korea	*Chosŏn*
Saudi Arabia	*Al-'Arabiyah as Suudiyah*
South Korea	*Tae Han Min'guk*
Sweden	*Sverige*
Thailand	*Muang Thai*
United Arab Emirates	*Al Imarat al Arabiyah al Muttahidah*

LET YOURSELF GO

no·mo·pho·bia (no-muh-FOH-bee-uh)

noun. The fear or anxiety associated with being without one's cell phone, or being out of cell phone contact.

From the English *no* and *mobile* and the Greek *phobia* ("fear")

The soul of a journey is liberty, perfect liberty, to think, feel, do just as one pleases. We go a journey chiefly to be free of all impediments and of all inconveniences; to leave ourselves behind, much more to get rid of others.

—WILLIAM HAZLITT,
"On Going a Journey," 1822

Technology, for all the many benefits it provides modern travel, also undercuts one of its primary features: the pure independence of the road. The first generation to have never known a time without smartphones has now begun traveling the world and digital tethers follow them everywhere they go.

Not only do these hyper-connected travelers feel beholden to various social media platforms, their social circles have come to rely on their near-constant access to the Internet as a guarantee of their well-being. Where letters once took months to reach a traveler's hometown, being out of contact for a mere few hours has suddenly become cause for concern.

Nomophobia can be harmful in that it prevents total immersion in the things a person is seeing and doing. Whether one worries that they might be missing something or that they themselves might be being missed, those distracting effects are the same. Luckily, there's a cure.

Recognize that the cord needs to be cut at both ends. Manage expectations early and often about how frequently you will be in contact. Explain that your choice is as much about mind-set as it is about convenience. To constantly shift between experiencing new surroundings and thinking of home is emotionally exhausting. A cell phone should be a lifesaving rope to be thrown as a matter of last resort, not a shackle that keeps you mentally chained to what's happening back home.

Travel is an inherently selfish act—and it should stay that way. Share all you want, but leave something for yourself. Looking down at a phone trying to post a picture of a sunset means you aren't watching the sun set. Let yourself go, disappear into the road, and don't resent a lack of reception—embrace that inaccessibility as the pure form of freedom that it is.

NO LOVE

W HEN TRAVELING, ONE should be particularly cautious of anything to do with romance or sex. Cultural norms surrounding these topics vary wildly around the world and are often heavily influenced by religion.

In some countries the following potential expressions of sexuality are simply frowned upon; in others they may be explicitly illegal and punishable by fines, deportation, imprisonment, and even death. Always research the specific laws of conservative countries before traveling and, when in doubt, err on the side of sexual modesty.

Interactions Between Genders	This might not only include overt public displays of affection, but even more innocuous hugging, touching of any kind, or being alone with a person of the opposite gender.
Apparel and Nudity	Not only are nudity and sexually suggestive clothing illegal in many areas, the very definition of these words vary greatly from country to country.
Homosexuality	Homosexuality remains unequivocally illegal in some countries, and culturally discouraged in many others. This topic should be treated with the utmost caution as even the suspicion of homosexuality can result in severe consequences in some areas.
Pornography	Pornography is officially banned in many areas of the world and what constitutes pornography is often open to wide-ranging interpretation. Literature and non-nude images are considered pornographic in some countries and possession of pornography can be "proven" through both physical and digital means.
Interaction Between Nationalities	Some countries have laws or deeply held customs concerning relationships between foreigners and native citizens. Romantic relationships are completely forbidden in some situations, in others dowries are expected or special licenses are required.
Age of Consent	Sexual age of consent laws vary greatly around the world from 12 (Angola) to 21 (Bahrain).
Relationship Status	Many religiously conservative countries do not allow unmarried couples to share a hotel room, among other restrictions.
Birth Control	Birth control methods should be planned in advance as some forms of birth control are difficult to obtain or illegal in certain countries.

B ELOW IS A list of major natural disasters, along with *warning signs* and advice.

When traveling in areas where natural disasters are common, stay informed about conditions and make all necessary preparations. Always err on the side of caution and evacuate the area if ordered to do so. The following instructions assume that safe evacuation is not possible.

EARTHQUAKE

There are no reliable indicators of an impending earthquake that can be regularly observed by humans without specialized equipment. Foreshocks, which are a series of smaller earthquakes that sometimes occur hours or days before a major earthquake, are considered the only potentially noticeable warning sign. However, foreshocks are not always present and should not be thought of as a dependable predictor of large earthquakes.

Seek shelter, remain indoors, avoid windows, and get to the lowest possible floor if in a multistory structure. Prepare for falling debris by crouching on the floor, surrounding yourself with padding, and protecting your head. Prepare for aftershocks, which can be unpredictable and last for weeks, if not months, depending on the magnitude of the initial earthquake.

TSUNAMI

Receding water, shaking ground, unusually large waves, rapidly rising tide, loud roar or rumble emanating from the ocean.

Immediately move inland to higher ground, avoid valleys. Do not return to the coastline; tsunamis are rarely a single massive wave but instead a series of deceptively powerful surges of seawater, meaning the danger can last for several hours.

TORNADO

Rotating funnel cloud, intense wind and rain immediately followed by periods of calm weather, loud continuous rumbling noise.

Seek shelter, remain indoors, avoid windows, and get to the lowest possible floor if in a multistory structure. Prepare for falling debris by crouching on the floor, surrounding yourself with padding, and protecting your head. Prepare for electricity outages.

AVALANCHE

Recent nearby avalanche activity, unstable or hollow snow, cracks in the snow, unusual sounds. Significant changes in weather like rising temperatures, strong winds, or recent snowfall can also signal an impending avalanche. Can occur without warning.

Continue moving and attempt to "swim" as much as possible to avoid being buried by debris. Attempt to grab passing trees. As the avalanche slows, keep your hands near your mouth and begin to dig out an air pocket. Spit to determine which way is up.

BLIZZARD

High winds, high humidity, freezing temperatures.

Remain indoors, continually stock water, conserve heating materials, prepare for electricity outages. If in a car: prevent carbon monoxide poisoning by ensuring exhaust pipe is clear. Turn on the engine intermittently for heat, and then back off to converse fuel. Alert others to your presence by turning on hazard lights or tying colored cloth on antenna. Stay hydrated and remain in car, do not venture out on foot. If on foot: seek any structural shelter. Remain hydrated, melt snow for water, but avoid eating snow if possible as this will lower your body temperature. Do nonstrenuous exercises to keep blood flowing to extremities.

FLOOD

Sustained rainfall, mud- or debris-filled rivers, overflowing rivers, dam or levee damage. Flash floods can occur with very little warning.

Move to higher ground as quickly as possible. Beware of downed power lines. Fast-moving water can be deceptively powerful: six inches (15 centimeters) can cause an adult to lose their balance; two feet (.6 meters) can move a vehicle.

ᵛᵛᵛ *continued* ᵛᵛᵛ

Drought, high temperatures, naturally dry terrain or vegetation, high winds, low humidity. Can occur without warning.

Shut off all sources of natural gas or propane. Fill whatever containers available with water. Remove all especially combustible objects (firewood, gas tanks) from area. Close, but do not lock, all windows and doors to prevent drafts. Turn off air-conditioning and turn on lights in anticipation of smoke. Stay low to the ground and breathe through a moist cloth to prevent smoke inhalation.

CYCLONE/HURRICANE/TYPHOON

Overcast skies, increasing winds, dropping barometric pressure, heavy rainfall.

Seek shelter, remain indoors, avoid windows, and get to the lowest possible floor if in a multistory structure. Prepare for falling debris by crouching on the floor, surrounding yourself with padding, and protecting your head. Prepare for electricity outages.

VOLCANO

Tremors, release of gas, increased surface temperature, emission of steam, ground swelling. Can occur without warning.

Avoid valleys and paths of least resistance down mountain. Avoid lava flows but also beware of equally dangerous mud flows and avalanches. Wear mask or use damp cloth to prevent breathing in volcanic ash.

THE ASSUMPTION OF RISK

The timorous may stay at home.

—JUDGE BENJAMIN CARDOZO,

Who was later appointed to the US Supreme Court, ruling in the 1929 case of *Murphy v. Steeplechase Amusement Co.* The plaintiff sued after hurting his knee on an amusement park ride called the Flopper. Cardozo ruled in favor of the amusement park, adding *"One might as well say that a skating rink should be abandoned because skaters sometimes fall."*

LINING UP AROUND THE WORLD

THE ENGLISH TRADITION of "queuing" dictates that people should line up one by one in an orderly fashion, each awaiting their turn. This staid and methodical method of organizing a crowd naturally influenced many other English-speaking nations and is now the norm in the United States, Canada, and Australia, among other countries. It is important for travelers to note however that such a systematic approach to lining up is not practiced everywhere.

Though there are some polite behaviors that are common throughout the world, such as deference to the elderly or disabled, for the most part there is very little agreed upon international line etiquette.

For instance, in many East African cultures, passively standing back is seen as a sign to both vendors and other customers that you are not yet ready to make a choice. In these scenarios, the onus is on the customer to vocally and aggressively demand service from the vendor, rather than quietly expect to be called upon.

In other cultures, such as China, allowing others to go before you is seen as a sign of submission that has significant class implications. By granting others priority, you are publicly acknowledging that they are above you in society. Thus, a hectic free-for-all ensues, each person hoping to be served first and therefore seen as more important than everyone else.

And yet in still other cultures, such as Japan, its sometimes not even necessary to stand in line. Outside a stadium at major sporting events for instance, one simply arrives, marks their place with tape or by leaving behind a small object, and leaves, confident that their fellow citizens will respect their reserved area when they return.

These cultural differences, combined with wide-ranging national definitions of what constitutes personal space, means that travelers should be prepared to encounter all different ideas of line etiquette when visiting other countries. Do not become upset if you think someone is "cutting in line" because, in their interpretation, there might not *be* any line. Simply recognize what everyone else is doing, whether that's forming a precise queue in an English train station or screaming to be heard in a rural Mongolian market, and join in.

GIVE ME SHELTER

1209 North Orange Street
Wilmington, Delaware 19801
USA

—The legal address of more than 250,000 American businesses, including Apple, Coca-Cola, Ford, Google, and Walmart. Large corporations register in Delaware to take advantage of the state's favorable corporate tax laws, among other benefits.

SOUNDS LOVELY

Some notable locations on the moon include:

Peninsula of Thunder	*Marsh of Decay*
Sea of Crisis	*Bay of Roughness*
Ocean of Storms	*Island of Winds*
Lake of Hatred	*Land of Sterility*

KNOW YOUR MARKET

WHITE MARKET
Legal and authorized
Shopping mall, food markets

GRAY OR BLUE MARKET
Technically illegal but generally allowed
Currency traders, counterfeit goods[1]

BLACK MARKET
Illegal and regularly punished
Drugs, weapons[1]

Travelers should note that in some situations the legality of a transaction is not a function of what is being bought but rather of who is doing the buying. Local law enforcement may target foreigners purchasing anything that is technically illegal, even if the market for such goods is not at all secretive or local people are openly buying or selling the very same items.

For instance, party-seeking travelers in Southeast Asia may encounter bars where illegal drugs are openly offered to patrons, replete with prices and descriptions printed on the menu. Though this might imply that it is therefore legal to purchase and consume these drugs, in many situations the official laws of the country still consider them to be illegal.[2] With this in mind, law enforcement may arrest travelers, who assumed they were simply enjoying the permissible pleasures of a liberal nation, and demand significant bribes in exchange for avoiding the often draconian penalties associated with drug use. This subjective approach to law enforcement is common in many countries around the world. Therefore, when in doubt, travelers should always ensure that whatever they are buying is completely legal under all applicable laws, regardless of the seemingly accepted nature of the market.

1 ››› The examples given are dependent on location and may not be considered illegal in all countries. See page 206 for more information on country-specific laws.

2 ››› See page 202 for more information on selective enforcement of laws and the Dutch concept of *gedogen*.

A MISREMEMBERED HERO

THE CREW OF the Navy Curtiss 4, commanded by Albert C. Read, were the **first to fly across the Atlantic Ocean**, in May 1919.

John Alcock and Arthur Brown were the **first to fly across the Atlantic Ocean without stopping**, in June 1919.

Charles Lindbergh was **the first to fly across the Atlantic Ocean without stopping, alone** in June 1927. Despite the fact that at least 70 people had already flown transatlantic flights, Lindbergh became much more famous than almost every other aviation pioneer and to this day is often incorrectly credited with other achievements. This is thought to have been caused by a combination of the intense American media coverage (his flight was one of the first to enjoy widespread live-radio reporting); his story (he was young, handsome, and knew how to capitalize on his fame through books and publicity tours); and the fact that he won the $25,000 Orteig Prize for flying nonstop between New York City and Paris (many aviation pioneers before Lindbergh didn't fly to or from such well-known cities).

LOCK IT UP

T HE SECURITY OF their possessions is the first thing on many travelers' minds. Here are some tips to help you decide which lock, or series of locks, will help protect you and your possessions.

DETER, NOT PREVENT

It is important to remember that the function of many locks, especially those used in travel, is as what security experts call a **deterrent**, rather than a **prevention** device. That is to say, very few of locks will actually *prevent* a dedicated thief, with enough time and the necessary equipment, from gaining access to a traveler's possessions. Instead, the fact that the traveler has any type of lock at all will *deter* them from attempting to break in, even if the lock itself would be fairly simple to disengage. Thus, even cheap, low-security locks serve the important purpose of convincing thieves to simply target other people who aren't using any sort of lock.

COMBINATION VERSUS KEY

While combination and key locks each have their particular pros and cons, the many advantages of combination locks are of particular usefulness to the traveler. Most importantly, combination locks leave the traveler with no small keys to worry about. These keys are easily lost in the chaos of travel and a variety of master keys, capable of opening many common travel key locks, are already in the hands of thieves around the world. Further, a combination lock can be shared by a group of trusted travelers much more easily than a key lock. For those worried about forgetting combinations, simply customize locks with personalized code hints. Lastly, if a thief does try to break a lock, it will likely be through brute force (smashing or cutting the lock) rather than trying to guess at the combination or pick the lock. Whether a given lock is combination or key is irrelevant if the thief is cutting through the bar, thus it is best to go with the more convenient combination lock.

BE APPROVED

In some situations, notably air travel, a traveler's plan for security will have to conform to regulations imposed by airlines and government agencies. For instance, the US Transportation Security Administration (TSA) only authorizes certain organizations to produce recognized locks, the most prominent of which is Travel Sentry:

Locks bearing this symbol can easily be opened by security officials using master keys if needed. They are generally very low security locks, although most luggage is inherently unsecure anyway.[1] While the use of recognized locks is not required by law, use of nonrecognized locks may result in significant damage to luggage or the locks themselves if the luggage requires inspection.

BE FLEXIBLE

Remember that you may need to lock a great variety of doors, windows, lockers, luggage, bikes, and much more, all with varying acceptable dimensions of suitable locks. Think about how you plan to travel when deciding which locks to bring: backpackers staying in hostel dorms will need more personal security than business travelers in luxury hotels. Below is a potential packing list of locks that will suit many travelers' needs.

	1 combination padlock
	For most lockers and doors. Make sure the neck isn't too thick to fit standard lockers. Heavy but worth the weight.
	1 cable combination lock
	For unusually shaped lockers, cabinets, windows, luggage and bike racks, and more. Thinner but adaptable.
	Multiple recognized small combination locks
	For luggage, and not just the larger pieces. As low-security as they are, a simple luggage lock on your day bag can serve as an effective deterrent against all manner of street thieves.

1 ››› Many types of luggage are made of material than can easily be cut into it. Additionally, sticking a ballpoint pen into the "teeth" of most zippers will force them apart and allow partial access to contents of the bag.

KEEP GOING

Lowly faithful, banish fear, / Right onward drive unharmed; / The port, well worth the cruise, is near, / And every wave is charmed.

— RALPH WALDO EMERSON,
American poet and essayist
Selected portion of "Terminus," c. 1866

LOCKED IN

THERE ARE 44 **landlocked** countries, or countries that have no access to the world's oceans. Of those, two are **double-landlocked**, meaning they are surrounded by landlocked countries and therefore citizens must travel through at least two other countries to reach the ocean.

LIECHTENSTEIN

UZBEKISTAN

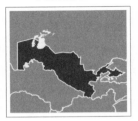

A PRIMER ON LATITUDE AND LONGITUDE

39°	21'	41.7132"	N
DEGREES	**MINUTES**	**SECONDS**	**DIRECTION**
76°	38'	2.0436"	W

Notes	*Other Common Formats*	
E/W of the prime meridian	Degrees decimal minutes:	39°21.695220' N, 76°38.034060' W
N/S of the equator		
60 seconds in a minute (60" = 1')	Decimal degrees:	39.361587, –76.633901 (–latitude = S, –longitude = W)
60 minutes in a degree (60' = 1°)	*Precision*	
1 degree of latitude = ~69 mi (111 km)	1 decimal place = a city	6 decimal places = a flower

ON COMMUNICATION

Americans who travel abroad for the first time are often shocked to discover that, despite all the progress that has been made in the last thirty years, many foreign people still speak foreign languages.

—DAVE BARRY,
American writer

WITNESSING THE DIVERSITY of language that the world has to offer is one of the great joys of travel. Exotic languages bombarding one's senses provides recurring confirmation that you are indeed somewhere excitingly unknown. And yet, for all their unique pleasures, different languages often also lead to frustration, especially when one is in urgent need of specific information. Even with every new smartphone translation app promising clear and easy communication in any language, communicating unassisted and in person remains an essential skill for travelers worldwide.

Here are some tips for effectively navigating the language barrier.

GIVE IT A TRY

The greatest enemy of clear language is insincerity.

—GEORGE ORWELL,
Politics and the English Language, 1946

Travelers who hail from English-speaking countries should feel lucky that their native tongue happens to be the most useful language to know when roaming the world. Though it lags behind Mandarin in number of fluent speakers, English has far wider global reach and is often the de facto common language in many international circumstances.

However, even though the language has permeated almost every culture on earth, travelers should never blindly assume a local person speaks English. At the absolute bare minimum, travelers should be aware of how to say a **greeting** and **thank you** in the local language. Words for **numbers, directions, food,** and **accommodation** are obviously also useful to know. But what is most important to remember is that, even with mangled grammar and a comically bad accent, the initial *attempt* to communicate is what's critical. Only after earnestly attempting to converse with a person in the local language is it appropriate to politely ask if the conversation might be switched to English. Locals will likely be happy to work with you to find an effective way

ˇˇˇ *continued* ˇˇˇ

to communicate. But assuming a local person will speak a foreign language while in their own country simply to accommodate a traveler who hasn't even made the effort to learn a single word of the local language may be seen as offensive.

NO SUGGESTIONS

Better a mysterious silence when one is in doubt,
than awkward indecision . . .

—MARY FRENCH SHELDON,
Sultan to Sultan: Adventures Among the Masai
and Other Tribes of East Africa, 1892

If you're speaking with someone without whom you share a common language it is important not to suggest answers to questions before they have a chance to speak. If you do, the person may agree with you simply because it is far faster and easier than explaining the alternative. For instance, if you say:

How many hours is the walk? Three?

The person may respond with *Yes* only because they know that this will be a satisfactory end to the conversation—even if the answer you proposed is not completely accurate. It is generally more effective to patiently wait for a reply without suggesting a potential answer. This will force the person to fully process the question and they may very well respond:

The walk is . . . nine hours.

BEING WRONG

There's no sense in being precise when you don't
even know what you're talking about.

—JOHN VON NEUMANN,
Hungarian-American mathematician

Travelers should realize that in certain societies local people, especially men, might be reticent to admit that they don't know the answer to a common question. To explicitly admit to a lack of knowledge, especially information that they might be expected to know, such as directions, can be seen as self-insulting or embarrassing. This carries a much more significant social stigma in some cultures than

Western travelers may be used to. In fact, in some areas it is more common for a person to provide incorrect information than to simply confess that they don't know. This often results in confusion or frustration because it is many travelers' assumption that if someone provides any answer to a question they must be reasonably sure that they are correct. This is simply not the case in many parts of the world and therefore it is best to ask numerous local people to verify important information and, if someone seems unsure initially, to take their answer with a grain of salt.

THIN ICE

BELOW IS A listing of minimum safe ice thickness for various activities. Note that the thickness of ice can differ greatly within a small area and ice is strongest closer to the shore. The chart below assumes new, clear black ice on a pond or lake, which is stronger than old cloudier, whiter ice. Never go out on the ice unless you are absolutely confident it is safe.

Minimum Clear Solid Ice Thickness

ACTIVITY	INCH	CENTIMETER
1 person on skis	2	5
1 person on foot	3	8
1 person ice fishing	4	10
Group single file	4	10
Snowmobile	5	13
Small car (2 ton/1.8 tonne)	8	20
Light truck (3 ton/2.7 tonne)	10	25
Medium truck (4 ton/3.6 tonne)	11	28
Heavy truck (8 ton/7.3 tonne)	12	30

COLORFUL SEAS

SEA	LOCATION	NAMING
White	Northwestern Russia	Covered by ice and snow for much of the year
Red	Between northeast Africa and the Arabian peninsula	A reddish cyanobacteria called *Trichodesmium erythraeum,* also known as "sea sawdust"
Yellow	Between China and the Korean peninsula	Gold-colored silt flowing from nearby rivers
Black	Southeastern Europe	The combination of its deep, dark waters and the fact that the sea was widely considered dangerous to navigate in antiquity may have influenced the sea's naming but the exact etymology remains disputed. Another theory contends that *black* comes from a medieval Turkish dialect meaning "north" while *red* comes from the same language and means "south."

GOING FOR A DRIVE

AN INTERNATIONAL DRIVING permit (IDP) is a supplement to a government-issued driver's license that is currently recognized by 170 countries.[1]

The document is a paper booklet about the size of most passports that is translated into 11 languages and is valid for one year from date of issuance or until the driver's license expires, whichever is earlier.

IDPs can be applied for through the government or authorized automobile associations of the traveler's country of residence. Two passport photos[2] are required to be submitted with the application and a small fee is usually charged. IDPs are only for use abroad; they are not valid in the traveler's country of residence.

It is important to note that an IDP should be thought of as a widely accepted translation of a government-issued driver's license, rather than a stand-alone permit. Additionally, a driver's license is required to apply for an IDP and must be carried with an IDP at all times for it to be considered valid.

Travelers should also be aware that carrying an IDP, along with a standard driver's license, is not always sufficient to legally drive in every country that recognizes IDPs. Some countries require that IDPs be exchanged for local driver's licenses upon arrival and others charge fees before granting visitors the right to operate a motor vehicle. This is often in addition to country-specific regulations regarding insurance, age minimums, gender,[3] length of stay, car rental policies, and other related issues. Travelers should always research the current policies of any country they plan on driving in.

Even if you don't plan on driving while abroad, an IDP can be a useful form of identification to have. Government-issued driver's licenses are rarely recognized as an acceptable form of identification and having an IDP, with its variety of translated languages, is sometimes useful in proving one's identity and communicating pertinent information.

Lastly, travelers should be cognizant that confusion and misinformation surrounding driving while abroad have made this an area of focus for scammers. Authentic IDPs can only be issued by approved organizations and should cost less than $30; any source claiming otherwise should not be trusted. Additionally, there is no "international driving license"; any document masquerading as such is fake.

....

1 ››› Countries that do not officially recognize modern IDPs:
Brazil, Burundi, China, Eritrea, Ethiopia, Iraq, Kiribati, Macedonia, Maldives, Marshall Islands, Micronesia, Mongolia, Nauru, Nigeria, North Korea, Palau, Samoa, Solomon Islands, Somalia, South Sudan, Timor-Leste, Tonga, Tuvalu, Vanuatu

2 ››› See page 170 for more information on passport photos.

3 ››› Saudi Arabia does not allow women to drive.

————◆————

FOUND IN TRANSLATION

W HILE STORIES OF international marketing translation failures abound,[1] corporations sometimes get linguistically lucky in bringing their products to a new market. After introducing Kit Kats to Japan, Nestlé executives were initially surprised to see surging sales of the candy every January. They soon realized that "Kit Kat" is reminiscent of the Japanese phrase *kitto katsu* ("surely win," colloquially meaning "good luck") and that the candy had become a popular gift for students taking exams. Nestlé quickly capitalized on this new tradition and today Kit Kats are extraordinarily popular in Japan, and available in dozens of flavors including grilled potato, salt watermelon, sweet bean paste, and wasabi.

....

1 ››› One notable controversy involved KFC trying to make inroads in China with their *"Finger-lickin' good"* slogan, but unfortunately translating it to *"We will eat your fingers off."* See page 243 for more international marketing mistranslations.

BLURRED LEGAL LINES

ge·do·gen (HEH-doh-hen)   *Dutch*

verb.   To knowingly tolerate or permit an activity that is technically
illegal.

The Dutch concept of *gedogen* is most notably illustrated through the
country's approach to cannabis, ecstasy, and other so-called soft drugs.
Though officially illegal, the use and sale of these drugs is permitted by
the Dutch government, and regulated and taxed accordingly. Issues
involving this type of "active tolerance" of illegality are often controversial, with a variety of compelling moral, financial, and political arguments to be made for both sides.

Travelers would be wise to familiarize themselves with the concept of *gedogen*, as this common tweak on standard legality is found
throughout the world, not just in the Netherlands. The line between
what is legal and what is illegal, though purportedly well defined, is in
reality quite blurred in some countries, which can make it difficult for
travelers to understand how local laws work. Add in widespread corruption, differing laws for natives and foreigners, and a myriad of cultural
considerations to this selective enforcement of laws and travelers are
often left with a confusing, semiofficial mix of law and custom.

The bottom line is that any law officially on the books can be
enforced at any time. The laws of a country are an evolving collection
of legal guidelines, not a precisely defined rulebook, and can be bent to
the to the will of the ruling government. If you are so inclined, check
with other travelers to see what technically illegal activities might be
culturally acceptable, but always be aware of the letter of the law, and
the potential consequences of breaking it.

HOME AWAY FROM HOME

A GOVERNMENT FREELY DECLARING an area of land to
be the sovereign territory of a foreign nation is extraordinarily
rare and almost only occurs when a member of a royal family gives
birth abroad. This allows the newest member of the royal family to
have technically been born on native soil, as occurred in the following examples:

JANUARY 1943, OTTAWA, INTERNATIONAL TERRITORY

The maternity ward of the Ottawa Civic Hospital was declared to be extraterritorial by the Canadian government, meaning that any births would occur in what was temporarily international territory. Therefore, newborn babies would derive citizenship from their mother, not from the country they are born in. This allowed Princess Margriet Francisca of the Netherlands to be born to Queen Juliana as a full Dutch citizen.

JULY 1945, LONDON, YUGOSLAVIA

The British government ceded the sovereignty of suite 212 of Claridge's Hotel in London to allow Crown Prince Alexander of Yugoslavia to be born to Queen Alexandra on native soil. Legend has it that a sprinkling of Yugoslavian dirt was even placed under the bed.

MARCH 1982, JOHANNESBURG, ALBANIA

The South African government declared the maternity ward of the Sandton Medical Clinic in Johannesburg to be Albanian territory for one hour, allowing Queen Susan to give birth to Prince Leka of Albania on Albanian soil.

A GOOD ADAGE

If possible, never cover any road a second time.

—Motto of Ibn Battuta, a 14th century Moroccan explorer who is widely considered one of history's greatest travelers. After leaving home alone at 21 for a planned 16-month journey to Mecca, he realized his love of exploration and didn't return home for 24 years. He eventually covered more than 75,000 miles (120,701 kilometers) in 44 countries between 1325 and 1354. He survived multiple shipwrecks, fought off repeated attacks from bandits and pirates, dined with the royalty of dozens of nations, and was married at least 10 times, among many other adventures.

INCOGNITO

SOME NOTABLE ALIASES that celebrities have used while traveling include:

Angelina Jolie . . . . *Miss Lollipop*
Jay-Z . . . . *Frank Sinatra*
Jessica Alba . . . . *Cash Money*
Johnny Depp . . . . *Mr. Oddpong*
Justin Bieber . . . . *Chandler Bing*
Justin Timberlake . . . . *Mr. Woodpond*
Marilyn Monroe . . . . *Zelda Zonk*
Michael Jackson . . . . *Mr. Doolittle*
Michael Jordan . . . . *Clark Kent*
Mila Kunis . . . . *Señor Pants*
Ozzy Osbourne . . . . *Harry Bollocks*
Paul McCartney . . . . *Apple C. Vermouth*
Sir Elton John . . . . *Sir Humphrey Handbag*
Slash . . . . *I. P. Freely*
Tom Hanks . . . . *Johnny Madrid*
Usher . . . . *Mr. Dinero*

DON'T MAKE YOUR MARK

Hadnakhte, scribe of the treasury,
came to make an excursion and amuse himself on the
west of the Memphis, together with his brother, Panakhti.

—VANDALISM WRITTEN IN HIERATIC SCRIPT
ON A TEMPLE WALL IN GIZA,
Egypt, c. 1244 BC

AS LONG AS travelers have explored the world, some have felt the need to leave some mark of their journey. Vandalism is as old as tourism itself and some of the world's most iconic landmarks have been irrevocably damaged by narcissistic visitors.

Relatively recently however, governments around the world have begun to crack down on graffiti. Tourists have been issued fines in excess of $20,000 and sentenced to serious jail time for writing or carving on historic sites. Never vandalize a national landmark—it is not only destructive and disrespectful, it is now officially illegal almost everywhere.

LIGHT VERSUS SOUND

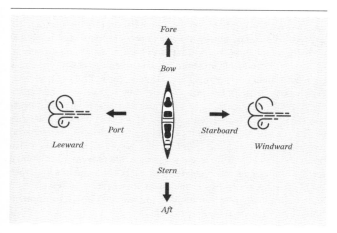

A STORM'S DISTANCE CAN be estimated by counting the seconds between when you see lightning strike and when you hear thunder. Divide by 5 for distance in miles and by 3 for distance in kilometers.

sec	2	4	6	8	10	12	14	16	18	20	22	24
mi	0.4	0.8	1.2	1.6	2.0	2.4	2.8	3.2	3.6	4.0	4.4	4.8
km	0.7	1.3	2.0	2.7	3.3	4.0	4.7	5.3	6.0	6.7	7.3	8.0

STUCK

R UBBING SOAP, LIP balm, candle wax, olive oil, glass cleaner, petroleum jelly, a crayon, or the tip of a graphite pencil on the "teeth" of a stuck zipper will help to unstick it.

KNOW YOUR WAY AROUND

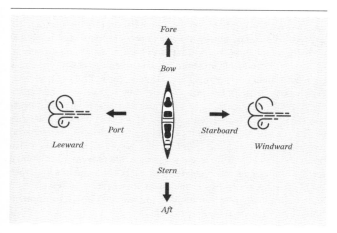

THE FLIGHT IS FULL

THE RECORD FOR the most passengers on a flight is **1,088**, set in May 1991 on a Boeing 747 operated by El Al airlines. The flight from Addis Ababa to Jerusalem was part of Operation Solomon, a secretive evacuation of Jewish citizens arranged by Israeli leadership to protect them from a rapidly deteriorating and potentially hostile government in Ethiopia. All seats were stripped from the plane to accommodate extra passengers and the actual number of people aboard may have been as high as 1,122, as dozens of unregistered children were allegedly snuck onboard.

Two babies were born during the flight and were granted Israeli citizenship. The nationality of children born during international travel is determined either by the nationality of the parents[1] or the location of the birth.[2]

....

1 ››› Based on the legal concept jus sanguinis (Latin for "right of blood"). Israeli law follows this principle.

2 ››› Other countries follow the legal concept of jus soli (Latin for "right of soil"). Under this principle, a vessel is considered the territory of the country in which it is registered, meaning any babies born aboard would become citizens of that country.

———————— ◆ ————————

FOLLOW ALL THE RULES

TRAVELERS SHOULD ALWAYS be cognizant of the fact that they are fully subject to all the laws of the country they are in.

Travelers should not expect any of the legal equality or political correctness they may be familiar with back home. A country's legal system is the product of millennia of nuanced cultural history and may be heavily influenced by religious extremism or radical political leadership. Some nation's laws are unequivocally sexist, racist, homophobic, or otherwise archaic in nature. Further, concepts like due process and the right to a legal defense simply do not exist in many countries around the world. Punishments, even for minor offenses, tend to be far harsher in less-developed countries and sentences are often carried out with a kind of swift, draconian justice. There is no international law that supersedes the regulations that a country chooses to govern by. If a traveler commits a crime on another country's sovereign soil and is convicted, there is often little the traveler's home government or the international community can do.

None of this means that you will encounter any legal difficulties while abroad, only that you should be aware that some societies live according to laws vastly different from what you might be used to. In addition to common regulations concerning things like drug use,[1] romance and sex,[2] photography,[3] politics and royalty,[4] or religiously prohibited activities, many countries also subscribe to other, less obvious rules about all manner of things.

These laws might run the gamut from charmingly strange to frighteningly strict, but all must be obeyed.

The following list is not meant as a complete collection of all the foreign laws that travelers should be aware of, but rather as an example of the types of lesser-known laws that are commonly enforced throughout the world.

» *Wearing camouflage clothing is against the law in* **Barbados**.

» *It is illegal to use a metal detector in* **Turkey**.

» *Smoking near a child in* **Latvia** *is considered physical abuse.*

» **Rwanda** *has banned plastic bags.*

» *In Svalbard,* **Norway**, *you are legally required to carry a gun when traveling outside of town limits to protect yourself from polar bear attacks.*

» *Arrests for witchcraft are not uncommon in* **Central African Republic**.

---

1 ››› See page 202 on the Dutch concept of *gedogen*.
2 ››› See page 187 for more information on laws surrounding romance and sex.
3 ››› See page 72 for more information on laws surrounding photography.
4 ››› See page 38 for more information on laws surrounding perceived insults to royalty and government officials.

THE NEW CUSTOMER SERVICE

T RAVELERS SHOULD NOTE that modern customer service is no longer primarily designed to serve the customer in person. Most large companies have made significant investments in serving the customer effectively over the phone and/or online and are generally not as focused on in-person interactions.

With this in mind, if you are at an airport and your flight has just been canceled, do not simply rush to the airline counter with the other stranded travelers to reschedule your flight. Immediately calling the airline's toll-free number or going to their website will likely get you much faster service.

THIS LAND IS MY LAND

Borders? I have never seen one.
But I have heard they exist in the minds of some people.

—THOR HEYERDAHL,
Norwegian explorer

LOOKING AT A precisely drawn modern map, one might assume the borders of the world are long agreed upon, meticulously researched, satellite-exact determinants of territory. This is decidedly not the case.[1] Most countries are currently engaged in territorial disputes over everything from city blocks to large islands. Though some of the disputes are innocuous quarrels between friendly national neighbors[2] over relatively valueless pieces of territory, many are much more serious. Below is a look at just some of the disputes that may alter the design of world maps in the years to come.

Notable Disputed Territories

	TERRITORY	COUNTRIES INVOLVED	DETAIL
Largest	Kashmir	China v. India v. Pakistan	Current estimates put control of this 86,000 mi^2 (222,739 km^2) region at: 45% India, 35% Pakistan, 20% China.
Smallest	Rockall	Denmark v. Iceland v. Ireland v. UK	Currently controlled by the UK, this minuscule island in the middle of the Atlantic measures only 8,442 ft^2 (784 m^2). The real value of Rockall is the fact that whoever controls it has a stronger claim to any oil reserves discovered nearby.*
Oldest	Gibraltar	Spain v. UK	Control over Gibraltar has been actively disputed since at least 1713. It is currently controlled by the UK, though it is largely self-governing.
Disputed by the highest number of countries	Spratly Islands	Brunei v. China v. Malaysia v. Philippines v. Taiwan v. Vietnam	Each country except for Brunei currently controls at least some portion of the islands.

* ››› See page 257 for more information about how national rights to oceanic natural resources are determined.

The only countries in the world not currently involved in a territorial dispute:

Albania · Andorra · Antigua and Barbuda · Austria · Bahrain
Belgium · Botswana · Bulgaria · Cabo Verde · Fiji · Germany · Grenada
Jamaica · Kiribati · Liechtenstein · Luxembourg · Maldives · Malta
Monaco · Mongolia · Montenegro · Nauru · Netherlands · Qatar
Samoa · San Marino · Saõ Tomé and Príncipe · Sri Lanka · Sweden
Switzerland · Tonga · Tunisia · Tuvalu · Vatican City

1 ››› Google Maps, for instance, alters the borders of their maps depending on the location of the person viewing them. For example, the region of Arunachal Pradesh is shown as a part of India when viewed from within India and part of China when viewed from within China.

2 ››› For instance, Canada and Denmark have been engaged in a relatively playful dispute over Hans Island, a tiny barren rock in the Nares Strait, for decades. A tradition has emerged in which Danes place a small Danish flag on the island, accompanied by a bottle of Danish schnapps, to claim the island for their homeland. Upon discovery, Canadians replace this claim with a Canadian flag, and bottle of Canadian Club whiskey, which remains in place until the Danes begin the cycle anew.

FULL-TIME TRAVELERS

ex·pat·ri·ate (eks-PEY-tree-eyt)

noun. People who have decided to live abroad, either for an indeterminate amount of time or permanently.
From the Latin *ex* ("out of") and *patria* ("homeland")

Living in the shadows of crumbled Western empires,
expats are social misfits who nevertheless bear the responsibility of being a
nation's first line of ambassadors overseas.

—CHUCK THOMPSON,
Smile When You're Lying, 2007

People become expats for all sorts of reasons, employment, relationships, and taxes chief among them. Yet, regardless of their origin story, almost all share a certain type of adventurous personality and an admirable readiness to fully immerse themselves in the unknown. They have proudly adjusted to their new circumstances and most are happy to impart their knowledge onto newcomers. Cherish expats as the valuable resource they are—you will rarely gain better insight into a foreign place than having a few strong drinks with a long-term expat.

AS FAR AS THE EYE CAN SEE

THE FOLLOWING EQUATIONS can be used to estimate the distance to the horizon. Note that these equations assume a clear sky, an unblocked horizon, and do not account for the effects of atmospheric refraction:[1]

IMPERIAL	METRIC
$d = 1.22 \times \sqrt{h}$	$d = 3.57 \times \sqrt{h}$
h = observation height in feet	h = observation height in meters
d = distance to horizon in miles	d = distance to horizon in kilometers

ALTITUDE REFERENCE	OBSERVATION HEIGHT		DISTANCE TO HORIZON	
	FT	M	MI	KM
Head sticking out of the water	0.5	0.2	0.9	1.4
Average eye level	5.5	1.7	2.9	4.6
A full-grown maple tree	30	9	7	11
Roof of an average 10-story building	100	30	12	20
Top of a Royal Caribbean Oasis–class cruise ship	236	72	19	30
Highest sand dunes in the Sahara Desert	500	152	27	44
Maximum altitude of an average helicopter	10,000	3,048	122	197
Typical skydiving altitude	13,000	3,962	140	225
Mount Kilimanjaro summit	19,341	5,895	170	274
Mount Everest summit	29,029	8,848	209	336
Commercial jet cruising altitude	35,000	10,668	229	369

....

1 ››› Atmospheric refraction is the bending of light caused by the varying densities in the earth's atmosphere. It allows the viewer to observe things that are actually slightly "past" or "over" what would normally be the horizon. This means, under certain weather conditions, that what the viewer is seeing may actually be as much as 20 percent farther away than the distances listed above.

KEEPING IT CHEAP

T HE 2016 BACKPACKER Index from PriceofTravel.com tracks the cost of budget travel in popular destinations around the world.

PRICE OF:
A dorm bed at a good and cheap hostel
3 budget meals
2 rides on public transportation
1 paid cultural attraction
3 cheap beers

CHEAPEST		MOST EXPENSIVE	
Pokhara, Nepal	$15.85	Zurich, Switzerland	$121.90
Hanoi, Vietnam	$17.12	New York City, United States	$113.10
Ho Chi Minh City, Vietnam	$18.29	Venice, Italy	$103.30
Goa, India	$18.63	Helsinki, Finland	$99.94
Chiang Mai, Thailand	$19.10	Boston, United States	$97.89

UNDER THE SEA

We must go see for ourselves.

—Motto of the *Calypso*, the ship of Jacques Cousteau, legendary ocean-ographer, conservationist, and filmmaker. Cousteau coinvented the equipment and practice of modern scuba diving and underwater photography, directed more than hundred films, won three Oscars, wrote dozens of books, and pioneered marine conservation.

THE ART OF HAGGLING

*Since our arrival on these coasts, [we] have learned that the cost
of everything from a royal suite to a bottle of soda water can be halved
by the simple expedient of saying it must be halved.*

—ROBERT BYRON,
The Road to Oxiana, 1937

THERE IS NO exact blueprint for a successful negotiation. There are however a variety of tactics that can get you a good price in almost any situation.

SET YOUR MIND

The single most effective thing a traveler can do when negotiating prices in a foreign market is to maintain a pleasant attitude. Haggling should be fun and interactions with vendors should be treated as the valuable cross-cultural interactions that they are. An outrageously high price should not be viewed as an insult, but as simply another play in a complicated game. Haggling is a deeply ingrained part of many cultures that is as much about socializing as it about the buying and selling of goods.

PLAN AHEAD

If you expect to spend a significant amount of money, it is best to plan ahead. Know the general range of prices, decide what specific items you'll be targeting, and talk with other travelers about their luck at the market.

CONCEAL LUXURIES

While there is no need to dress in tattered clothing, wearing a nice watch or using an expensive cell phone in front of a vendor may identify you as a relatively rich foreigner probably willing to pay higher prices.

HIDE YOUR EXCITEMENT

Do not act overtly excited when you first come across that perfect souvenir, this gives the vendor obvious leverage. Casually ask the price and try to convey minimal emotion concerning your interest in their product.

BEWARE OF VENDORS BEARING GIFTS

A cup of tea, a sample of food, a trinket "to remember a new friend by": just because these are offered does not mean they are free. These might be used to guilt you into a purchase, they might be secretly added onto to the final price of an item, or they might actually be free—make no assumptions and be clear about your intentions before accepting.

DON'T MAKE THE FIRST OFFER

The vendor may ask what you think an item is worth, or otherwise goad you into being the first to actually state a number. Never do this as you have almost nothing to gain. Either you'll offer too high a price, which the vendor will use to their obvious advantage, or you'll offer too low a price, which will result in the same type of negotiation that would have occurred anyway. Further, the mere fact that you have thought about a potential price shows the vendor you are at least somewhat interested in the item.

START LOW

But not too low. This is one of the most common mistakes that travelers make. If you're after something that you think is worth 20 units of local currency and a vendor starts at 40 units of local currency you may be inclined to counter with 1, under the logic that you will both compromise equally and end up around 20. However, though the vendor starting high is an accepted part of the haggling ritual, counteroffering an extremely low price may be seen as offensive. This communicates to the vendor that you either don't adequately recognize the value of their product, or you are not seriously considering a purchase and are wasting their time.

COMBINE WHEN POSSIBLE

This might mean teaming up with other travelers or buying everything at once, but always remember that the more you buy, the better per unit price you can negotiate.

If one of the items you are interested in is relatively cheap, it might be best to save this tactic for the end of the negotiation. Don't reveal your interest in the cheaper product until you reach a "final" price on the more expensive items. Then propose you'll pay that price under the condition the vendor include the cheaper item.

FIND A PROBLEM

A small chip in the wood, an errant brushstroke on the painting—any imperfection can help lower a price. However, be very careful not to offend the vendor, who may have also created the product. You want to communicate that, though you are interested and impressed by the product, you feel this tiny imperfection should lower the price.

BECOME A TRADER

Before sending a rarely used item home or discarding it altogether, always consider its trade value. Trading is a common practice in many parts of the world and travelers often carry items that are unavailable or

▾▾▾ *continued* ▾▾▾

prohibitively expensive for local peoples. Don't expect to trade your way into a free room at a luxury hotel; however, in a market setting you might be surprised by the high value even seemingly basic items command.

WALK AWAY

When you can't agree on a price, walking away can be a very effective strategy. But be careful not to misuse this classic tactic. Many travelers walk away too early, looking over their shoulder and expecting a vendor to chase after them. Others leave in an angry huff, which only serves to further alienate the vendor.

This method should only be employed after serious negotiations, when the vendor has given their "final" price. Thank the vendor and leave apologetically, as if you're deeply remorseful a deal could not be made. Be aware that most customers try some version of this tactic so for it to be effective, you need to commit fully. Don't look back and be prepared to immediately accept or reject a price if the vendor does indeed track you down.

SWITCH CURRENCIES

In certain economic situations, offering to pay in other currencies, such as dollars or euros, can be very appealing to vendors. Note that this is generally only done for expensive items. Be sure you understand the exchange rate[1] and double-check your figures.

EMPTY YOUR WALLET

A classic haggling tactic for good reason. Separate your money into different pockets and prepare a wallet[2] that only has the maximum amount of money you are willing to pay for a given item.

BE CHARMING BUT DON'T BE CHARMED

Don't think of a vendor as an opponent you want to defeat, but rather as a friend you want to persuade. Smile often, hilariously mispronounce a few local phrases, lightly joke around, and feign outrage when quoted a high price. You want to seem attentive and confident, but also unfailingly friendly. The negotiation is a game and vendors appreciate those who play with the right mix of wit, humor, and graciousness.

But as you endear yourself to the vendor, be aware that they may also try to psychologically influence you. You will hear many a sob story: tales of wives pregnant with triplets, sons whose school must be paid for, daughters in need of medical operations. These stories are rarely true; just as the traveler has a variety of haggling tactics at their disposal so too does the vendor.

It is every traveler's personal choice how much to conflate shopping with charity. The simple reality is that street and market vendors are often poorer members of a society who have become heavily reliant on tourists for income. This is not to say you should pay an unfair amount for a mass-produced tchotchke, only that you should be cognizant of relative disparities in income levels. Some travelers are too quick to boast about their conquests in arguing over inconsequential amounts of money with desperately poor people. There is no shame in paying a generous price to a friendly vendor for a treasured souvenir.

1 ››› See page 253 for more information on exchange rates.
2 ››› See page 43 for more information on the two-wallet system.

THE EMOTIONS OF ADVENTURE

res·fe·ber (RACE-fay-ber)   *Swedish*

noun. The unique combination of anxiety and excitement one often feels before the beginning of a journey.
From the Swedish *resa* ("travel") and *feber* ("fever")

Resfeber is the feeling you get when you buy a plane ticket to a place you've never been, see a long-awaited train pull into a station, or board a ship that will take you across an ocean. It is the personal realization that you are about to be thrust into the unknown, and all the frightening and beautiful things that come with it. It is the friction that results from abject fear meeting pure excitement. The only cure is to go.

THE WORKING WORLD

LARGEST EMPLOYERS IN THE WORLD	EMPLOYEES (MILLIONS)
United States Department of Defense	3.2
Chinese People's Liberation Army	2.3
Walmart	2.1
McDonald's	1.9
United Kingdom National Health Service	1.7

RELATIVELY DANGEROUS LARGE ANIMALS

SELECTIVE REPORTING BIAS is the phenomenon in which people believe something to be far more common that it actually is because the few incidents that do occur receive an inordinate amount of attention. There is perhaps no more effective example of this than animal attacks. Based on media coverage, one might expect that tigers and lions regularly prey on helpless explorers. These frightening and powerful animals may be tailor-made villains but the simple reality is that they almost never attack humans.

Consider the poor, misconstrued shark. You are far more likely to be killed by a falling coconut, a toddler, or a vending machine than a shark. Every year, 10 times more people are bitten by other people in New York City than are bitten by sharks worldwide. Yet, through a combination of natural fear, pop culture villainy, and the aforementioned selective reporting bias, sharks are on the forefront of many travelers' minds when swimming off an unfamiliar coast. And while it is true that sharks have attacked humans[1] in the past, there are a variety of other animals more worthy of your concern.

Though it is extraordinarily uncommon for *any* large animal to attack a human, below is guide to defending yourself against the creatures a person might realistically encounter in the course of their travels.

GENERAL BEST PRACTICES

» Never come between a parent animal and its offspring or between a hungry animal and its food.

» Avoid cornering animals; always leave a frightened or surprised animal an obvious escape route.

» Some animals remain motionless or "play dead" as a defense mechanism. Do not approach or touch a potentially dangerous animal, no matter how it appears.

» Animals of many different species have adapted to completely rely on humans for food. Whether through indirect means like eating garbage or being fed directly, this behavior has been reinforced for hundreds of generations in some cases. Recognize that these animals are now totally dependent on finding food in this way, have no other source of nourishment, and will pursue these food sources as aggressively as they would hunt in the wild. If an animal is displaying threatening behavior and you are carrying food, they are almost undoubtedly more interested in the food than in you.

» The threat of disease is generally much more dangerous than the animal itself. Seek medical attention immediately if you are bitten by any wild animal.

» Mosquitoes, bees, flies, spiders, scorpions, worms, snails, locusts, hornets, ants, and various small marine animals are far more dangerous to humans than any large animal in the world. Wear insect repellent, confirm the safety of any potential swimming area, shake out shoes before putting them on, and beware of diseases transferable through insect bites.

BEAR

COMMONLY FOUND IN
*Asia, Europe, North America,
South America*

....

SIGN OF IMMINENT ATTACK
*Swinging head from side to side,
snorting, continual staring*

WHAT TO DO IF ENCOUNTERED

Make your presence known by speaking in a noticeable but calm voice. Remain still, ready any deterrents (such as pepper spray), while assessing the bear's movements. Make yourself appear as large as possible and begin to slowly back away while talking continually. Do not run and do not to turn your back on the bear.

If the bear begins charging, remain still, stand your ground, and begin yelling. Most initial charges are bluffs and, regardless, attempting to run will likely have far worse consequences. If the bear makes contact or remains focused on you, clasp your hands on the back of your neck, lay facedown with your backpack on, and "play dead." Most bear interactions with humans are defensive: they simply want

ˇˇˇ *continued* ˇˇˇ

to ensure you are not a threat to their cubs or food source. However, if the bear does not leave the area and begins attacking, immediately fight back with any weapons available while making as much noise as possible.

BUFFALO

COMMONLY FOUND IN
Africa, Asia

SIGN OF IMMINENT ATTACK
Head held high, snorting, horn thrashing

WHAT TO DO IF ENCOUNTERED

Be prepared for the buffalo to charge at any time and without warning, especially if the animal is injured or alone. Do not attempt to stand your ground; immediately run toward the safety of a tree or other obstacles. If there is no safe area in sight, as a matter of last resort, look to judge the animal's position and move sideways at the last possible moment to avoid being gored.

CROCODILE

COMMONLY FOUND IN
Africa, Asia, Australia, North America, South America

SIGN OF IMMINENT ATTACK
Hissing, snapping

WHAT TO DO IF ENCOUNTERED

In water: Do not splash water or make unnecessary noise, swim to the shore as quickly and quietly as possible. ***On land:*** Run from the water's edge in a straight line, do not waste time zigzagging. If bitten, attack the animal's eyes, ears, nostrils, or throat.

ELEPHANT

COMMONLY FOUND IN
Africa, Asia

SIGN OF IMMINENT ATTACK
Coiled trunk, ears close to head

WHAT TO DO IF ENCOUNTERED

Remain downwind if possible and back away slowly while avoiding eye contact. Elephants are known to employ bluffs, known as "mock charges," in which they test perceived threats by fanning out their ears, trumpeting, and swinging their legs in a show of intimidation. If the elephant is exhibiting these behaviors, stand your ground and do not show your back to the elephant.

If the elephant displays the aggressive behavior detailed above, it is likely preparing to actually charge. Run in a zigzag pattern, toward large obstacles. If you fall or are knocked down, curl into a ball, protect your head with hands, and don't struggle or attempt to stand up until the animal leaves the area.

HIPPOPOTAMUS

COMMONLY FOUND IN
Africa

SIGN OF IMMINENT ATTACK
Snorting, bellowing, opening mouth (which may look like yawning)

WHAT TO DO IF ENCOUNTERED

In water: Continually make your presence known by splashing the water.
On land: Run, being sure not to put yourself between the hippo and the water, and aim for groups rocks or trees that will help slow down the charging hippo. If bitten, attack the animal's eyes, nostrils, and throat.

ⱽⱽⱽ *continued* ⱽⱽⱽ

HYENA

COMMONLY FOUND IN
Africa, Asia

SIGN OF IMMINENT ATTACK
*Baring teeth, snarling, whooping
(loud rallying call to other hyenas)*

WHAT TO DO IF ENCOUNTERED

Do not turn your back to the hyena and run unless there is a nearby tree you can climb. Attempt to surprise and intimidate the animal by shouting, spreading your arms, and stamping your feet. Hyenas are notoriously opportunistic hunters and scavengers—sacrifice any food you may be carrying by throwing it to far from you, but making sure it lands in full view of the hyenas.

MONKEY, BABOON, AND CHIMPANZEE

COMMONLY FOUND IN
Global

SIGN OF IMMINENT ATTACK
Baring teeth, grunting

WHAT TO DO IF ENCOUNTERED

Monkeys, baboons, and chimpanzees are normally only aggressive around humans they think have food, so immediately discard any and all food. Remain calm, show your empty palms to indicate you have no more food, and slowly back away without showing your teeth or making direct eye contact.

MOOSE AND ELK

COMMONLY FOUND IN
Asia, Europe, North America

SIGN OF IMMINENT ATTACK
Maintaining eye contact, lowered head, stomping feet, pinned back ears, whipping head back and forth

WHAT TO DO IF ENCOUNTERED

Back away while seeking a tree, rock, or other obstruction to hide behind. Turn and run if you have considerable distance between yourself and the animal. If you fall or are knocked down, curl into a ball, protect your head with hands, and don't struggle or attempt to stand up until the animal leaves the area.

SNAKE

COMMONLY FOUND IN
Global

SIGN OF IMMINENT ATTACK
Hissing, coiling, raising up

WHAT TO DO IF ENCOUNTERED

Back away slowly and carefully. Be aware that snakes can strike very quickly within a limited range. If bitten, remain calm and immediately call for help.[2]

vvv continued vvv

WILD DOG

COMMONLY FOUND IN
Global

SIGN OF IMMINENT ATTACK
Baring teeth, snarling, raised hackles

WHAT TO DO IF ENCOUNTERED

Avoid eye contact, don't show your teeth, and don't turn your back or attempt to run. Stand up straight and remain motionless with your hands at your sides while assessing escape options and the intent of the animal. If dealing with a large dog, or a pack of dogs, throw away any food you may be carrying without making any sudden movements.

If the dog does not lose interest or begins to try to bite, speak aggressively in a loud, deep voice while remaining careful not to make eye contact.

If bitten, attack the animal's eyes, nose, or throat.

1 ››› Perhaps they're out for revenge. Sharks kill an average of four humans each year. Humans kill more than 10,000 sharks every hour.
2 ››› See page 51 for more information on snakebites.

THE CONSEQUENCES OF DISAGREEMENT

TRAVELERS SHOULD NOTE that the significance of conversation is not equally valued throughout the world. Free speech is not an inalienable global right; it is one protected by select governments. Honest discussion, and even dissent, concerning topics like politics and religion is respected in only a few nations and condemned in many. In some parts of the world, words alone can have much more severe consequences than travelers may be accustomed to.

Remember that one person's oppressive dictator may be another's beloved king; one person's violent uprising may be another's noble revolution; one person's cult may be another's religion. Outside media outlets sometimes frame news in a way that might be offensive to local people and it's important to stay cognizant of this divide in viewpoints. The fact that you may only be repeating a certain perspective is often no excuse—any spoken opposition to certain cultural institutions will often be treated seriously. At home, freely speaking one's mind might result in a respectful disagreement. Doing so abroad can not only lead to arrest, but may offend people to the point of physical retaliation. Speak your mind freely if you wish, but be aware of this difference in potential consequences.

ROUND, THE WORLD

I have always read that the world comprising the land and water was spherical, and the recorded experiences of Ptolemy and all the others have proved this . . . But as I have already described, I have now seen so much irregularity that I have come to another conclusion respecting the Earth, namely, that it is not round, as they describe, but of the form of a pear, which is very round except where the stalk grows, at which part it is most prominent; or like a round ball, upon part of which is a prominence like a woman's nipple . . .

—CHRISTOPHER COLUMBUS,
in a 1498 letter to King Ferdinand and Queen Isabella

THOUGH THE EXACT size of the earth was debated, the fact that the earth was some sort of spherical shape was common knowledge in almost every society since at least the time of the ancient Greeks. The myth that people believed the earth to be flat seems to have been largely caused by a heavily fictionalized biography of Columbus written by Washington Irving in 1828.

ON TIME

TIME TO GET ORGANIZED

AS THE 19TH century drew to a close, the need to standardize time around the globe became increasingly apparent. A rush of technologies, from trains to telegraphs, had suddenly connected the world like never before and the use of localized and often arbitrary ways of determining the time soon presented a number of problems.

An elegant solution was proposed: divide the world into 25 time zones of an hour difference each, most 15 longitudinal degrees wide.[1] Greenwich, slightly southeast of central London, was chosen as the prime meridian, the definition of 0° longitude, in part because its Royal

vvv *continued* vvv

Observatory was already an internationally renowned center for astronomical research and timekeeping. By midway through the 20th century these standards were in use by the majority of the countries in the world.

But while this relatively simple concept was quickly implemented and remains the theoretical basis for the system used today, the practical application of time zones is not so straightforward.

ANYTHING BUT STANDARD

The international history of time zones is like the international history of measurement standards or outlet types or which side of the road to drive on. These types of nationalized decisions are never based simply on ease of use or international compatibility. Instead they are the product of countless successive political administrations around the world, each fueled by wildly divergent motivations. Thus the theoretically straightforward system detailed above has become significantly more complicated.

The Democratic Republic of Congo uses two time zones, while China, a country four times larger, uses only one. Many countries at least partially observe Daylight Savings Time, but more than a hundred don't. Some countries and territories now use half-, or even quarter-hour, time zone increments. Australia uses both vertical and horizontal time zones. Egypt has changed its official time zone multiple times in the past few years, while Spain has been content to use what most experts agree to be the wrong time zone for more than 70 years. This is to say nothing of the hundreds of cultural and religious-based methods of timekeeping still in use in many parts of the world. The long and short of it is that the world's time zones are, predictably, a mess.

PRESENT TIME

Today the world's clocks are officially based on **Coordinated Universal Time** (UTC), an incredibly precise successor to Greenwich Mean Time (GMT) that is based on the movement of atoms.[2] The prime meridian remains unchanged and local time zones are defined by the difference (or offset) between the two.[3] For example, New York City is UTC–5, or 5 hours "behind" UTC, and Sydney is UTC+10, or 10 hours "ahead" of UTC. See the next page for a map of time zones around the world.

1 ››› Twenty-five, and not 24, time zones were needed because 0 GMT is a time zone. It was decided that GMT+12 and GMT–12 would be only 7.5° wide and thus:
(23 time zones of 15° each) + (2 time zones of 7.5° each) = 360°.

2 ››› The terms Greenwich Mean Time and GMT are still commonly used and are now considered interchangeable with UTC.

3 ››› See page 1 for the Country Directory with a complete listing of time zones by country.

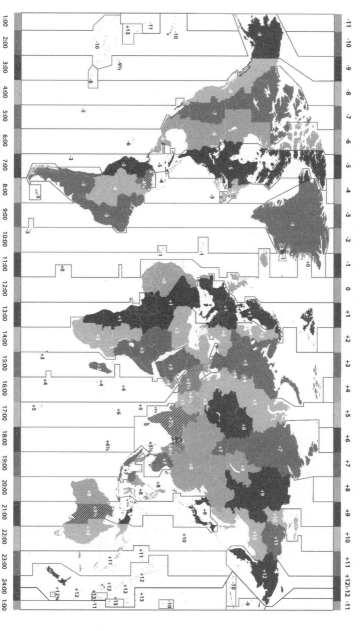

Worldwide Map of Local Time Zones

"WASTING" TIME

aso·lar·e (Ah-so-LARR-eh)   *Italian*

verb. To spend time in a pleasant but unproductive or aimless way

---

> *How beautiful it is to do nothing, and then rest afterward.*
> —Spanish proverb

Many travelers are naturally inclined toward constant activity. After braving the inconveniences of long flights, border crossings, and bumpy bus rides, they feel a need to justify those efforts by remaining constantly busy in their task of taking advantage of these new surroundings. They are not here to *be*, they are here to *do*, and often carry checklists to that effect. While this is a perfectly natural and understandable approach to travel, travelers would do well to remember the Italian concept of *asolare*.

Asolare might mean spending the day drinking rich local coffee in a town square or leisurely wandering crooked alleyways with no set destination. It might consist of enjoying either the sun of an exotic beach, or appreciating the air-conditioning of a darkened movie theater. The point is that one's itinerary shouldn't be thoroughly dictated by guilt, external or otherwise. Travel is personal and one's journey needn't ever be justified to others. It is permissible to simply exist in a foreign paradise.

TEATIME

THE UNITED KINGDOM'S power grid is specifically designed to account for millions of citizens simultaneously brewing tea during commercial breaks of popular television events. The largest ever instance of the phenomenon, which is known as a TV pickup, occurred on July 4, 1990, at the end of a penalty shootout between England and West Germany in the World Cup semifinal, when an additional 2,800 megawatts of power were needed to ensure the grid wouldn't be overloaded by the huge number of citizens all turning on electric kettles at virtually the exact same time.

AIR RAGE

THE FIRST DOCUMENTED case of air rage occurred in 1947 on a flight from Havana, Cuba, to Miami, Florida, when a heavily intoxicated man attacked another passenger with a bottle of alcohol and then proceeded to bite a flight attendant who tried to intervene. Drunk and violent though he was, he was not charged with a crime because commuter air travel was so new that no one had seriously considered how to prosecute crimes committed onboard. The 1963 Convention on Offences and Certain Other Acts Committed on Board Aircraft in Tokyo determined that the laws of the country in which the plane is registered would take precedence in such matters.

GLOBAL GRAFFITI

THE SINGLE-MOST PREVALENT graffiti phrase in the world is probably *KILROY WAS HERE*. Originally popularized by American soldiers in World War II and propagated by countless tourists, the phrase now appears in thousands of locations around the world, often accompanied by the figure seen above.

The exact origin of the phrase remains disputed, but likely derives from an American shipyard inspector from Massachusetts named James J. Kilroy. Kilroy would write the phrase on different parts of ships during their construction to indicate he'd completed his inspection, assuming his markings would later be painted over. As the war continued, there was no time to paint the ships before sending them to Europe, meaning thousands of servicemen encountered the mysterious phrase without any explanation. It soon became a running joke to write the expression wherever they were fighting and the cartoonish figure became a sort of unofficial mascot among the enlisted troops.[1] The tradition subsequently spread to the general public and today the phrase and accompanying drawing can be seen at virtually every major tourist attraction where widespread graffiti is present.

---

1 ››› Both Hitler and Stalin allegedly commanded subordinates to investigate who this "Kilroy" was and how he'd managed to travel so extensively and be involved in so many major battles.

BRAGGING RIGHTS

T HE EUROVISION SONG Contest is an extraordinarily popular international singing competition, the latest iteration of which featured performers from 40 countries. Each country sends a contestant or group who performs an original song live in whatever language they choose.[1] A portion of the estimated 200 million total viewers vote via phone, text, or digital app on which song they liked best in each round of the competition, though they are not allowed to vote for the contestant from their own country. These public votes are combined with the results from a national jury of music industry professionals to determine the national vote of each country. The national votes are then tallied to determine a winner, whose country gets to host the event next year. Notable past winners have included ABBA (representing Sweden in 1974) and Céline Dion (representing Switzerland in 1988).

NO. OF WINS	COUNTRY
7	Ireland
6	Sweden
5	France, Luxembourg, United Kingdom
4	Netherlands
3	Denmark, Israel, Norway
2	Austria, Germany, Italy, Spain, Switzerland, Ukraine
1	Azerbaijan, Belgium, Estonia, Finland, Greece, Latvia, Monaco, Russia, Serbia, Turkey, Yugoslavia

1 ››› Contestants do not need to be citizens of the country they represent.

———————◆———————

CLASSIC INSPIRATIONS

The motives of my voyage were a certain intellectual restlessness,
a passion for novelty, a curiosity about the limits of the ocean
and peoples who might dwell beyond it.

—LUCIAN OF SAMOSATA,
Greek satirist, *True Fictions*, 150

A GOOD TRIP

He had fought a prince, jilted a princess,
intoxicated the Doge of Venice, carried off a Duchess from Madrid,
scaled the walls of a convent in Italy, narrowly escaped the inquisition
at Lisbon, and concluded his exploits by a duel in Paris . . .

—SIR JONAH BARRINGTON,
on the Grand Tour of Beauchamp Bagenal, a legendary Irish traveler and politician

THE PRINCESS IN question is thought to have been Charlotte of Mecklenburg-Strelitz, who later married King George III and became Queen of Great Britain and Ireland.

AN IMPORTANT MONTH IN THE HISTORY OF HOT AIR BALLOONING

THE FIRST HYDROGEN-FILLED hot air balloon was designed by Jacques Charles and launched on August 27, 1783, from Paris. The balloon traveled north for about 45 minutes before landing near the village of Gonesse, where it was immediately attacked by frightened villagers who believed it to be some kind of monster.[1]

A little over three weeks later on September 19, 1783, the Montgolfier brothers launched the first hot air balloon to carry passengers from the palace of Versailles in front of King Louis XVI, Marie Antoinette, and 130,000 onlookers. Though the king had originally proposed using criminals, it was later decided that a duck, a rooster, and a sheep would be the first test pilots. Sheep were thought to be physiologically similar to humans and, as animals known to be able to fly and survive at different altitudes, the duck and rooster were used as controls for the experiment. The balloon rose to roughly 1,500 feet (457 meters) and flew about 2 miles (3.2 kilometers) in 8 minutes. The sheep, the duck, and the rooster were found to be perfectly fine, paving the way for the first human hot air balloon flight a little over two months later.

---

1 ››› In reporting on the incident, a Parisian newspaper called *Mercure de France* ridiculed the villagers' naïveté with the sardonic quip: "The creature, shaking and bounding, dodged the first blows. Finally, however, it received a mortal wound, and collapsed with a long sigh."

THE COST OF POPULARITY

If we don't want to end up like Venice,
we will have to put some kind of limit in Barcelona.

—Barcelona Mayor Ada Colau Ballano in 2015 on plans to reduce tourism by limiting new hotel construction and closely regulating short-term rental properties. Though far smaller than Barcelona, Venice has seen its native population plummet as tourism has made the city increasingly expensive and crowded. Barcelona is among the first major global destinations to begin actively discouraging tourism, not for environmental reasons, but solely for the good of its residents.

◆

AIR AND SEA DISTRESS CALLS

BELOW IS A list of internationally recognized air and sea distress calls, along with their origin and colloquial meaning. These calls are traditionally repeated three times and followed by all relevant information about the status of the passengers and vessel. Note that issuing fake or unwarranted distress calls is a serious crime, punishable by fines and jail time in most countries.

SECURITAY
From the French word *sécurité* meaning "safety"

"We have important safety information that we need to communicate."

PAN-PAN
From the French word *panne* meaning "breakdown"

"We have an urgent situation onboard,
but there is no immediate danger to the life of the passengers
or to the safety of the vessel."

MAYDAY
From the French word *m'aider* meaning "help me"

"We require immediate assistance,
we are in a state of emergency in which the life of the passengers
and/or the safety of the vessel is directly threatened."

A MAN ABOUT TOWN

ba·cheque (BA-check) *Lingala*

noun. A local operator who knows the city or area well.

Though they may be unfamiliar with the word, the concept of a *bacheque* will be familiar to anyone who has traveled extensively in developing countries. A *bacheque* is a loosely defined profession that might be best described as a mix of concierge, translator, tour guide, fixer, middleman, and hustler. A *bacheque*'s office is the streets: they know everyone, they can get anything, and can generally make things happen in places where business is conducted in a far different manner than travelers may be used to.

A good *bacheque* can be an extremely useful contact for a traveler to have. Some economies are so fraught with cultural sensitivities, or warped by corruption, that navigating the local bureaucracy without assistance is almost impossible for an outsider, especially one who does not speak the language. Travelers should be aware however, that *bacheques* do not offer their unique blend of services free of charge. The *bacheque* always gets a cut, even if their exact form of payment is not apparent. Kickbacks from expensive restaurants and hotels they lead travelers to, overcharging for transportation, exchanging currency at inflated rates—this is how many less trustworthy *bacheques* make their money. Be vigilant: an honest *bacheque* should be rewarded with a handsome tip, a deceitful one should be disregarded as a common con man.

DON'T TAKE IT FOR GRANTED

Experts estimate that of the entire world's population:

» *94 percent have never flown on an airplane*

» *75 percent are lactose intolerant*

» *66 percent have never seen snow in person*

» *45 percent have never consumed alcohol* [1]

1 ››› Aged 15 and older.

A PRIMER IN VEXILLOLOGY

THE FOLLOWING CUSTOMS regarding the display of flags are widely understood throughout the world. Note that the desecration of the national flag, or any item bearing the image of the flag, is considered a serious crime in many countries.

Half-mast[1]	A time of mourning or remembrance
Upside down[2]	Distress
Knotted[3]	Distress
Black flag	Danger; the ending of a truce; also traditionally used by pirates
Red flag[4]	Warning
White flag	A request to communicate; a truce
Removal of flag	Surrender

1 ››› The flags of Iran, Iraq, and Saudi Arabia feature Islamic text that is considered sacred by Muslims, therefore these flags are never flown at half-mast.

2 ››› The flag of the Philippines being flown upside down specifically indicates the country is at war.

3 ››› Due to the fact that it can be difficult to easily tell whether some flags are upside down or not, knots are sometimes tied into flags to indicate distress. At sea, any particularly irregular display of flags is generally interpreted as a sign that the crew may be in danger.

4 ››› The term *red flag* has evolved into a widely used idiom used to designate a specific issue that may foretell future problems. The exact origin of this phrase is unclear, but red flags have been used for hundreds of years to signal war, disaster, or general caution in many different cultures.

BLACK SHEEP

EXPERTS BELIEVE THAT Kim Jong-un was selected as Supreme Leader of North Korea only after his older half-brother Kim Jong-nam angered their father Kim Jong-il by being arrested at a Japanese airport in May 2001. Jong-nam, who was considered the heir apparent at the time, was attempting to secretly visit Tokyo Disneyland using a fake Dominican Republic passport that listed his name as "Pang Xiong." This particularly delighted media outlets in neighboring China, as *pang xiong* translates to "fat bear" in Mandarin.

TRAVELERS SHOULD BE aware that in many parts of the world the offering of tea, coffee, or other drinks to a guest in one's home carries deep cultural meaning and should always be accepted, with very few exceptions.

The offering of a drink is a symbolic gesture of welcome and by accepting you are graciously affirming your friendship while humbly acknowledging your host's hospitality. To decline such an offer would generally be considered deeply offensive. If the beverage being offered is not to your taste, try to drink it slowly as it will likely be immediately refilled when empty.

GUIDE TO POWER

AN INCOMPATIBLE WORLD

MORE THAN A century ago, as public use of electricity spread across the globe, countries developed wildly different standards for this new technology with little thought to international compatibility. As a result, the world's power grids are now a convoluted mess of different voltages, each accessed by maddeningly dissimilar outlets, and will likely remain that way for the foreseeable future. Countries are now so financially invested in their current infrastructures that any significant change or standardization is highly unlikely. Below is a guide to navigating the complex world of international electricity.

BE COMPATIBLE

Safely accessing electricity primarily depends on two factors: **voltage** and **outlet/plug type**.

FACTOR	APPLICABLE DEFINITION	CORRESPONDING DEVICE(S)
Voltage (V)	A measure of the potential energy between the outlet and plug	Converter, Transformer
Outlet/Plug Type	The physical shape of the outlet and corresponding plug	Adapter

✦✦✦ *continued* ✦✦✦

It is crucial that travelers consider both voltage and outlet/plug type when using electricity in an unfamiliar country. For instance, though an outlet might be physically compatible with a plug, if it outputs a higher voltage than the device was designed for, serious damage can occur.

The compatibility of a third factor, **frequency (Hz)**, is no longer considered critically important as most modern consumer electronics are designed to work at both 50 Hz and 60 Hz. However, some devices that utilize large motors and/or precise nondigital clocks can be affected by conflicting frequencies and should be checked before use.

The information provided in this section applies only to AC (alternating current), as opposed to DC (direct current), power. AC is the standard for consumer power in every country in the world.

Note that the electricity supply of some developing countries is highly unstable, meaning power outages, power spikes, and inconsistent voltages are commonplace. It is best practice to unplug devices during power outages, as the power may spike when coming back on. Surge protectors can also help protect devices against unpredictable power supplies.

GUIDE

STEP 1: CHECK THE VOLTAGE

» *Compare the local voltage[1] to the device specifications, which are usually found on the plug itself.*

» *Note that many modern devices such as cell phones and battery chargers are now dual or multi-voltage (often shown as "110V–240V" or something similar), meaning they will work with a wide range of voltages.*

If the voltages are compatible, skip ahead to **Step 3**.
If the voltages are not compatible, continue to **Step 2**.

STEP 2: CHANGE THE VOLTAGE

» *If the device is not dual voltage or is otherwise incompatible, you will need to manipulate the local voltage to match the specifications of your device. This is done through the use of a converter or transformer, which can either "step up" (increase) or "step down" (decrease) the local voltage.[2]*

» *Always carefully research which type of converter or transformer is necessary and read all instructions before using. Many converters and transformers are designed to only be used for short periods (less than two hours) at a time.*

Use a converter if your device is electrical. This includes devices with mechanical motors, like an electric shaver, or devices with heaters, like a hair dryer.

Use a transformer if your device is electronic. This includes devices with computer chips and/or circuits, like cell phones and GPS trackers.

STEP 3: CHECK THE PLUG

» *After confirming the voltages are compatible, the next step is ensuring the physical shape of the plug matches the local outlet type. A matching plug and outlet type should be obvious, and the plug should fit the outlet with little to no resistance.*

If the plug and outlet type are compatible, skip ahead to **Step 5**.
If the plug and outlet type are not compatible, continue to **Step 4**.

STEP 4: CHANGE THE PLUG

» *Adapters are small, inexpensive, and sold either by individual type or as universal adapters that work with multiple outlet types. See the next page for information on outlet/plug types around the world to determine necessary adapters.*

Use an adapter if the plug does not easily fit into the outlet.

STEP 5: PLUG IN

» *When using a device abroad for the first time, or to take extra precaution, periodically monitor the device to ensure the plug or outlet is not unusually hot and that no smoke or unusual smells are emanating from the area.*

---

1 ››› Found in the Country Directory on page 1.
2 ››› While they may be necessary for certain single voltage devices, few travelers still carry converters or transformers. These products can be both expensive and heavy and most travelers find it far easier and more cost efficient to simply travel only with dual or multi voltage devices.

∨∨∨ *continued* ∨∨∨

OUTLET TYPES AROUND THE WORLD

Below is an overview of all outlet types in use today, along with their corresponding plug types. Also included is whether the connection is **grounded** or **ungrounded** when being used with corresponding plug type and which *additional plugs types are safely compatible* with each outlet type.[1] Note that some outlets, especially in popular tourist locales, are combination or "universal" outlets, which accept multiple plug types.

For a detailed list of outlet types by country, please consult the Country Directory, page 1.

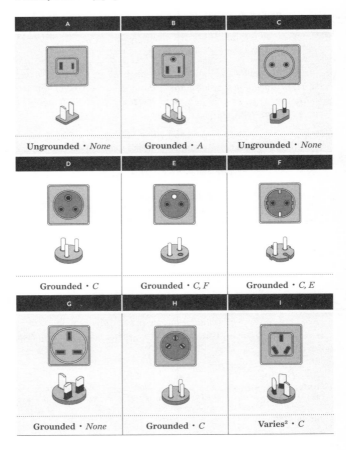

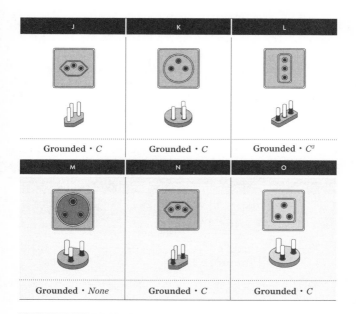

J	K	L
Grounded · *C*	Grounded · *C*	Grounded · *C*[3]

M	N	O
Grounded · *None*	Grounded · *C*	Grounded · *C*

1 ››› A grounded plug is one in which a third prong is included to "ground" the connection, or connect it directly to the earth. This provides an extra level of safety for some high-voltage or metal-encased devices by providing an outlet for electrical charge in the event of a malfunction. Some ungrounded (two-prong) plug types can safely be used with multiple outlet types.

2 ››› The ungrounded type of the I plug has two pins, the grounded type has three.

3 ››› Only certain types of the L outlet accepts C plugs, all others accept only L plugs.

THANK YOU, SIR

The vice president of the United States will gladly carry your bags for you.

—VICE PRESIDENT RICHARD NIXON

To famed trumpeter Louis Armstrong in New York's Idlewild Airport in 1958.

NIXON HAD SPOTTED the musician and, after a photo op, learned that Armstrong was waiting in line for customs. The future president then invited Armstrong to bypass customs, even kindly offering to carry the older musician's suitcases. It was later revealed the bags contained three pounds of marijuana.

HAVE A DRINK

W HEN CONSIDERING HOW much water to bring on a walk or hike, always err on the side of caution. Bring as much as you can comfortably carry and more than you think you'll need. Do not assume you will find drinkable water in the wilderness and bring along a tested and trusted filtering system if you plan on hiking in remote areas for extended periods of time or in extreme conditions. Necessary water consumption levels vary greatly by person, exertion, elevation, and temperature. Below is a general guide for a sole individual hiking in hot conditions.

Amount of Drinking Water to Bring

HOURS		2	4	6	8
Volume	Ounce (US)	51	101	152	203
	Quart (US)	1.6	3.2	4.8	6.3
	Liter	1.5	3	4.5	6
Weight	Pound	3.3	6.6	9.9	13.2
	Kilogram	1.5	3	4.5	6

THE MOST IMPORTANT MEAL

A VARIETY OF NATIONAL breakfast traditions have gained popularity throughout the world and are now often advertised to travelers in popular tourist locales. This guide is provided not to imply that this is what every citizen of these countries regularly eat, but rather to preview what you will be served should you order such a breakfast.

AMERICAN
Eggs, bacon, sausage,
hash browns, toast, coffee

ENGLISH
Tea, sausage, bacon, eggs, mushrooms,
beans, tomato, hash browns, toast

AUSTRALIAN
Vegemite, toast, cereal, yogurt,
fruit, coffee

JAPANESE
Rice, miso soup, soybeans,
fish, pickles, juice, tea

ISRAELI
Eggs, salad, cheese, bread,
jam, olives, juice, coffee

FRENCH
Croissants, other assorted
pastries, jam, coffee

GESTURES OF NOTE

Below is a list of potentially offensive or confusing common gestures and the areas in which their meaning may most commonly be misinterpreted. Note that this is not a complete list of all inappropriate physical movements, but rather only covers typical Western gestures whose intended meaning might become lost in translation.

Hand Gestures

HAND GESTURE	DESCRIPTION	LOCATION
THUMBS-UP	*A deeply offensive insult in some countries, indicates immaturity or dissatisfaction in others*	Greece, Middle Eastern and West African countries
PALM OUT	*Implies that someone should be punished in a disgusting way*	Greece, Pakistan
THUMB BETWEEN FINGERS	*Depending on location, may be seen as an insult or a sexual reference*	Indonesia, Turkey, Russia
FINGERS CROSSED	*Offensive reference to the female anatomy*	Vietnam
OK	*Depending on location, may reference a person's genitals or imply someone has no worth*	Brazil, France, Turkey, Venezuela
HANDS IN POCKETS	*Can imply boredom or a lack of respect, especially in formal settings or when speaking to an older person*	South Korea, Turkey
BLOWING YOUR NOSE	*Blowing your nose in public is considered disgusting or rude in many countries*	China, Japan, Saudi Arabia

HAND GESTURE	DESCRIPTION	LOCATION
FORWARD CHIN SCRATCH	*Rudely implies you're not interested in something or you want someone to leave*	Belgium, France, Italy, Tunisia
COME HERE	*A gesture reserved only for dogs in some countries*	Japan, Philippines, Singapore
ONE HANDED	*Giving or receiving an object with one hand implies dismissiveness or disinterest*	Japan, South Korea
FINGER HORNS	*Used to indicate a man's wife is being unfaithful*	Brazil, Italy, Spain, Portugal
INWARD V	*Rude gesture indicating you deeply dislike someone*	Australia, Ireland, New Zealand, United Kingdom

Body Gestures

GESTURE	DESCRIPTION
	Buddhism teaches that the head is where the spirit resides and this has significant effect on the cultural norms of countries throughout southern Asia. Never touch another person's head and note that this extends to babies and small children. While it may be normal to lightheartedly ruffle a child's hair in the West, this would be considered extremely inappropriate to a traditional Buddhist parent in a country like Thailand.
	Cultural norms surrounding eye contact vary greatly by culture. In Asia, persistently meeting someone's eyes is usually considered impolite; in parts of Africa continual eye contact is seen as a sign of aggression; yet in other areas staring at strangers is culturally acceptable and continual eye contact is interpreted as an indicator of confidence. This is to say nothing of how gender affects these customs, or how travelers might be stared at in some area simply due to the novelty of their physical appearance or dress. In general, it is best to err on the side of politeness and avoid maintaining eye contact with strangers.

	In India as well as parts of Africa and the Middle East, the left hand is traditionally reserved for unclean purposes, including bathroom activities. Thus you should avoid touching someone, shaking hands, eating, or receiving a gift with your left hand when traveling in these areas.
	The feet are considered a particularly unclean part of the body in many cultures, especially in Asia. Be wary of showing the soles of your feet, or using your feet to point or pick something up. Further be careful to never step on anything of cultural importance, such as a newspaper showing the picture of a national leader or currency adorned with the image of royalty, as this will be considered extraordinarily offensive.

WHO TO CALL

The most widely used **emergency phone numbers** in the world are:

112[1] · *119* · *911* · *999*

Using one of these four numbers will connect you to some sort of emergency services in more than 80 percent of countries.

Travelers should be aware that in many countries even deactivated cell phones without a service plan can still be used to call emergency services. However, while this means that you should be able to connect to emergency services from any functional cell phone (even one that has been disconnected for lack of payment), this does not mean that you will be able to use a cell phone in an area without reception.

In the event of an emergency, make sure any satellite navigation functionality is enabled to assist emergency personnel in locating you.

While emergency services are primarily designed to receive calls, emergency organizations around the world are continually adding text functionality. Voice and text are transmitted via different frequencies in most countries, and text utilizes far less bandwidth, so if you are having trouble connecting by phone, try sending pertinent information to an emergency number via text. Note that text functionality requires registration in some countries.

....

1 ››› *112* is the standard emergency number for almost all cell phone carriers, meaning it will automatically redirect to local emergency services when necessary. For instance, calling *112* from a cell phone in Sydney will automatically redirect to *000*, the official emergency number of Australia.

CARGO CRUISING

T HERE IS AN understandable appeal to the idea of traveling aboard a cargo ship: a unique, relaxing, grittily authentic ride from port to port seems like the perfect antidote to the chaos of airline travel or the structured ridiculousness of cruise ships. However, while it is still possible to travel by cargo ship, it is no longer as easy as strolling down to the docks and hitching a ride.

Traveling aboard a modern cargo ship is an expensive mode of transport that requires careful planning. Cargo ships that offer transport service, which are increasingly rare, generally carry a maximum of 12 passengers[1] and trips need to be booked at least two months in advance through specialized travel agents. Expect to pay a minimum of $100/day, with all food included. Due to insurance and work permit policies, working aboard a cargo ship in exchange for free board is almost never an option. Interested parties should remember these are working ships on which the comfort of the passengers is always a secondary concern to the timely delivery of the cargo.

....

1 ››› Ships carrying more than 12 passengers are legally required to have a physician onboard.

RIDE SHARING

n·get·em (en-GEHT-em)   *Indonesian*

verb. For a bus to search for more passengers.

The Indonesian slang word *ngetem* describes an important aspect of overland travel in many developing countries, namely that empty buses do not travel far. Most buses will not depart for their final destination until they are entirely full of either passengers or cargo. Regardless of departure time, regardless of ticket price, regardless of trip length, regardless of weather: buses will either remain parked, circle the city seeking passengers, or frequently stop to try and sell tickets to pedestrians. This is a standard practice that will not be influenced by one upset traveler.

Further, it is important to note that "full" is an extraordinarily culturally relative word. It is not at all unusual for buses to carry twice their intended number of passengers, in addition to significant amounts of cargo, which often include livestock. It is widely understood that a ticket only guarantees a ride on a bus, not a specific, reserved seat. Safety considerations, like seatbelts, are largely ignored and breakdowns due to overloading are common. Wait by the road for a safer, less crowded bus if you wish, but realize that you may be waiting a long time.

MARKETING MISTAKES

Some notable product slogans that have been lost in translation include:

COMPANY	COUNTRY	INTENDED MEANING	COLLOQUIAL TRANSLATED MEANING
Coors	Spain	*"Turn it loose!"*	*"Suffer from diarrhea!"*
Ford	Belgium	*"Every car has a high-quality body."*	*"Every car contains a high-quality corpse."*
Minnesota Valley Canning Company	Saudi Arabia	*"Jolly Green Giant"*	*"Intimidating Green Ogre"*
Parker Pens	Mexico	*"It won't leak in your pocket and embarrass you."*	*"It won't leak in your pocket and make you pregnant."*
Pepsi	China	*"Come alive with the Pepsi Generation!"*	*"Pepsi will bring your ancestors back from the dead!"*
Perdue Chicken	Mexico	*"It takes a tough man to make a tender chicken."*	*"It takes an aroused man to make a chicken affectionate."*
Procter & Gamble	Russia	*"Shampoo and conditioner in one bottle."*	*"Shampoo and an air conditioner in one bottle."*
Schweppes	Italy	*"Schweppes Tonic Water"*	*"Schweppes Toilet Water"*

ON BRIBERY

. . . every lock in Spain is to be picked with a silver key,
and every difficulty smoothed by a properly administered bribe . . .

—RICHARD FORD,

A Handbook for Travellers in Spain, 1847

SOME COMMON TERMS FOR BRIBERY[1]

Note that spelling, pronunciation, and colloquial meaning may vary.

TERM	COMMONLY USED IN	APPLICABLE TRANSLATION
Ashaan ad-dukhaan	Egypt	*"Something for your cigarettes"*
Baksheesh	Multiple countries	*"Gift"*
Chai	Multiple countries	*"Tea"*
Fakelaki	Greece	*"A small envelope"*
Finjaan 'ahwa	Syria	*"A cup of coffee"*
Gaseoso	Angola	*"Soft drink"*
Gum eun don	South Korea	*"Black money"*
Kenopenz	Hungary	*"Oil money"*
Kitu-kidogo	Kenya	*"Small things"*
Komshaw	Multiple countries	*"Present"*
Mordida	Multiple countries	*"Bite"*
Pot-de-vin	France	*"A glass of wine"*
Rasplata	Romania	*"Reward"*
Rusvet	Turkey	*"Pie"*
Schmiergeld	Germany	*"Greasing money"*
Spintarella	Italy	*"A little shove"*

THE COST OF DOING BUSINESS

Travelers should be aware that cultural viewpoints on bribery vary greatly from country to country. People from developed countries tend to view bribery in any form as a shameful sin, an obstacle to fairness and democracy. Yet in many parts of the world bribery is an accepted facet of everyday life. Whether part of a longstanding cultural tradition or the inevitable result of a corrupt government, bribery often isn't considered a complex issue of morality but rather a simple issue of salary. Bribes are thought of as an efficient way to circumvent corrupt government bureaucracies or an ultra-local informal system of taxation or as a surreptitious bonus to ensure prompt service, not as an immoral act of greed.

WHO GETS BRIBED

Bribery is borne of circumstance, not guilt or convenience. The simple, constant truth is that bribes are paid to those who are able to exploit positions of power; any extraneous factors can be disregarded.

Many travelers are inclined to rely on black-and-white concepts of justice or fairness that don't really apply in these situations. Claiming "I've done nothing wrong" doesn't matter: you're not paying for forgiveness. Saying "but this is your job" won't inspire some desperately poor bureaucrat to suddenly realize the error of their ways and abandon any thoughts of corruption. Whether it's a cop claiming some obscure law has been violated or a border official refusing to approve a visa application, all that matters is that a situation exists in which one person has significant power over another and they are choosing to exploit it.

ON LEGALITY

Ethics and finances aside, some travelers worry that paying a bribe will get them into legal trouble, either abroad or when they return home. In most situations, the paying of a bribe is technically illegal but almost never prosecuted. Remember that the official being bribed is likely experienced in dealing with travelers and knows how to conduct the transaction quickly and privately.

Some countries do have laws outlawing their citizens from paying bribes to foreign officials while abroad. However, these laws are generally designed to prevent companies from bribing foreign governments, rather than to prosecute private citizens who pay relatively small bribes while traveling. Citizens of developed countries are almost never prosecuted by their home governments for paying bribes in the course of normal tourism or travel.

ᵛᵛᵛ continued ᵛᵛᵛ

Minimize Leverage

Corrupt officials can only extract bribes when they have the leverage necessary to do so. Properly monitoring the amount of risk you're willing to undertake will help to minimize the amount of money you may need to pay in bribes.

Being pulled over for driving a motorbike in Zanzibar without a Tanzanian license is frustrating, but ultimately a relatively low-stakes situation that may therefore result in a small bribe. Carrying illegal drugs in the Philippines, a crime that is technically punishable by death, is an extremely serious situation in which corrupt police officers have a massive amount of leverage, meaning the resulting bribe, if possible at all, will be much higher.

Be Prepared

When visiting a country in which travelers are regularly forced to pay bribes, prepare yourself for the possibility by carrying small bills, separating money into multiple pockets,[2] and talking to other travelers about the expected cost of local bribes. Also be aware that corrupt officials may be interested in expensive jewelry or electronics.

Know Who You're Dealing With

The first thing to do in a potential bribery situation is to ensure the people you're dealing with are who they say they are. There are a number of scams predicated on con artists impersonating police officers or government officials.[3] Beware of unofficial uniforms or vaguely defined "inspectors."

Once you confirm the legitimacy of the officials, focus on identifying the most senior official present and try to speak with them in private. You want to avoid having to bribe multiple people.

Remain Calm

As if the circumstances weren't already stressful enough, some officials try to intimidate travelers into complying with their demands by acting standoffish, offended, or angry. It is absolutely critical to remain calm. Act friendly to the point of seeming naïve, and apologetic if you've broken any local laws. Acknowledge the authority of the officials and remain polite regardless of their attitude or tactics.

Don't Rush

Travelers who have spent long periods of time in heavily corrupt countries know that the paying of bribes can quickly evolve from a scary and memorable encounter to a repetitive and time-consuming nuisance. Officials rarely ask for a bribe directly and tend to enjoy lecturing foreigners on the complexities of their rule-breaking before getting around to asking for a bribe. No matter how frustrated you may be by the time being spent, to say nothing of the money, allow the official to complete their speech before attempting to move the conversation forward.

Don't Make the First Move

Regardless of how obvious the official's intent may be, never directly offer a bribe. It is essential that you preserve plausible deniability. Discussion of the bribe itself should always be shrouded in euphemisms, whether it's one of the common words for bribery detailed previously or some other locally appropriate term.

The best possible scenario is for the official to blatantly solicit a bribe. At the very least, indirect reference to a payment should result relatively organically from the discussion itself, not from an explicit offer from the traveler.

If the conversation stalls, with neither party wanting to initiate discussion of a bribe , the following are common phrases used to begin the negotiation:

> *"May I pay the fine here and now?"*
> *"I'm sure there must be some other way to settle this matter."*
> *"I'm leaving the area soon,*
> *I'd like to get this figured out before then, if possible."*
> *"Can I make a donation to your organization?"*

Negotiate

While this is heavily dependent on leverage, it is often possible to negotiate the cost of a bribe. Play the part of a friendly but clueless tourist who's earnestly trying, but failing, to navigate the intricacies of this wonderful country. Do not attempt to minimize the seriousness of any local laws you may have broken as this will only offend the official.

Remaining careful to not be too explicit, keep the conversation focused on the amount you can afford to pay to resolve the situation. This is the part of the process where preparation comes into play. There is no more effective negotiating tactic than an empty wallet.

Pass It

Once the amount of the bribe has been decided on, the official will direct you exactly how to physically hand over the money. They will likely have a preferred method of exchange, perfected over years of experience. Whether this is a simple handoff, money placed in an envelope or notebook, or passed literally "under the table," the key here is discretion. Remember that, just as you don't want to bribe multiple officials,

▾▾▾ *continued* ▾▾▾

the official you're bribing doesn't want to have to share the money with the entire department. Note that in some cultures it's customary to hand someone money using both hands and this includes bribes.

Repeat Customers

A bribe is usually a transaction between a traveler and a single official or group of officials, nothing more. It's not a national "get out of jail free" card and corrupt officials often work independently of one another. One of the reasons it's important to remain calm and carefully negotiate a bribe, as opposed to frenziedly handing over some sum of cash, is that you may end up paying multiple bribes for the same offense.

In paying a bribe, try to negotiate whatever future protections you think might be possible, but realize most officials won't provide any assurances. Follow the instructions they provide and immediately come up with a plan to eliminate whatever leverage resulted in the bribe in the first place.

Move On

As costly, stressful, and frustrating as paying bribes can be, don't let it affect your outlook on a country. Only a fool would judge an entire nation's people based on the conduct of one corrupt official. Simply settle the matter in as little time and for as little money as possible and move on with your trip, now armed with the experience to avoid paying bribes in the future.

THE WORLD'S MOST AND LEAST CORRUPT COUNTRIES[4]

MOST CORRUPT	LEAST CORRUPT
North Korea, Somalia	Denmark
Afghanistan	Finland
Sudan	Sweden
Angola, South Sudan	New Zealand
Iraq, Libya	Netherlands, Norway

1 ››› Some sources consider *facilitating payments* or *grease payments* to be technically distinct from bribes. Along that line of thinking, a grease payment involves something to which you are rightfully entitled (like paying extra simply to expedite a visa process) and a bribe involves you normally wouldn't be entitled to (like paying to escape prosecution for a crime you've committed). For the purposes of this section however, both will be referred to as bribes.

2 ››› See page 43 for more information on the two-wallet system.

3 ››› See page 140 for more information on these types of scams.

4 ››› According to Transparency International's *2015 Corruptions Perceptions Index*.

At the time of this writing, the three highest unclimbed mountains in the world are:

NAME	LOCATION	RANGE	ELEVATION	WORLD RANK
Gangkhar Puensum	Border of Bhutan and China	Himalaya	24,840 ft (7,571 m)	40
Four unsuccessful attempts were made before Bhutan banned all mountaineering in 2003 in deference to local religious beliefs that spirits inhabit the summit.				
Muchu Chhish	Northeast Pakistan	Karakoram	24,452 ft (7,453 m)	60[1]
A British team attempted to summit this peak in 2015 but failed due to multiple avalanches, among other issues.				
Labuche Kang III East	Tibet	Himalaya	23,786 ft (7,250 m)	94
Labuche Kang is in one the most inaccessible regions of the Himalayas and is considered extremely technically difficult. An American climber died trying to summit its western peak in 2010; summiting the eastern peak has never been attempted.				

1 ››› Some sources consider Muchu Chhish to be a part of the Batura Muztagh subrange, not a stand-alone mountain. Thus, this world ranking is intended only to compare to its elevation to the rest of the world's highest mountains, not to define its status in the mountaineering community.

ANTARCTIC OWNERSHIP

NO COUNTRY OWNS Antarctica.[1] The Antarctic Treaty of 1959, now signed by 53 countries, dictates the continent can only be used for peaceful scientific purposes and that any country is permitted to conduct research, provided they make their results publicly available.

1 ››› Some countries, like Argentina and Australia, technically still maintain claims to different portions of Antarctica. However, many of these claims are not widely recognized and all were suspended when the treaty was enacted.

FAKE OUT

THE FIRST THING to recognize when considering the purchase of a brand-name item being sold in a touristy area is that, unless it is being sold at an authorized store, it is fake. Though this is sometimes immediately obvious from the quality of the item, vendors will almost always try to convince travelers that they somehow acquired a large amount of expensive designer label products to sell on the street at incredible discounts. Never be fooled, understand that you will be buying a lower-quality item at a much cheaper price, and don't hold out hope you will come across an authentic product among the counterfeits.

The legality of buying counterfeit goods abroad concerns two elements: the actual purchasing of the product, and getting the product through customs upon returning home.

ON BUYING

This issue is heavily dependent on location. In some European countries, notably France and Italy (where, not coincidentally, many of the most-counterfeited brands are based), the purchase of counterfeit goods can result in significant fines, upward of $10,000. These are often deterrent fines: consumers are rarely prosecuted but if they are, they are punished harshly as an example to others. Other countries are far less strict about the purchasing of counterfeit products and they are sold openly with little to no fear of reprisal.

ON BRINGING IT HOME

Many countries allow travelers to bring a small number of counterfeit items through customs, assuming they are for personal use and not resale. Even in countries where importing any amount of counterfeit goods is technically illegal, customs officials are generally focused on more serious crimes. Yet, like the penalties associated with purchasing counterfeits, every once in a while they may make an example out of an unlucky traveler. Always confirm the latest laws and customs regulations as these are always subject to change.

If you decide to buy counterfeit goods, always pay cash. Vendors of counterfeit goods are often already criminals simply by virtue of their profession[1] and so using a credit card may give an unsavory character a good chance to steal your financial information. Avoid purchasing electronics as it is far more difficult to determine quality. Insist on testing anything that can be tested, whether it's the sound quality of headphones or the tensile strength of a handbag. If specific labels aren't of particular importance, look for knockoffs rather than counterfeits as they're often cheaper and, legally, far less risky.

KNOCKOFF

An imitation that does not use trademarked materials like labels or logos.

COUNTERFEIT

A virtually exact copy that uses trademarked materials to intentionally confuse or deceive consumers.

Very, very few travelers who buy and bring home counterfeit or knockoff items ever face repercussions, though specifics are obviously important. You will not be prosecuted for bringing a pair of counterfeit sunglasses through US customs. However, trying to import a suitcase full of fake Gucci handbags into Italy will likely land you in a serious amount of trouble.

1 ››› The selling of counterfeit goods is illegal in far more countries than the buying of counterfeit goods is.

ENVIRONMENTAL MATH

+ A **carbon footprint** is the total amount of harmful greenhouse gases produced by an individual, activity, or organization. As it applies to travel, a carbon footprint refers to the measurable impact a specific mode of transportation, such as a plane flight, has on the environment.

− A **carbon offset** is the equivalent reduction in greenhouse gases needed to theoretically nullify the production of greenhouse gases by an individual, activity, or organization. In the realm of travel, a carbon offset generally refers to the amount of money needed to fund environmental efforts that will compensate for the amount of greenhouse gases produced by a trip.

= Some transportation companies now automatically calculate the carbon footprint of a passenger's trip and offer the customer the option of paying a carbon offset, thus effectively making their trips **carbon neutral**.

[This was a] rare act.

—A spokeswoman for Eastern China Airlines commenting on the story of a Chinese man who exploited a loophole in one of the airline's policies at Xi'an Xianyang International Airport. After discovering that the purchase of first-class, fully refundable ticket granted him access to the VIP lounge and its extensive buffet for a preflight meal, he realized he could essentially eat for free as long as he was scheduled to fly somewhere. He was discovered after the airline noticed he'd rescheduled the same flight more than 300 times. He eventually received a full refund.

ON FINANCES

The heaviest baggage for a traveler is an empty purse.

—ENGLISH PROVERB

PREPARE TO SAVE MONEY

TO MINIMIZE INCONVENIENCE and needless expense, it is best practice to arrange one's finances well in advance of a trip. With such a variety of membership programs and bonus features, the credit card market has become an extremely complex space but, suffice it to say, all credit cards are not created equal. Research card conditions to see what international service fees are charged and, depending on length of trip, consider getting a new credit or debit card specifically for travel. Once you've selected your credit cards, alert the applicable companies that you will be traveling so your cards aren't canceled due to unusual activity. Be sure to carry multiple cards of multiple types as ATMs in many countries are notoriously unpredictable.

Which credit and debit cards to use, and when to use them, depends heavily on the specific finances of a traveler. But as ubiquitous as credit cards have become in developed countries, much of the world's economy is still based in cash. Assume that you'll need to pay cash for most purchases, especially in developing countries, and be sure to keep a reserve stash of dollars hidden in your bag for emergencies. When you need to exchange currency, be sure to consider all factors to ensure you receive the highest possible value for both your money and time. Below is a guide to navigating the complicated world of currency exchange.

TIME IS NOT MONEY

The only thing more valuable to a traveler than a full wallet is an open schedule. Many travelers spend entirely too much time searching for a favorable exchange rate when they actually have little financial incentive to do so.

The amount of time you devote to exchanging money should be a simple function of the amount being exchanged and the stability of the exchange rate. Pick your battles. If you plan on staying in a country for an extended period of time, research historical exchange rates, talk to other travelers, find a favorable rate, and exchange a large sum of money. However, if you've just arrived and only need enough money for a hot meal and a place to sleep, don't waste your day visiting banks and arguing with currency traders. The rates offered by a currency trader at a bus park near the border will undoubtedly be less favorable than at a bank in the capital city. But if you're only exchanging $50, that difference in rates will not be worth losing a day of exploring over. Move on, this is not what you came for and there is much else to do.

WHERE TO TRADE

Where and when one should exchange money is heavily dependent on the infrastructure and economic stability of a country. In theory, the market for a currency should be dictated purely by supply and demand. The value you might hope to receive for the supply of currency you possess should be exactly determined by how much demand exists for that currency. In practice, government manipulation of currency values, international banking fees, and banking withdrawal charges results in that theoretically simple market splintering into a variety of submarkets, each with their own advantages and disadvantages.

OFFICIAL

The most important thing to recognize when trading currency through official means is that exchange rates may be artificially inflated or deflated for reasons having nothing to do with supply and demand. Some governments heavily manipulate their currency through various financial techniques, and this has a more significant effect on the exchange rates offered by official mediums of exchange.

The following options are all birds of the same feather in that they are beholden to those official exchange rates. For instance, credit card

v v continued *v v*

transactions are calculated using exchange rates determined by large international banks, not whatever the "going rate" might be on the street, to say nothing of additional banking fees. Thus, the following official mediums of exchange may be more secure and convenient, but you might not be receiving the highest possible value for your money.

MEDIUM OF EXCHANGE	POTENTIAL ISSUES	TYPICAL EXCHANGE RATE
Bank	Fees; sometimes do not allow non–account holders to exchange currency	↑ *Sometimes dissatisfactory*
ATM	Fees; not available everywhere	
Credit cards	Fees; not accepted everywhere or for smaller purchases	*Frequently very unfavorable*
Currency exchange companies	Fees; not available everywhere	↓

UNOFFICIAL

Street currency traders often offer more competitive exchange rates at the cost of security and, sometimes, legality. Trading currency through unofficial means is technically illegal in many countries, but enforcement varies greatly. Additionally, any transaction where large amounts of cash is involved may be targeted by criminal elements. Be sure to talk to other travelers and research local laws to accurately calculate whether a more favorable exchange rate is worth the risk involved.

If you do choose to trade currency through unofficial means, here are some tips on doing so safely.

Separate

Separate the currency you plan on exchanging from any of other money you might have on you. Prepare a safe hiding place to put the money you receive.

Know the Money

Be generally familiar with what the local currency looks and feels like. Though some counterfeiting techniques can only be detected by experts, many are obvious to the informed amateur.

Know the Math

Street currency exchanges can be loud, hectic affairs, naturally made stressful by the relatively large amounts of money being dealt with.

When you're already concerned about your personal security and the legality of the transaction, it can be difficult to properly double-check necessary calculations.

Further, because some foreign currencies are individually worth such small amounts, exchange-rate math can be particularly confusing for travelers not accustomed to dealing with such high multiples. For instance, a traveler new to Malawi with a single $100 bill to trade might engage in a hasty currency exchange near the border and receive dozens of colorful bills totaling 7,000 Malawi Kwacha. This not only physically feels like a lot of money to the traveler but, knowing the exchange rate to be about 700 to 1, they may initially believe the math to be correct and gratefully declare the transaction to be complete. However, they should have double-checked their figures: $100 is actually worth 70,000 Malawi Kwacha and by the time the traveler realizes this deceit the currency trader will be long gone.

Know the Job

While you should be careful that you aren't scammed, you should also realize that street currency traders work for profit. They are not public servants required to offer a fair market rate; they are businesspeople who expect to be negotiated with. Do not be offended or act impolitely when offered what you consider to be an unfair exchange rate. Engage in a negotiation if you want to; move on if you do not.

RAINBOW BEACHES

COLOR	COMMON CAUSE	NOTABLE EXAMPLE
Black	Basalt	Vik Beach, Iceland
Green	Olivine	Papakōlea Beach, Hawaii, US
Orange	Limestone	Porto Ferro, Sardinia, Italy
Pink	Coral	Pink Sand Beach, Eleuthera, Bahamas
Purple	Manganese garnet	Pfeiffer Beach, California, USA
Red	Iron	Kokkini Beach, Santorini, Greece
White	Quartz	Hyams Beach, New South Wales, Australia

Shape	Oblate spheroid		COSMIC ADDRESS
Equatorial circumference	24,901 mi	40,074 km	Universe ↓ Observable Universe ↓ Laniakea Supercluster ↓ Virgo Supercluster ↓ Local Group ↓ Milky Way Galaxy ↓ Orion Arm ↓ Solar System[3] ↓ Planet Earth
Natural satellites	1 (Moon)		
Artificial satellites	1,419 (operational)		
Axial tilt	23.44°		
Rotational direction	West to east		
Equatorial rotational speed	1,040 mph	1,674 km/h	
Earth orbital speed	67,027 mph	107,870 km/h	
Solar system orbital speed	490,000 mph	788,579 km/h	
Galactic speed	2,237,000 mph	3,600,103 km/h	
Total speed at which everyone on earth is continually moving through the universe[1,2]	-2,795,067 mph	-4,498,226 km/h	

1 ››› As is indicated, those who live near the equator are up to moving 1,040 mph (1,674 km/h) faster than those living nearer to the poles due to the equatorial rotational speed of earth.

2 ››› Interstellar and intergalactic speed measurements are fundamentally relative in that, because all observable objects are in motion, there is no universal frame of reference. There is no stationary object within the universe to measure speed against. Thus, the solar and galactic speeds provided above measure only how fast these objects are moving toward other stars and galaxies—which are also moving. Recent discoveries have even indicated the entire universe itself may be simultaneously expanding and "moving," though toward, from, or through what remains unknown.

3 ››› As unimaginative as it may sound, the official name of the solar system in which earth is located is indeed simply "the Solar System."

MAKE IT A HABIT

IT IS BEST practice to routinely shake out your boots every morning to dislodge whatever might have crawled into them during the night.

SOVEREIGNTY OF THE SEA

The United Nations Law of the Sea Convention dictates the
following rights to the world's oceans:

Exclusive Economic Zone	Coastal country has sole rights to all natural resources	200 nautical miles (230 mi/370 km)
Contiguous Zone	Coastal country can enforce laws related to customs, immigration, pollution, or taxation	24 nautical miles (28 mi/45 km)
Territorial Waters	Coastal country's sovereign territory, though foreign ships must be allowed safe passage	12 nautical miles (14 mi/22 km)

Coastline

Where "international waters" technically begin is occasionally a matter of dispute, but is generally agreed upon to be anything outside of a country's territorial waters. Contrary to popular belief, sailing in international waters does not provide total legal immunity for any crimes committed. Instead, ships in international waters are subject to all laws and regulations of whichever country's flag they fly.[1]

....

1 ››› This is an admittedly imperfect system, as in many situations no other country can enforce laws aboard that ship. Thus, nefarious ship owners have been known to purchase the right to fly the flag of landlocked countries, such as Mongolia, knowing the Mongolian government would likely never spend the resources necessary to prosecute a crime on a ship sailing in international waters on the other side of the world.

————◆————

MAKE IT YOUR OWN

CUSTOMIZE ANYTHING IN your bag that looks generic: things like phone chargers and toothbrushes can easily be mixed up.

The tried-and-true travel tip of adding a colorful identifier to a piece of luggage can help save time in a variety of travel situations.

Note that in parts of Asia, travelers are expected to remove their shoes before entering buildings. If you wear a popular brand of flip-flops or sandals, be sure mark them with a unique design. This will allow you to easily locate your shoes in the pile, which often become massive, disorganized mounds of hundreds of pairs in popular tourist locales.

COUNTRY INTERNET CODES

A COUNTRY CODE top-level **domain** (also known as a ccTLD or country Internet domain) is the unique two-letter domain extension reserved for use by a geographic region or sovereign state. The first country Internet domains were registered in 1985 by the United States, the United Kingdom, and Israel (.us, .uk, and .il, respectively). Since then, many more countries have registered their own country Internet domains, each enacting regulations about who can operate websites using them. Some restrict their use to citizens or businesses within the country, others license them for varying amounts of money, and Central African Republic (.cf), Gabon (.ga), Equatorial Guinea (.gq), and Mali (.ml), allow anyone to use their country Internet domains, free of charge.[1]

As the Internet has evolved into the massive information network it is today, certain domains have dramatically in1creased in value based solely off the spelling of a country's name. Below is a list of some of the most commercially viable country Internet domains currently in use.

ccTLD	COUNTRY	COMMONLY USED TO REFERENCE
.ad	Andorra	Advertising industry
.am	Armenia	AM radio stations
.be	Belgium	*be*
.bz	Belize	Business
.co	Colombia	Corporations
.dj	Djibouti	Music disc jockeys
.fm	(Federated States of) Micronesia	FM radio stations
.in	India	*in*; Internet industry
.is	Iceland	*is*
.it	Italy	*it*; information technology industry
.md	Moldova	Medical industry
.me	Montenegro	*me*

ccTLD	COUNTRY	COMMONLY USED TO REFERENCE
.mu	Mauritius	Music industry
.to	Tonga	*to*
.tv	Tuvalu	Television industry

1 »» These countries allow for free registration to promote use of the Internet among citizens and raise global awareness about their country's Internet presence.

THE WANDERING PHILOSOPHER

I seemed to be possessed by the spirits of wanderlust,
and they all but deprived me of my senses.
The guardian spirits of the road beckoned,
and I could not settle down to work.

—MATSUO BASHŌ,
The Narrow Road to the Deep North, 1694

BORN TO A low-ranking samurai and his wife in 1644, Matsuo Bashō is now considered one of Japan's most influential poets and an unrivaled master of haiku. Historians believe he undertook at least four major trips through Japan, including a 1,200-mile (1,931-kilometer) walk in 1689 that formed the basis for *The Narrow Road to the Deep North*, his masterpiece. In works like *Journals of a Weather-beaten Skeleton* (1685), *Notes in My Knapsack* (1688), and *Monkey's Raincoat* (1691), he wrote haiku about everything from the philosophical wonders of travel:

Traveler's heart,
Never settled long in one place,
Like a portable fire.

To its most banal inconveniences:

Fleas and lice biting,
Awake all night,
A horse pissing close to my ear.

EMBASSIES[1] **ARE THE** channels governments use to do their international bidding. One of their many functions is assisting travelers with a variety of travel, medical, and legal issues such as replacing lost passports, arranging medical care, helping travelers find legal representation, and evacuating citizens during emergencies.

THE POLITICS OF INTERFERENCE

It is important to note that embassies and their employees are high-profile extensions of their home government and, as such, their actions can have wide-ranging political ramifications. For instance, an embassy sending military personnel to assist a traveler would be much more complex than potentially saving the life of a single citizen. It would be an extremely serious geopolitical decision that could be interpreted as tantamount to a declaration of war. In short, embassies are simply resources for travel information and assistance, not dedicated defenders of citizens abroad. Think of embassies like an international network of well-connected friends who may be able to help out in an emergency, not as a protective older sibling always ready to jump in the middle of a fight.

YOU'RE NOT HOME

Contrary to popular belief, embassies are actually not considered territory of the representative country. They are merely a designated part of the host country that has been granted a special exemption from certain laws and regulations. Though citizens of the host country may not enter an embassy without permission, some employees of the embassy are not subject to local laws through diplomatic immunity, and an attack on an embassy is considered an attack on the representative country, the embassy itself is not "part of" or "on the soil of" the country it represents.

NOWHERE TO GO

No nation has an embassy in every country in the world. For example, at the time of this writing the United States maintains no formal diplomatic relations, and thus no embassy, with the nations of Bhutan, Iran, and North Korea. And in addition to matters of hostile geopolitics, there are issues of simple practicality. Though the two countries enjoy a cordial political relationship, the US has no official presence in the tiny island nation of Saint Lucia and all diplomatic business is handled through a shared embassy in nearby Barbados. These sorts of situations are typical throughout the world of international relations, meaning it is not unusual for travelers to find themselves in a country in which their home nation does not have an embassy.

If you find yourself in need of an embassy in a country where your home government has no official representation, the first thing you should do is to get in contact with the embassy of your government in the closest nearby country. Embassy personnel there will be experienced in dealing with similar situations. They will likely direct you to the local embassy of an allied government to whom they have outsourced embassy services. These types of agreements have become increasingly common as many governments have little interest in funding entire embassies in countries with whom they don't have highly developed diplomatic relations. If you know you'll be traveling in countries for extended periods of time where your home government is not represented, research whether an official, wide-ranging relationship is already in place. For instance, Australia and Canada regularly rely on each other's embassies in many countries and all EU member states are required to provide embassy services to all EU citizens. Through the use of these diplomatic alliances most governments are able to provide assistance to their citizens no matter where they happen to be in the world.

....

1››› The precise terminology used to refer to diplomatic missions varies from country to country and may also include *consulate, consulate general, high commission, permanent mission,* and other terms. Specific services offered by each are dependent on the country in question. While normally reserved for a major diplomatic mission in a capital city that houses a country's ambassador, for purposes of this work the term *embassy* will be used to describe any diplomatic mission, regardless of official capacities.

————————◆————————

THE TRAVELING KIND

Like the characters in Chekhov, they have no reserves—
you learn the most intimate secrets. You get an impression of a world peopled
by eccentrics, of odd professions, almost incredible stupidities, and,
to balance them, amazing endurances.

—GRAHAM GREENE,
English author, *The Lawless Roads*, 1939

PARENTS JUST DON'T UNDERSTAND

SOME PARENTS HAVE trouble understanding a young person's motivation for travel. The parent often thinks back to a time when the world was a slightly scarier place and wonders how a few months of travel will affect potential career prospects. The young person's desire to explore is often fueled by largely inexpressible ideas coupled with a seeming lack of regard for the future. And thus an argument inevitably ensues. It may comfort any traveler currently engaged in such a philosophical argument to know that this is an age-old tradition. As long as there have been travelers exploring the earth, there have been worried parents anxiously awaiting their return home.

Below are excerpts from a letter a 22-year-old Charles Darwin wrote to his father, Dr. Robert Darwin, about his desire to join a South American expedition aboard the HMS *Beagle*. This trip would eventually lead to Darwin's theory of evolution and thus could arguably be considered the single-most important journey of the past 500 years.

But in 1831, Charles was simply another newly graduated student, trying to convince a pessimistic father to permit and fund a grand international adventure. In his letter, Charles included a list of his father's specific stated objections and, knowing his deep disapproval of his plan, also enlisted his uncle Josiah Wedgwood to help convince his father of the value of this potential journey. Included in this reprinting are the counterpoints that Wedgwood later sent to help persuade Dr. Darwin.

My dear Father,
I am afraid I am going to make you again very uncomfortable.
But upon consideration, I think you will excuse me once again
stating my opinions on the offer of the Voyage . . .

[DR. ROBERT DARWIN'S OBJECTIONS,
ALONG WITH JOSIAH WEDGWOOD'S COUNTERPOINTS.]

» **Disreputable to my character as a Clergyman hereafter.**
I should not think that it would be in any degree disreputable to his character as a Clergyman. I should on the contrary think the offer honourable to him; and the pursuit of Natural History, though certainly not professional, is very suitable to a clergyman.

» *A wild scheme.*

I hardly know how to meet this objection, but he would have definite objects upon which to employ himself, and might acquire and strengthen habits of application, and I should think would be as likely to do so as in any way in which he is likely to pass the next two years at home.

» *That they must have offered to many others before me, the place of Naturalist.*

The notion did not occur to me in reading the letters; and on reading them again with that object in my mind I see no ground for it.

» *And from its not being accepted there must be some serious objection to the vessel or expedition.*

I cannot conceive that the Admiralty would send out a bad vessel on such a service. As to objections to the expedition, they will differ in each man's case, and nothing would, I think, be inferred in Charles's case, if it were known that others had objected.

» *That I should never settle down to a steady life hereafter.*

You are a much better judge of Charles's character than I can be. If on comparing this mode of spending the next two years with the way in which he will probably spend them, if he does not accept this offer, you think him more likely to be rendered unsteady and unable to settle, it is undoubtedly a weighty objection. Is it not the case that sailors are prone to settle in domestic and quiet habits?

» *That my accommodations would be most uncomfortable.*

I can form no opinion on this further than that if appointed by the Admiralty he will have a claim to be as well accommodated as the vessel will allow.

» *That you should consider it as again changing my profession.*

If I saw Charles now absorbed in professional studies I should probably think it would not be advisable to interrupt them; but this is not, and, I think, will not be the case with him. His present pursuit of knowledge is in the same track as he would have to follow in the expedition.

» *That it would be a useless undertaking.*

The undertaking would be useless as regards his profession, but looking upon him as a man of enlarged curiosity, it affords him such an opportunity of seeing men and things as happens to few.

The letter was ultimately successful. Robert Darwin relented and allowed Charles to undertake what was supposed to be a two-year jour-

▼▼▼ *continued* ▼▼▼

ney. Charles returned five years later, having conducted fieldwork in some of the world's most unusual ecosystems and circumnavigated the planet. With him he brought the knowledge and experience that would eventually challenge the very foundations of all life on earth.

BUGS IN THE BED

CIMEX LECTULARIUS
Actual size

CIMEX LECTULARIUS
Magnified 5X

BEDBUGS ARE SMALL, fast, and typically more active at night, all of which makes them difficult to see with the naked eye.

TEST YOUR ROOM

Before moving luggage into the room,[1] thoroughly inspect the blankets, sheets, headboard, mattress pad, mattress and surrounding area with a flashlight. Note that bedbugs can reside in almost any material, from cotton sheets to a wooden desk. It would be rare to see an actual bedbug; instead look for any rust- or black-colored stains or dots. These are bloodstains, indicators that a bedbug has fed in that location. True to their name, the large majority of bedbugs are found within about 10 feet (3 meters) of the bed.

TEST YOURSELF

Though people can have a wide range of reactions to bedbugs, the most common symptoms are red bite marks in groups of three, often in a straight line. These bites can take a few days to appear and may cause swelling or itching. Bedbugs do not transmit disease.

If you've been bitten, you will need to ensure you eradicate bedbugs from your clothes and possessions. While bedbugs don't live on humans like lice or fleas, they can infest many of the items in a traveler's bag. Wash all clothes at the highest acceptable temperatures, in excess of 110°F (43°C) is recommended. Separate all potentially infested nonwashable items into plastic bags and carefully check for remaining bedbugs.

---

1 ››› Another option is putting your luggage in the bathtub, one of the least likely places to find bedbugs.

The would-be explorer must now shift for himself. A book, however complete, can be of no further use to him; he must learn from that hardest of taskmasters, "experience," how to meet difficulties and dangers on their own ground and to grapple with them on equal terms without the aid of the vast powers of science and civilisation to help him in overcoming them.

And yet, if these few pages have drawn aside the curtain, so as to show just a glimpse of the interior life of this great mysterious land, and if these few words of advice and direction have served to make the path of the wanderer a little bit smoother or not quite so intricate; or even if the stay-at-home who reads these same pages as he sits by his comfortable fireside, disturbed only by the rain which patters on the window panes or drips on the roof, has been able to picture to himself the great continent as it stretches in undisturbed solitudes far from the roar and traffic of the great city, and to put himself for one short hour in the place of the wanderer in all his successes and disappointments, and can feel with him in the dull strain of anxiety or the quick sigh of relief—if these things are brought about, then I think that this book will not have been written in vain.

—W. O. CAMPBELL

Through Patagonia, 1901

INDEX

AAirpass (American Airlines), 24
ABBA, 228
accommodations
    oldest hotel, 169
    overbooking, 176–177
    scams related to, 144–147
Adams, Ansel, 72
Adams, Douglas, 138
Adventurers Club, 88
advisories, 92–93
African animals, 50–51
Agloe, New York, 137
air distress calls, 230
air-to-ground communication, 26
air travel, 231
    air rage, 227
    around-the-world tickets (RTW
        tickets), 156–157
    London-to-Sydney itinerary
        (1939), 66
    longest and shortest flights, 55
    most passengers on a flight, 206
    safety of, 128
    Skytrax, 109
    supersonic flights, 119
    turbulence, 167
airlines
    fictional, for media, 60
    Great Lounge War, 179
    overbooking, 176–177
    pilots who fall asleep, 128
    pregnancy policies, 167
    proof of onward travel for, 42
    ticket prices, 38
Alcock, John, 193
alcohol, 231
Aldrin, Edwin "Buzz," 160–161
Alexander, Crown Prince of
        Yugoslavia, 203
aliases, of traveling celebrities, 204
Alpers, Ernest, 137
altitude sickness, 46–49
America (airship), 26
American Airlines, 179
Amundsen, Roald, 88
Andersen, Hans Christian, 36
animals. See wildlife
Antarctica, 24, 249

Apollo 11 astronauts, 160
Apollo 13 astronauts, 134
Arabian Oryx Sanctuary, 61
arctic tundra, mirages in, 82
Armstrong, Louis, 81
Armstrong, Neil, 160
Arnold, Walter, 120
around-the-world tickets, 156–157
asolare, 226
ATMs, 146, 252
Australia, 93, 94, 191
avalanches, 189

baboons, 220
baby technique (pickpocketing), 151
bacheques, 231
Backpacker Index, 211
backpacks, preventing theft of, 26
Ballano, Ada Colau, 230
Banda, Hastings Kamuzu, 176
banned products, 139
Barcelona, Spain, 230
Barrington, Sir Johan, 229
Barry, Dave, 197
Bashō, Matsuo, 259
beaches, colors of, 255
bears, 217–218
bedbugs, 264
beverages
    alcohol, 231
    amount of drinking water for
        activities, 128
    offerings of, 233
    safety of drinking water, 85, 116
    saying "cheers," 128
big bill scam, 144–145
Big Five, 136
births during international travel,
        202–203, 206
Bislama, 131
black market, 192
black rats, 91
Black Sea, 200
blizzards, 189
blue market, 192
blue zones, 169
body gestures, 240–241
Bolivia, 78

boots, shaking out, 256
border crossings. *See also* visas
    differences among, 81
    having your own pens for, 80
    proof of onward travel for, 40–42
    and unstamped passports, 172
border restrictions, in Schengen Area, 130
border run, 77
borders, 208–209
bowline knot, 159
breakfast traditions, 238
bribery, 244–248
bribes, 81
British passports, 43
broken glass scam, 148
Brown, Arthur, 193
Brown, H. Jackson, Jr., 55
buffalo, 218
Burnett, Edward, 119
Burton, Sir Richard, 86
bus trips, 242–243
Byron, Robert, 212

Calypso, 211
cameras, 72–75
Campbell, W. O., 267
Canada, 25, 93, 191
capitals
    of countries, 2, 4, 6, 8, 10, 12, 14, 16
    of independent states, 18
    of territories, 18, 20, 22
car rentals
    damaged rental scam, 143
    overbooking, 176–177
carbon footprint, 251
carbon neutral trips, 251
carbon offset, 251
Cardozo, Benjamin, 190
cargo ship travel, 242
cartography, 102–103. *See also* maps
celebrity aliases, 204
Charles, Jacques, 229
Charlotte of Mecklenburg-Strelitz, princess, 229
"Cheers," 128–129
chimpanzees, 220
China, 83, 191
Churchill, Winston, 161
circumnavigation, 108–109
cities, most expensive, 83

Claridge's Hotel, London, 203
climbing
    altitude sickness, 46–49
    unclimbed mountains, 249
clock times, 224
cloud, uploading photos to, 75
clumsy thief technique (pickpocketing), 152
Collins, Michael, 160
Columbus, Christopher, 223
combination locks, 194, 195
commonwealth realms, 107
communication, 197–199. *See also* language(s)
    by phone (*See* phone calls)
    significance of free speech, 222–223
Continental Airlines, 179
Coordinated Universal Time (UTC), 224
Coriolis force/effect, 66
corruption, 244–248
cosmonauts, 70
counterfeit currency, 179
counterfeit goods, 250–251
countries
    borders of, 208–209
    commonwealth realms, 107
    date formats of, 51
    endonyms and exonyms for, 185
    general information on, 1–18
    international dialing prefixes, 104–105
    Internet censorship and surveillance by, 181
    landlocked, 196
    measurement systems of, 51
    monarchies, 105–107
    most corrupt, 248
    notable national flags, 58
    population density rankings, 118
    pronouncing names of, 36–37
    queuing etiquette in, 191
    in Schengen Area, 130
    side of road for driving in, 135
    territories associated with, 18–23
    travel freedom ranking of, 46
    very small, relative size of, 101
country codes
    of independent states, 18
    of specific countries, 2, 4, 6, 8, 10, 12, 14, 16

country Internet codes, 258–259
Cousteau, Jacques, 211
Crandall, Robert, 24
credit card scams, 146
credit cards, 252–254
crime
    digital attacks, 153–154
    pickpocketing, 141, 151–153
    prequalifiers for, 141, 142
    scams, 141–150
    theft, 26, 39, 117, 141, 194–195
    tips for avoiding, 140
crocodiles, 218
currency
    exchange rates, 252–254
    foreign, acceptance of, 179
    of independent states, 19
    royalty pictured on, 38
    small goods given instead of change
      for, 95
    of specific countries, 3, 5, 7, 9, 11,
      13, 15, 17
    street traders for, 254–255
    of territories, 19, 21, 23
    of United States, 137
    in unstable economies, 95
    Zimbabwean dollars, 40
currency confusion scam, 148
currency conversion scam, 145
customer service, 207
customizing possessions, 257
customs, 90–91, 160
cut bag scam, 143
cut infections, 117
cyclones, 190

damaged rental scam, 143
danger
    from large animals, 216–222
    perception of, 35
    travel advisories, 92–93
    when confronted with criminals,
      143
Darwin, Charles, 262–264
Darwin, Robert, 262–263
date formats, 51
debit cards, 252
declining requests/pitches, 44–45
DEET (diethyltoluamide), 52–53
Delaware, incorporating in, 192
deserts, mirages in, 82

deterrents, theft, 194
Dhaka, Bangladesh, 118
diethyltoluamide (DEET), 52–53
digital attacks, 153–154
Dion, Céline, 228
directions, nautical, 205
Disraeli, Benjamin, 130
distance to horizon, estimating, 210
distress calls, 230
diving, 58–59
dogs, wild, 222
double-landlocked countries, 196
dream rental scam, 144
Dresden Elbe Valley, 61
driving
    damaged rental scam, 143
    international driving permits,
      200–201
    side of road for, 135
dromomania, 37
drop bear, 94
drug dealer scam, 148
drugs, legality of, 202
durian, 60

early checkout scam, 145
Earth
    facts about, 256
    shape of, 223
earthquakes, 188
Eastern China Airlines, 252
Eberhardt, Isabelle, 163
El Al Airlines, 206
electric service, 233–237
    in independent states, 19
    in specific countries, 3, 5, 7, 9, 11,
      13, 15, 17
    in territories, 19, 21, 23
electronic devices
    digital attacks, 153–154
    drying out, 64–65
    finding chargers for, 237
    governments' monitoring of,
      180–181
    smartphones, 186
elephants, 219
Elizabeth II, Queen, 43
elk, 221
embassies, 92, 260–261
emergency phone numbers, 241
Emerson, Ralph Waldo, 184, 195

employers, world's largest, 215
endonyms, 185
Enrique of Malacca, 108–109
etiquette
    queuing, 191
    tipping, 90
European rabbits, 91
Eurovision Song Consent, 228
exchange rates, 252–254
    currency confusion scam, 148
    for Zimbabwean dollars, 40
exonyms, 185
expatriates, 209
Explorers Club, 87–88

fake ATMs, 146
fake demo scam, 145
fake ticket agent scam, 147
Fellows, Charles, 70
fernweh, 36
fight technique (pickpocketing), 152
film production, in India, 155
finances, arranging, 252–255
first date scam, 149
first-night effect (FNE), 175
flags, 58, 232
flip-flops, 39
floods, 189
food(s)
    American items in foreign grocery
        stores, 63
    availability of, 24
    durian, 60
    new, 84
    snacks, 24
    specificity of menus, 127
    spicy dishes, 119
forced purchase scams, 146
Ford, Richard, 244
free speech, 222–223
friendly tour guide scam, 149
Frost, Robert, 162–163
Fucking, Austria, 117

Gall, James, 103
gedogen, 202
Gerbner, George, 125
gestures, 239–241
giant African land snail, 91
Gibbon, Edward, 183
Gimbels, 26

gold ring scam, 150
goods, counterfeit, 250–251
graffiti, 204, 227
grand tours, 183
gray market, 192
Great Lounge War, 179
Greene, Graham, 126, 261
Greenland National Park, 37
Greiter, Franz, 120, 121
Gubin, Mark, 157
guidebooks, rankings in, 97

hacking, 153–154
haggling, 212–215
Haise, Fred, 134
Hall, Mary, 141
hand gestures, 239–240
Handler, Daniel (Lemony Snicket),
    170
Hawes, William, 70
Hazlitt, William, 186
health/medical issues, 110–117
    altitude sickness, 46–49
    bedbugs, 264
    cut infections, 117
    drinking water, 116
    financial protections for, 117
    infectious diseases with
        vaccinations, 113
    malaria, 113–115
    motion sickness, 132
    motorbike, scooter, motorcycle
        accidents, 117
    pharmaceutical packing, 116–117
    psychological symptoms involving
        travel, 125
    seasickness, 132–133
    sunburn protection, 120–124
    vaccinations, 110–113
    wildlife injuries, 50–51
hero technique (pickpocketing), 153
Heyerdahl, Thor, 207
hidden charges scam, 147
Hillary, Sir Edmund 88
hippopotamus, 219
Hobo Code of Ethics, 71
Hong Kong, 83
Höppl, Siegfried, 117
hot air ballooning, 229
Howe, Lord Geoffrey, 61
hurricanes, 190

Huxley, Aldous, 92
Hyena, 220

Ibn Battuta, 203
ice thic ss, for safety, 199
ichigo ichie, 184
illegal actions
    concerning royalty, 38
    photography, 73
illegal transactions, 192–193
Imperial Airways, 66
independent states, 16, 18, 19
India, 155
inferior mirages, 82
*Information and Directions for
    Travellers on the Continent*
    (Starke), 97
ink technique (pickpocketing), 151
insect repellent, 52–53
instant escape technique
    (pickpocketing), 153
International Certificate of
    Vaccination of Prophylaxis
    (ICVP), 112–113
international dialing prefixes, 104–105
international driving permits (IDPs),
    200–201
International Union for Conservation
    of Nature (IUCN), 32
international waters, 257
Internet
    censorship and surveillance of,
        180–181
    connections for, 154
Inuit people, 25
invasive species, 90–91
Irving, Washington, 223
islands on lakes on islands on lakes on
    islands, 25
Israeli passport stamp, 172
"It's Greek to me," 30–31
IUCN Red List, 32–33

Japan, 191, 201
Java, Indonesia, 118
jellyfish stings, 50
Jerusalem syndrome, 125
Juvenal, 43

Kaaba, Mecca, Saudi Arabia, 157
Kelly, Scott, 154

Kerouac, Jack, 135
Kiddo (cat), 26
Kilroy, James J., 227
"Kilroy was here," 227
Kim Jong-nam, 232
Kim Jong-un, 232
Kit Kats, 201
Kitchiner, William, 116
Kitlineq Island, Canada, 25
kiwis, 39
knockoff goods, 251

lactose intolerance, 231
landlocked countries, 196
language(s), 197–199
    declining things, 44–45
    endonyms and exonyms, 185
    foreign, stress in trying to speak, 40
    mai pan rai, 178
    most widely understood words, 84
    multiple, terms for people who
        speak, 26
    phrases for misunderstandings in,
        30–31
    product slogans, 243
    proficiency in, 34–35
    saying "smile" in, 72
    in Vanuatu, 131
    words designating outsiders, 27–29
    words/phrases for "cheers," 128–129
    writing systems, 54–55
latitude, 196
law enforcement, 193
Le Sueur, Alec, 84
Lee, Laurie, 129
leeches, 50
legal issues
    attacks during air travel, 227
    bribery, 245
    concerning royalty, 38
    counterfeit goods, 250–251
    drug enforcement laws, 202
    enforcement of local laws, 206–207
    photography, 73
    with transactions, 192–193
    vandalization/graffiti, 204
Leka, Prince of Albania, 203
Liechtenstein, 196
light scale scam, 146
Lindberg, Otto G., 137
Lindbergh, Charles, 193

Living Poor (Thomsen), 34
Livingstone, David, 85
locks, 194–195
London, England, 83
longevity zones, 169
Longfellow, Henry Wadsworth, 82
longitude, 196
Lovell, Jim, 134
Luanda, Angola, 83
Lucian of Samosata, 228
Luigi Amedeo, Prince of Italy, 70

Magellan, Ferdinand, 108, 109
mai pan rai, 178
mailing souvenirs, 182
malaria, 113–115
Malawi, 176
map technique (pickpocketing), 151
maps
    trap streets on, 137
    types of projections, 102–103
Margriet Francisca, Princess of the
        Netherlands, 203
Masefield, John, 85
Mean World syndrome, 125
measurements, 51
medical issues. *See* health/medical
        issues
Mercator, Gerardus, 102
Meri, Lennart, 102
Metallica, 24
metric system, 51
mirages, 82
Mitchell International Airport, 157
monarchies and monarchs, 105–107.
        See also royalty
monkeys, 220
Montgolfier brothers, 229
Moon, 134, 192
moose, 221
More, Sir Thomas, 76–77
Most Traveled People, 89
motion sickness, 132
motorbike/motorcycle accidents, 117
mountains, unclimbed, 249
Muir, John, 69
*Murphy v. Steeplechase Amusement
        Co.,* 190

National Geographic Society, 87
natural disasters, 188–190

nautical directions, 205
Nepal, 58
Nestlé, 201
Netherlands, 202
New Guinea, 100
New York City, 83
New Zealand, 39
ngetem, 242–243
Nisiyama Onsen Keiunkan hotel,
        Japan, 169
Nixon, Richard, 81
nomophobia, 186
North Pole, 56

Oceanic Airlines/Airways (fictional), 60
old woman technique (pickpocketing),
        152
omertà, 158
Operation Solomon, 206
Orwell, George, 197
Ottawa Civic Hospital, Canada, 203
outsiders, words designating, 27–29
overbooking, 176–177

packing, 70–71
parachuting through thunderstorm,
        139
paradises, 158
Paraguay, 58
Paris syndrome, 125
Parrish, Donald M., Jr., 89
Parry, Sir William, 25
passport(s), 170–175
    British, 43
    numbers on, 174
    for pets, 168–169
    photographs for, 170–171
    protecting, 173–175
    of Ramses II, 160
    for Schengen Area, 130
    secondary, 173
    stamping of, 172–173
Peace Corps, 34
Peary, Robert, 170
Peru, 75
Pes, Gianni, 169
Pet Travel Scheme (PETS), 168–169
Peters, Arno, 103
petition technique (pickpocketing), 152
pharmaceutical packing, 116–117
Philippines, 25

phone calls
    emergency phone numbers, 241
    international dialing prefixes,
        104–105
photographs, passport, 170–171
photography, 72–75
Pickhardt, Otto C., 161
pickpocketing, 151–153
picture technique (pickpocketing),
    152
population densities, 118
postal services, 182
Poulain, Michel, 169
pregnancy, airline policies concerning,
    167
prevention, theft, 194–195
prices
    Backpacker Index, 211
    haggling, 212–215
    in most expensive cities, 83
    selective, 76
    specificity of, 126
product slogans, 243
proof of onward travel, 40–42
psychological symptoms involving
    travel, 125

Qantas Airways, 66
qibla pointers, 157
queuing etiquette, 191

Ramses II, 160
Rand McNally, 137
Rankin, William, 139
ranking/rating systems
    for air travel, 109
    for restaurants, 164–165
    for sights, 97
Read, Albert C., 193
Red List (IUCN), 32–33
Red Sea, 200
relationships with fellow travelers, 184
resfeber, 215
restaurants
    rankings, 164–165
    specificity of menus, 127
rip-off scam, 143
riptides, escaping, 30
rivers, navigating, 166
"The Road Not Taken" (Frost),
    162–163

Robinson, Arthur H., 103
romance, 187
Rondôna tribes, 99–100
Roosevelt, Theodore, 88
Root, Amos Ives, 159
Ross, Sir John, 25
Rothstein, Steve, 24
Royal Geographical Society, 86
Royal Menagerie, Tower of London,
    119
royalty, 38
    declaring sovereign territory for
        births in foreign nations,
        202–203
    passports for, 43
RTW tickets, 156–157
Rules of 3, 96

Sacheuse, John, 25
safaris, 50–51
St. John Baptist de la Salle, 31
Samoa Air, 38
SanDisk, 74
Sandton Medical Clinic,
    Johannesburg, South Africa,
    203
scams, 141–150
Schengen Area, 130
scooter accidents, 117
Scotland, 94
Scott, Robert Falcon, 86
scuba diving certification, 58–59
sea distress calls, 230
seas, 133, 200
seasickness, 132–133
seasons, shoulder, 75
selective pricing, 76
Sentinelese, 99
Serrano, Juan, 108–109
Seven Seas, 133
Seven Summits, 134
Seven Wonders of the World, 67–69
sexuality, expressions of, 187
Shakespeare, William, 30
sharks, 216
Shaw, George Bernard, 35
Sheldon, Mary French, 198
shipping souvenirs, 182
shipwreck categories, 138
Shlim, David, 49
shopping scams, 144–147

shoulder seasons, 75
show technique (pickpocketing), 153
singing competition, 228
Skunk Works, 119
Skytrax, 109
slow service scam, 147
smartphones, 186
smiling, 72, 131
snacks, 24
snakebites, 51, 221
snakes, 221
snow, experience with, 231
South Pole, 57
souvenirs, mailing, 182
sovereignty of the sea, 257
space travel, physical changes from, 154
specificity, 126
speeding violations, 120
Starke, Mariana, 97
Steinbeck, John, 45
Stevens, Thomas, 70
Stevenson, Robert Louis, 165
storms, distance of, 205
street currency traders, 254–255
street game scam, 148–149
street salesmen, 44–45
street scams, 148–150
stuck zippers, 205
sudden closure scam, 149
sudden technique (pickpocketing),
    151
summits, 134
sunburn protection, 120–124
sunglasses, 39
superior mirages, 82
supersonic flights, 119
survival times
    Rules of 3 for, 96
    in water, 65
swarm technique (pickpocketing), 151
Swigert, Jack, 134
Switzerland, flag of, 58

taxes, entry/exit, 81
taxis, 143–144, 149
temperature measurements, 51
territorial disputes, 208–209
territories, 18–23, 104–105
Thatcher, Margaret, 61
theft. *See also* crime
    backpacks, 26

flip-flops or sunglasses, 39
of Fucking, Austria, signs, 117
locks for preventing, 194–195
of passport, 175
pickpocketing, 141, 151–153
Theroux, Paul, 158
Thicknesse, Philip, 142
Thompson, Chuck, 209
Thomsen, Moritz, 34
Thoreau, Henry David, 142
threatened species, 32–33
ticket scalpers, 147
time issues
    clock times, 224
    specificity of given times, 126, 127
    "wasting," 226
time zones, 223–225
    of countries, 3, 5, 7, 9, 11, 13, 15, 17
    of independent states, 19
    of territories, 19
tipping etiquette, 90
tornadoes, 188–189
tour group traitor technique
    (pickpocketing), 152
tourism
    local costs of, 230
    unconventional types of, 96
tourist police scam, 150
tourists
    separate pricing for, 76
    urban local beast myths told to,
        94–95
tours
    grand tours, 183
    overbooking, 176–177
traffic jams, 83
Trans World Airlines (TWA), 179
transatlantic flights, 26, 193
transportation scams, 143–144
trap streets, 137
travel
    feelings accompanying, 215
    longing for, 36
    proof of onward travel, 40–42
    specificity of given times, 126, 127
    talking to others about, 31
travel advisories, 92–93
travel clubs, 86–89
travel code, 34
travel freedom rankings, 46
Travel Sentry, 194

travelers
  choices for, 162–163
  full-time, 209
  parents' misunderstanding of, 252
  registration/enrollment programs, 92
Travelers' Century Club, 89
tribes, uncontacted, 98–100
tsunamis, 188
Twain, Mark, 132
two-wallet system, 43
typhoons, 190

ultraviolet index (UV index; UVI), 123
uncontacted tribes, 98–100
United Airlines, 179
United Kingdom, 93, 226
United Nations Educational,
    Scientific, and Cultural
    Organization (UNESCO),
    61–63
United States
  currency of, 137
  embassies of, 260–261
  jackalope, 95
  queuing etiquette in, 191
  reciprocal visa policies, 78
  travel advisories of, 93
  travel warnings about, 177
unlockable locker scam, 144
unzip and grab technique
    (pickpocketing), 152
Utopia (More), 76–77
Uzbekistan, 196

vaccinations, 110–113
vandalism, 204
Vaniman, Melvin, 26
Vanuatu, 131
Vatican City, 58
Venice, Italy, 230
victim scam, 150
Victoria Island, Canada, 25

visa run, 77
visas, 77–81
  applications, 77, 170–171
  denial of, 78–80
  photos, 170–171
  proof of onward travel, 40–42
  reciprocal policies, 77–78
  for Schengen Area, 130
  and travel freedom rankings, 46
volcanoes, 190
von Neumann, John, 198
Vulcan Point, Philippines, 25

wallets, 43
warning technique (pickpocketing), 153
water
  direction in draining of, 66–67
  drinking water, 85, 116
  survival times in, 65
Wedgwood, Josiah, 262–263
Wellman, Edith, 26
Wellman, Walter, 26
white market, 192
White Sea, 200
wild dogs, 222
wildfires, 190
wildlife
  Big Five, 136
  dangerous, 216–222
  dealing with injuries from, 50–51
windfall scam, 150
wonders of the world, 67–69
words, most widely understood, 84.
    See also language(s)
World Heritage Sites, 61–63
Wright brothers, 159
writing systems, 54–55

Yellow Sea, 200
yoko meshi, 40

zoos, admissions fees for, 119

ACKNOWLEDGMENTS

IN WORKING ON this book, I have been the recipient of more generosity than any one person rightfully deserves. Far more people than can possibly be listed here have contributed their time and efforts to this project and I will forever be in their debt. To all those omitted, especially friends throughout Baltimore, Washington D.C., New York, and Texas, know that I won't ever forget your support over the past years.

To my agent, Cindy Uh of Thompson Literary Agency: thank you for taking a chance on an unpublished wannabe with an offbeat idea. Through every step of this process, you've helped me focus my passion while fiercely protecting the integrity of my work. Thanks too to Meg Thompson and everyone else at the wonderful Thompson Literary Agency for their expertise and support.

To my editor, Lisa Tenaglia of Black Dog & Leventhal: as a first-time writer working in a little-known genre, I could not have asked for a kinder and more gifted editor to work alongside. You carefully considered every idea, provided countless insights, and have been an absolute pleasure to work with. Your patience and intelligence made this book enormously better; thank you for everything. Thanks also to everyone at Black Dog & Leventhal, as well as Hachette, especially J. P. Leventhal, Maureen Winter, Michelle Aielli, Kara Thornton, Odette Fleming, Mike Olivo, and Ankur Ghosh, for their hard work.

To Paul Kepple and Max Vandenberg at Headcase Design: thank you for approaching every page of this project with creativity and expertise. You skillfully adapted this wildly divergent mix of ideas and introduced a myriad of superb new design innovations. In short, your excellent work turned my jumble of concepts into a gorgeous book. Thank you.

To all the friends I've met abroad, especially: Ally, Katia, Nishal, Damion, Tim, Scottie, Ryan, Sanna, Sarah, Craig, Anja, Clara, Marloes, Mark, Daragh, Gerry, Danilo, Mike, Gabe, Laoise, Tom, Adi, Pete, Ronnie, Allison, Molly, Rachel, and Lizzie: I love you all. Keep going. I'll see you back out on the road.

To Al in Tabora, Tanzania: we met at the Golden Eagle hotel. After a few terrible days of traveling, I had begun to question why I went out exploring at all. You invited me to a holiday celebration, introduced me to your lovely family, and we talked for hours. I have never forgotten the kindness you showed me that day and I never will. People like you are the reason I travel. Thank you.

To Katrin and Nikolas: we met in southern Uganda and I stayed at your home in Kigali. Your instant, almost reflexive, generosity personifies what I love about exploring. Wherever you are now, thank you.

To the von Klencke family of Hämelschenburg, Germany: you have always been such gracious hosts to myself and my family. Your generous invitations have inspired many a European trip, to say nothing of Henry's and my adventure in Russia. Thank you for your continual kindness and hospitality.

To Kathy Hudson and Greg Otto: you two have been incredibly supportive of me, and are always ready with a kind word or a key piece of advice to help me navigate this unconventional path. Thank you.

Thanks also to: Charlie Totten and Lauren Marks, Andrew Williams, Eli Dresner, Mac and Ann Williams, the entire Bozman crew, Michael Carrington, the whole Friendsgiving crew down in the district, Scott Pressimone, C. Alexander "Sandy" London, Brian Kevin, Stacy Schiff, and the staffs of the public libraries of Baltimore, Brooklyn, and Boothbay Harbor.

To Peter and Abby Jackson: for help with marketing and design, and for always being positive, encouraging friends.

To Matt and Sarah Pope: for being incredibly supportive friends who have helped this book in far too many ways to list here.

To Matt Owens: for being an extraordinarily kind and loyal friend, as well as a true tech mastermind.

To Isaac Boltansky: for your thoughtfulness and friendship over the past two decades. You have always been a trusted source of advice, as well as an exceedingly generous and caring friend.

To Nick Silbergeld: this book wouldn't have happened without you, plain and simple. The Brooklyn days of Halloween Dog, shooting pool, and dive bars were not only incredibly fun, they were critical to the creation of this book. Thank you.

To Nick and Kate Colvin: you two have been the most unbelievably supportive, thoughtful, incredible friends along every step of this long journey. Since the very beginning, you've encouraged me in every pursuit and helped me immensely in following this dream. Thank you.

To Meg: for innumerable meals, gifts, introductions to helpful friends and contacts, and so many other generosities. You are one of the most selfless people I've ever known and have been a constant source of love and encouragement.

To Burge: for always being unfailingly positive, optimistic, and supportive.

To Drum: I can't possibly do justice to all the ways you've helped both me and this book. Ideas were formed over late night New York City dinners, pages were begun when I was living in your apartment, and you've always been an incredibly close friend and advisor. You are an integral part of why this book exists and I'll never forget your kindness, generosity, and friendship.

To Colin: you're the best brother a guy could ask for and one the most truly thoughtful, kind people I know. I'm proud of you in everything that you do, thank you for your unwavering support.

To Molly: your compassion and dedication to helping people is a continual inspiration to me. You're the greatest sister in the world and I can't thank you enough for your love and encouragement.

To Mom and Dad: thank you for everything. I am, by far, the luckiest person I know and that is entirely because of you two. You have fully supported me in everything I have ever done and I love you more than I'll ever be able to express. Thank you.

This book was written in loving memory of Jeff Rice, Nancy McFadden, Dorothy McFadden, John McFadden, Betty Jane Rice, and Romney "Bud" Rice.

ILLUSTRATION CREDITS

ABOUT THE AUTHOR

Tonight is the night that I am going to travel. I have to go through pirate ships, in haunted houses, and through pumpkin patches. This will be an adventure. I hope I come back sometime but I do not care when.

I'm going to pack good things—food, weapons, and things like that, but I hope I do not have to brush my teeth. I am Evan the Adventurer.

I'm going to go to candy stores on the way because I might run out of candy. I am going to be a farmer for Halloween. This note is from Evan Rice.

—A LETTER BY THE AUTHOR,
age 6½, written with the help of his mom, October 1992

EVAN S. RICE has spent more than two years on the road, traveling alone through 32 countries on six continents. He's loved everywhere he's ever been and doesn't play favorites, but thinks more people should check out **Colombia**, **Malawi**, **Mozambique**, and northern **Malaysia**. While traveling, he enjoys collecting **knockoff Rubik's cubes** and **beer labels**. His preferred mode of transport is by **train**. On long rides, he can be found passing the time **reading** and watching **sci-fi movies**. He continues to worry about running out of candy. Some of the best candies he's come across in his journeys are **Crunchies** (UK), white chocolate **Sublimes** (Peru), **Prince Polos** (Poland), and **Mogul Duos** (Argentina).

Selected travel highlights include:

» *Hiking in* **Patagonia**

» *Sampling street food in* **Penang**

» *Bartending in* **Buenos Aires**

» *Voice acting in* **Livingstone**

» *Relaxing in* **Santa Marta**

» *Exploring in* **Siem Reap**

» *Homestaying in* **Ivanovo**

» *Studying in* **Perth**

» *Partying in* **Ko Pha Ngan**

» *Trekking in* **Bwindi**

When not out exploring, he lives in **Baltimore, Maryland,** which he considers the greatest city in the world.

TheWayfarersHandbook.com

 thewayfershandbook   evan.s.rice

 wayfarershandbook   evan_s_rice

BornLost.com

USEFUL INFORMATION

CONVERSIONS	TEMPERATURE	
	$C°$	$F°$
1 centimeter (cm) ≈ .39 inches (in)		
1 meter (m) ≈ 3.28 feet (ft)	100	212
1 meter (m) ≈ 1.09 yard (yd)		
1 kilometer (km) ≈ .62 miles (mi)	90	194
1 nautical mile (nmi) ≈ 1.85 kilometers (km)	80	176
1 nautical mile (nmi) ≈ 1.15 miles (mi)		
1 sq. meter (m²) ≈ 1.20 sq. yards (sq yd)	70	158
1 sq. kilometer (km²) ≈ .39 sq. miles (sq mi)		
1 hectare (ha) ≈ 2.47 acres (ac)	60	140
1 milliliter (ml) ≈ .20 US teaspoons (tsp)	50	122
1 milliliter (ml) ≈ .07 US tablespoons (tbsp)		
1 liter (L) ≈ 33.81 US fl. ounces (fl oz)	40	104
1 liter (L) ≈ 4.17 US cups (c)		
1 liter (L) ≈ 2.11 US pints (pt)	30	86
1 liter (L) ≈ 1.06 US quarts (qt)		
1 liter (L) ≈ .26 US gallon (gal)	20	68
1 imperial teaspoon (tsp) ≈ 1.20 US teaspoons (tsp)	10	50
1 imperial tablespoon (tbsp) ≈ 1.20 US tablespoons (tbsp)		
1 imperial fl. ounce (fl oz) ≈ .96 US fl. ounces (fl oz)	0	32
1 imperial cup (c) ≈ 1.18 US cups (c)		
1 imperial pint (pt) ≈ 1.20 US pints (pt)	-10	14
1 imperial quart (qt) ≈ 1.20 US quarts (qt)		
1 imperial gallon (gal) ≈ 1.20 US gallons (gal)	-20	-4
1 gram (g) ≈ .035 ounces (oz)	-30	-22
1 kilogram (kg) ≈ 2.20 pounds (lb)		
1 metric ton (t) ≈ 1.10 US tons (ton)	-40	-40

SPEED								
Kilometers per hour (km/h)	20	40	60	80	100	120	140	160
Miles per hour (mph)	12	25	37	50	62	75	87	99
Knots (kn)	11	22	32	43	54	65	76	86

INTERNATIONAL MORSE CODE

SOS: · · · − − − · · ·

COMMON EMERGENCY RADIO FREQUENCIES

121.5 MHz: civilian aircraft distress · **243.0 MHz:** military aircraft distress
406.0 MHz: international distress frequency · **156.8 MHz** (Channel 16 VHF):
maritime emergency · **500 kHz:** old emergency Morse code frequency
2182 kHz: maritime emergency